THE SUFFERIN

The Suffering Self is a controversial interdisciplinary study of the spread of Christianity across the Roman empire. Judith Perkins shows how Christian narrative representation in the early empire worked to create a new kind of human self-understanding – the perception of the self as sufferer. Drawing on feminist and social theory, she addresses the question of why themes of martyrdom and bodily suffering were so prevalent in early Christian texts.

This study crosses the boundaries between ancient history and the study of early Christianity in the context of the Greco-Roman world. Perkins draws parallels with suffering heroines in Greek novels and in martyr acts and examines representations in medical and philosophical texts.

The Suffering Self is important reading for all those interested in ancient society, or in the history of Christianity.

Judith Perkins is Professor of Classics and Humanities at Saint Joseph College, West Hartford, Connecticut.

THE SUFFERING SELF

Pain and Narrative Representation in the Early Christian Era

Judith Perkins

London and New York

First published 1995
by Routledge
11 New Fetter Lane, London EC4P 4EE

Simultaneously published in the USA and Canada
by Routledge
29 West 35th Street, New York, NY 10001

© 1995 Judith Perkins

Typeset in Garamond by
Florencetype Ltd, Stoodleigh, Devon

Printed and bound in Great Britain by
TJ Press (Padstow) Ltd, Padstow, Cornwall

British Library Cataloguing in Publication Data
A catalogue record for this book is available from the British
Library

Library of Congress Cataloguing in Publication Data
Perkins, Judith
The Suffering Self : Pain and Narrative Representation in the
Early Christian Era / Judith Perkins.
p. cm.
Includes bibliographical references and index.
1. Suffering–Religious aspects–Christianity–History of
doctrines–Early church, ca. 30–600. 2. Pain–Religious
aspects–Christianity–History of doctrines–Early church,
ca. 30–600. 3. Identification (Religion)–History of
doctrines–Early church, ca. 30–600. I. Title.
BR195.S93P47 1995 94–42650
272′.1–dc20

ISBN 0–415–11363–6 (hbk)
ISBN 0–415–12706–8 (pbk)

Brewster
Sine qua non

CONTENTS

PERMISSIONS

Portions of this book have been previously published as follows:

Material from Chapter 1 was published in *Arethusa* 15 (1985) 211–230.
Material from Chapter 4 was published in *Latomus* 53 (1994) 837–847.
Portions of Chapter 5 were published in *Arethusa* 25 (1992) 145–155
and in *The Search for the Ancient Novel* (1993) ed. James Tatum, Johns
Hopkins University Press 296–307. Chapter 7 was published in the
Harvard Theological Review 85 (1992) 245–272 (Copyright 1992 by the
President and Fellows of Harvard College. Reprinted by permission.)
Chapter 8 was published in *Greek Fiction* (1993) ed. John Morgan and
Richard Stoneman, Routledge 255–271.

I would like to thank the following for permission to reprint copyright
material:
The Clarendon Press for *The Acts of the Christian Martyrs* (1972) ed. H.
Musurillo.
E. J. Brill for *Aelius Aristides, The Complete Works* (1981–86) ed. C. H.
Behr.
The University of California Press for *Collected Ancient Greek Novels* ed.
B. P. Reardon.
Akademie-Verlag for *Galen: On Prognosis (Corpus Medicorum Graecorum
5.8.1)* (1979) ed. V. Nutton.
Westminster John Knox Press for *The New Testament Apocrypha* (1992)
ed. Wilhelm Schneelmelcher and Edgar Hennecke.
Harvard University Press and the Loeb Classical Library for:
The Apostolic Fathers (1917) K. Lake.
Epictetus Works (1925) W. A. Oldfather.
Lucian (1936) A. M. Harmon.
The Correspondence of Fronto (1919–20) C. R. Haines.
Marcus Aurelius: The Communings with Himself (1924) C. R. Haines.

Thanks are due to Douglas Edwards, Brigitte Egger, and Robert Dobbin
for permission to quote from their unpublished Ph.D dissertations.

ACKNOWLEDGEMENTS

A book that has taken this long to produce has incurred many debts. I owe a great deal to several institutions: the National Endowment for the Humanities for supporting my participation in a 1979 summer seminar, "The Social World of Early Christianity," directed by Wayne Meeks, and for granting me in 1990–1991 a Fellowship that afforded me time to write; to the Wesleyan Humanities Center for providing space and stimulating discussion; and to Saint Joseph College for awarding me sabbatical leave to finish this project. Many generous scholars have shared their knowledge with me. I owe Wayne Meeks, Richard Pervo, Brigitte Egger, and Kent Rigsby particular gratitude for their generosity. Special thanks are also due James Tatum for his editing and considerably improving what is now Chapter 5; Allen Ward for his help on Chapter 4; and Jay Francis for allowing me to read his book *Subversive Virtue* while it was still in typescript. My colleagues at Saint Joseph have provided invaluable support: Father John Stack and Julius Rubin never wearied of endless discussions of religion, and Dennis Barone read the entire manuscript. I must also thank at Saint Joseph Sister Dorothy O'Dwyer and Jane Cunningham for their help with the production of the book.

I especially thank two friends who have challenged my thinking and my expression of it for what now seems a whole lifetime: Penelope Laurans Fitzgerald and Cornelia Clark Cook. My greatest debt, finally, is owed to those who, I fear, have experienced real pain because of my theoretical interest in suffering: my mother, Barbara Bailey, my children, Alexander, Austin, and Laela, and especially my husband, Brewster, to whom this book is dedicated.

INTRODUCTION

James Joyce referred to moments of sudden unexpected insight as
"epiphanies." Coming upon a segment of a speech that Lucius
Apuleius delivered to the senate of Carthage near the middle of
the second century A.D., I had one of those epiphanic moments.
Apuleius was a figure centrally placed in his second-century society,
interested in philosophy and religion, an eminent orator in a culture
that celebrated oratorical ability, author of the novel, the
Metamorphoses. What caught my attention in this instance was how
he chose to present himself to his audience in Carthage. Rain had
interrupted Apuleius' speech thanking the Carthaginians for
awarding him a public statue, and an injury to his ankle extended
the delay. Apuleius resumed his speech by comparing himself to a
poet who had died before being able to complete an interrupted
recitation.

> For my recitation was as I am sure you remember interrupted
> by rain . . . I put it off to the morrow and it was nearly with
> me as with Philemon. For on the same day I twisted my
> ankle so violently at the wrestling school that I almost tore
> the joint from my leg. . . . However it returned to its socket
> though my leg is still weak with the pain. But there is more
> to tell you. My efforts to reduce the dislocation were so great
> that my body broke out in a profuse sweat and I caught a
> severe chill. This was followed by an agonizing pain in the
> bowels which only subsided as its violence was on the point
> of killing me. A moment more and like Philemon I should
> have gone to the grave and not to my reading, should have
> finished not my speech, but my destiny.
>
> (*Florida* 16, Butler's (1909) translation)

1

Apuleius carefully crafted his comparison, playing on verbal similarities in the Latin, but his graphic description of his bodily symptoms strikes a modern reader as rather excessive, perhaps even disgusting. This eminent orator, however, can be trusted to know what would attract his audience and engage their interest. It was his choice to represent himself so graphically as a body in pain, a sufferer that precipitated my moment of "epiphany."

I had been seeing a similar representation of the human self offered in many other texts of the second century, but had not focused on these other examples as representations *qua* representations. One expects to find persons being described as bodies experiencing pain, as sufferers in the discourses of martyrs, doctors, and Asclepius worshipers. Medical discourse by its nature is full of such images, and the second century is a period of a pronounced general interest in medicine as the prominence of the doctors Rufus, Soranus, Aretaeus, and Galen testified (Nutton 1985: 24). Glen Bowersock pointed to the emphasis on the body and its health in the extant correspondence between Marcus Aurelius and his tutor, Fronto, as signaling a general and popular concern (Bowersock 1969: 59–75). And Aelius Aristides' extensive recording in his *Sacred Tales* of his numerous symptoms of ill-health and his interactions with the god, Asclepius, as well as the expansion of the shrines of the god, testify to a widespread focus on health during this period. Representations of sick or suffering bodies had appeared to me as natural in these narratives, part of their effort to convey the reality they described. Encountering Apuleius, however, presenting himself as a person in pain, so out of context, almost gratuitously, to claim attention, forced me to recognize that his image of himself as a sufferer was purposefully chosen, one selected from any number of other possible self-representations he might have presented. With this recognition, I suddenly realized that what I had been accepting as simply realistic presentation in texts was, in fact, part of an extensive formulation in the culture of the second century that represented the human self as a body in pain, a sufferer. That I had not realized this sooner only testifies again to the inherent magic of discourse that lulls us into forgetting to look past its projection of reality and to ask questions like: why is this subject being treated now? why in this particular manner? what purpose is served for their authors and readers by these kinds of discourses?

The power of discourse inheres precisely in this remarkable ability it has to set its agenda and mask the fact that its representation both has an agenda and that there could be other representations and other agendas. Every representation is by its very nature partial and incomplete. A representation of "reality" must leave something out, even as it puts something in. A culture's discourse represents not the "real" world, but rather a world mediated through the social categories, relations and institutions operating in the specific culture. Another way of saying this is that every representation reflects some cultural "interest," and, therefore, discourses in a society never just float free. They are informed by, and they help to constitute, the society's particular preoccupations and intentions. In this study I want to identify a particular preoccupation in the discursive climate of the early Roman empire. From a number of different locations, narratives were projecting a particular representation of the human self as a body liable to pain and suffering. This representation challenged another, prevailing, more traditional Greco-Roman image of the self as a soul/mind controlling the body. I intend to try to locate the "triumph" of Christianity within the discursive struggle over these representations. It would be around one of these represented "subjects," the suffering self, that Christianity as a social and political unity would form and ultimately achieve its institutional power.

Although discourses do not represent "reality," they do have very real effects. In every society, persons come to understand themselves, their roles and their world through their culture's discursive practices and the "reality" these practices bring into cultural consciousness. It is my contention in this study that the discursive focus in the second century on the suffering body contributed to Christianity's attainment of social power by helping to construct a subject that would be present for its call. It is in this sense that I say that the "triumph" of Christianity was, at least in part, a triumph of representation. In the Hellenic world from the fifth century B.C. on, the prevailing cultural discourse presented a conception of the human self as a rational mind/soul exerting control upon a body whose needs and desires inhibited the mind/soul's attaining the perfection that was imaged in the rational order of the cosmos. In the early empire another self-conception surfaced in a number of texts from different cultural points – that of a mind/soul joined to a body liable to pain and suffering, in need of outside attention and direction. It is this latter representation that will come to prevail in the ideology, the "thought-world," of Christianity. But texts from the late first and early second centuries A.D. demonstrate that this conception of the self as sufferer was already circulating in the cultural discourse of the period. I wish to argue in this book that this emergent cultural subject, and the ideological shift it gives hint of, helped to enable the growth of Christianity. Before proceeding to outline my argument, I should locate my work in its own cultural matrix and indicate how certain contemporary critical interests have influenced its development.

Contemporary critiques of the notion of a transcendent and universal human nature have been a catalyst for redirecting historical inquiry into new areas. A number of modern theorists, in particular Michel Foucault, have offered that concepts of what constitutes "human nature" change over time, as human subjects learn to apprehend themselves in new and differing ways. Humans do not possess a nature; rather, they acquire one through the various self-understandings and self-representations their cultures offer them. Donald Morton and Mas'ud Zavarzadeh have summarized this perspective:

> (post)modern critical theory does not conceptualize the subject as a stable entity but argues that the parameters of the subject vary according to the current discursive practices in any historical moment. In this view the human does not possess a timeless essence, a consciousness that places him beyond historical and political practices; rather he is considered to be produced by these practices or as an effect of these discourses.
>
> (Morton and Zavarzadeh 1991: 4)

Cultural discourse "produces" humans in the sense that human subjects come to understand themselves through the categories and representations of "being human," operating and present in their particular culture. What makes up the "reality" for any culture is similarly recognized as a constituted category and liable to change. For humans also acquire their sense of the "real" through the frameworks and classifications provided in their societies. In Janet Wolff's words: "the social world cannot be conceptualized as having some independent existence, but rather has to be understood as a provisionally stable and constantly reconstituted complex of discourses, processes and institutions" (Wolff 1992: 711).

These assumptions about human subjects and the social worlds they inhabit have effected a changed focus in historical study. How discourses work to produce certain "subjectivities," i.e., "historical forms of consciousness," and create the social worlds around these is now a subject for historical inquiry (Johnson 1986–1987: 43). Historians see that the importance of such topics for understanding the workings of past cultures and this new focus has opened (for historical analysis) texts traditionally excluded from historical study. The recognition that literary, religious, and technical discourses all contribute to generating a cultural world has revealed that the traditional distinctions made between historical documents and other texts was essentially arbitrary.[1] If historians wish to approach an understanding of the dynamics of a past period, they must incorporate the testimony of many different kinds of discourses. In Leonard Tennenhouse's words, "the history of a culture is a history of all its products" (Tennenhouse 1982: 141). Clifford Geertz also pointed to the necessity of casting a wide net in the study of cultures: "God may not be in the details but the 'world' – everything that is the case – surely is" (Geertz 1992: 133).

These details, comprising the "world," are supplied by the amalgam of particularities and specificities embodied in the culture's various productions. Within this framework of historical analysis, all sorts of discourses become important repositories for historical understanding as well as important vehicles for historical change. Recent historical analysis has expanded to accommodate this recognition.[2]

Studies of how power operates in societies, for example, no longer concentrate exclusively on the roles of kings or emperors or the actions of armies or states, but focus instead on the discursive practices through which persons in a society learn to apprehend themselves and their roles in certain ways.[3] Foucault noted that power did not actually reside in the mechanisms of domination alone:

> The analysis, made in terms of power, must not assume that sovereignty of the state, the form of law, or the overall unity of a domination are given at the outset; rather these are only the terminal forms power takes.
>
> (Foucault 1980: 92)

In Foucault's view, power radiated from innumerable points: "power is everywhere not because it embraces everything, but because it comes from everywhere" (1980: 93). Power for Foucault was, as Linda Peterson explained:

a whole complex of forces; it is that which produces what happens. Thus even a tyrannical aristocrat does not simply wield power, for he is empowered by "discourses" – accepted ways of thinking, writing and speaking – and practices that amount to power.

(Peterson 1992: 419)

It is these "accepted ways of thinking, writing and speaking," and the social worlds they produce and the kinds of power they make possible, that have become a subject of historical inquiry. This focus has shifted historical attention from an examination of major actors in the historical scene, or from major events in the past, to an investigation of how various discourses in a historical period work to produce particular "subjectivities," i.e., particular forms of self-understandings and particular social worlds that generate certain kinds of social power. The dominant power in a society is recognized as being sustained through the domination of a particular social discourse.

One of Foucault's major perceptions was his predication of the relationship between power, as he defined it, and knowledge – that they implied each other. In his work on prisons and mental hospitals, he sought to demonstrate his contention that, as Vincent Leitch summarized, "there is no power relationship without the correlative constitution of a field of knowledge, nor any knowledge that does not presuppose and constitute at the same time power relations" (Leitch 1992: 131; Foucault 1965, 1977). Foucault's work suggested that the question one should ask about any emerging complex of discourses is: where is the power in this knowledge? As Averil Cameron noted in her study of Christian rhetoric, the development and control of a given discourse "may provide a key to social power" (Cameron 1991: 1).

With respect to the discourse around the body occurring in the early centuries of the Roman empire, Foucault had initiated an answer to the question "what were the effects of power generated by what was said?" (Foucault 1980: 11). Identifying a new emphasis on the body in the late Republic and early Roman empire in his *History of Sexuality*, Foucault located this attention on the body within a more general concern for the care and cultivation of the "self" prevalent during the period. He connected the "turn to the body" to the development of a notion of the self as an individual, "an object of knowledge and a field of action," and the beginning of a subjectivity that saw this self as needing attention and care (Foucault 1988: 42).

What struck me as particularly significant about this discourse around the body was that the body depicted as "attended-to" was so often a sick or suffering one (Foucault 1988: 56–57). If a society's reality is, as we have said, a social construct produced from the array of its discursive practices, this emphasis shows a new prominence for the suffering subject in the period. That is to say, a new knowledge was growing up around this subject, for knowledge is, in Edward Said's words, "the making visible of material" (Said 1979: 127). Suffering may be everywhere, but if it is not brought to cultural consciousness, in effect, it has no existence, that is, there is no knowledge of it. Perceptions of reality are filtered through culturally given categories and where there is no category, i.e., no cultural knowledge, perception is impeded. A simple example can demonstrate how knowledge regulates perception. Recall what happens when we learn the meaning of a new word – suddenly the word seems to turn up everywhere. This common experience substantiates the chilling recognition that our earlier ignorance of the word had hidden its existence from us although it must have been right in front of our eyes.

This example of the learned word enacts in microcosm how "not being aware" can hide from observers what is quite literally right in front of them. In cultural terms, those belonging to the category of sufferers, the sick, the deformed, the poor, had little existence in cultural representation throughout most of Greco-Roman antiquity before the early empire. That is not to say that humans were not in pain or did not suffer before this period, but that their pain and suffering did not have significant cultural visibility and in that sense they did not have substantial existence within cultural consciousness. But the concerted discursive attention on bodies and their health and pain that I am going to document in this study changed that situation.

In the late Hellenistic period and the early Roman empire, the suffering body became a focus of significant cultural concern and this gave rise to the creation of a new subjectivity – the self as sufferer. The representation I opened with, where Apuleius presented himself as a sufferer, corresponds to other similar self-representations in the period. Consider, for example, this short letter to Marcus Aurelius from his tutor, Fronto: "I have been troubled, my Lord, in the night with widespread pains in my shoulder and elbow and knee and ankle. In fact I have not been able to convey this news to you in my own writing" (*Ad Marcum Caesarem* 5.73; Fronto 1919–1920: 1.187). Narratives such as those of Apuleius and Fronto are examples of a subjectivity under construction. In both discursive examples each man posited himself as a certain kind of subject – a sufferer. Such narratives contributed to and helped constitute the creation of a particular cultural self-apprehended identity, that is, a subjectivity. Texts such as Apuleius' and Fronto's offered for public consumption and identification the image of the self as a sufferer and indicate how inhabitants of the early empire were coming to apprehend themselves as sufferers. And as Steven Cohan and Linda Shires have explained, this is precisely how ideology and narrative work:

> ideology retains its power as a real medium of imaginary understanding; it makes you the subject *of* as well as *to* the representation of meaning . . . a narrative text does not simply represent subjectivity to readers or viewers; more importantly, it also signifies their subjectivity for them.
>
> (Cohan and Shires 1988: 137, 149)[4]

To individuals in a culture, representations offer consciousness of themselves as certain kinds of subjects. In the early empire inhabitants were coming to experience themselves as sufferers.

To return to the question opening this section: whose power was in this new knowledge of the self as a sufferer? My answer – Christianity's power. The effects of this new knowledge of sufferers can be seen in the institutionalization of the Christian church. From its earliest periods, Christianity's growth correlated with the constitution of a category of sufferers, in particular, with the poor and the sick. As heirs and inhabitants of a Christian thought-world, it is difficult to remember that these in fact are cultural categories, and essentially absent from the classificatory systems of the earlier Greco-Roman world. As J. H. W. G. Liebeschuetz has noted, "the idea that the poor, the sick and the old ought to be helped because they were there and even God's creatures is not classical" (Liebeschuetz 1979: 187).[5] It is perhaps even more important to note that such categories of people were, in essence, not even "there" in any significant way in the cultural representation of the ancient world and, therefore, in the culture's consciousness. Like the new word before it is learned, the poor, the sick and the old hardly existed as subjects of knowledge for the classical world.

8

In these terms, the discursive project in the early empire – to construct a subjectivity of sufferer with all the subcategories this assumes – becomes significant for the growth and institutionalization of Christianity. Without the preparation of a subject already underway in the cultural discourse of the early empire, the defining elements of Christianity as we know it may not have emerged. But Christian discourse was able to join other types of discourses to produce the subjectivity it needed to exist as an institution. One key to Christianity's success was its ability to produce the kind of subjecthood necessary to form the basis of its political and social unity and to continue to develop and control the discourse that produced such a subject (Eagleton 1990: 24). It is through such mechanisms that institutions acquire and maintain power. By producing certain kinds of subjects, discursive practices can, in Steven Cohan and Linda Shires' words, control "the dissemination of certain knowledges, thereby ensuring the domination of certain social interests" (Cohan and Shires 1988: 141). Christianity significantly altered the "accepted ways of thinking, writing and speaking" about the human subject in the discourse of the early empire. And this discursive shift made possible, as Foucault said it always does, new forms of power in the society.

The production and maintenance of this new cultural subject, and the power this gave rise to, profoundly changed ancient society. In his article "What Difference Did Christianity Make?," Ramsay MacMullen bracketed off what seems to me to be the most important evidence for answering the question posed in his title. MacMullen insisted that any test of difference "must show Christians not just talking but doing" (1986: 324). But the basis for Christianity's difference is located precisely in its talk. MacMullen suggested that Christianity failed to make much difference in the Roman empire because it failed to affect social practices such as slavery or judicial savageness. But the major difference Christianity made was itself, its own institutionalization, and the new categories it introduced into cultural consciousness. These instigated major differences – a new power institution became a force in the social arena (Lane Fox 1987: 22). Christianity was only able to create itself as an institution because cultural "talking," its own and others, had prepared a subject ready for its call – a subject that apprehended itself as a sufferer.

My study focuses on the effects certain kinds of writing had on history; my focus is writing itself as a historical agent as it enabled the institutional formation of Christianity, and not on historical events or figures as such (Bender 1987: 1–9). Nevertheless, at this point it might be helpful to glance at a few suggestive examples from recent historical studies that display the "real" power effects for Christianity in this production of a subjectivity of sufferer. Wayne Meeks (1993), for example, pointed to the importance of the poor for the early institutionalization of Christianity. By the middle of the third century, the Church in Rome already supported 1,500 people (Eusebius 6.43), and the need to manage such charitable operations may have acted as a primary impetus for the early formation of the Church. As Meeks noted:

> Peter Lampe has speculated that it was the need to coordinate charitable efforts, that first led to a central organization of the otherwise "fractionated" house-communities of Christians in Rome. If that is true, then the practice of giving was actually one factor that propelled the institutionalization of the church . . .
>
> (Meeks 1993: 108, citing Lampe 1987: 334–345)

In his penetrating study *Power and Persuasion in Late Antiquity*, Peter Brown (1992) demonstrated how aggressively bishops in the fourth century sought power and authority in the cities in their role as "lovers of the poor." The bishops' authority thus rested on their connection with a category whose visibility in the Roman cities derived from the perception of the subjectivity of "the sufferer." In Brown's words,

> In the name of a religion that claimed to challenge the values of the elite, upper-class Christians gained control of the lower classes of the cities. By the end of the fourth century their authority rested on a newly created constituency.
>
> (Brown 1992: 78)

This same "love of the poor" provided a reason for the Church's accumulation of wealth.

As they were made visible, that is, made subjects of knowledge, the poor also became subject to control. Once the poor were enrolled on Church registers, Brown pointed out they "became stabilized and could not move to other cities" (Brown 1992: 98). This situation provides a perfect demonstration of Foucault's theory that new knowledge implies new power which, in turn, entails new institutions. The construction of the subjectivity of the sufferer brought into Greco-Roman cultural consciousness in new ways all those belonging to this category, the poor, the sick, the deformed, which, in turn, enabled the Church to acquire and consolidate wealth and power in their name.

The category of the suffering sick, like that of the poor, also furnished an opportunity for the acquisition of social and political power. Brown described how in fifth-century Alexandria, for example, the patriarch acquired for his use what nearly amounted to a civil militia for he "commanded, in effect, a hand-picked force of some five hundred men with strong arms and backs, the *parabalani*, who were nominally entrusted with the 'care of the bodies of the weak' as stretcher-bearers and hospital orderlies" (Brown 1992: 102). As hospitals arose in response to the new cultural/social category of the sick, power for those controlling these institutions followed.

T. D. Barnes, in his study of Athanasius, provided an example of how, before the middle of the fourth century, even a churchman from a "low-class origin" had come to accumulate and wield considerable power as a result of his oversight of services for the poor (Barnes 1993: 176–180). Constantine exiled Athanasius, bishop of Alexandria, on the basis of his enemies' accusation that he was "threatening to prevent the grain from being sent from Alexandria to Constantinople (*Apologia contra Arianos* 87.1)" (Barnes 1993: 179). This accusation shows that the bishop of Alexandria controlled the imperial subsidies of grain designed for widows throughout the Egyptian provinces and had obtained both power and opportunities of patronage from this office. In fact, Athanasius appears to have had so much power to control the supply of grain that he had disrupted the grain trade that Constantine needed to maintain the urban peace in Constantinople. Athanasius sought to rebut the charges by asking how a poor private citizen such as he could have obtained so much power. Eusebius, bishop of Nicomedia, however, testifying to the inherent power growing up around the services provided for sufferers, "swore that the bishop of Alexandria was rich, influential, and unscrupulous (*Apologia contra Arianos* 9.3/4)" (Barnes 1993: 24). These examples display how bishops through their offices of caring for sufferers had come to control wealth and influence. The subjectivity it helped to produce and maintain provided the Church with its institutional impetus and power.

The triumph of Christianity was, in part at least, a triumph of a particular representation of the self. Through a number of discursive

11

practices, individuals began to think of themselves as bodies liable to pain and suffering. As sufferers, categories of people came to be viewed as "us," and were afforded a cultural attention and community concern that they had not had in the traditional Greco-Roman world.[6] Peter Brown pointed out a detail from Theodoret's *Historia Religiosa* (*Patrologia Graeca* 1384) that indicates how deeply this self-understanding permeated thinking in some localities. Theodoret describes a group of young girls in fourth-century Syria playing a game; some girls dressed in rags as monks while others acted as sufferers seeking exorcism. In other words, one group played at being poor and the other at being possessed (pretending to be sick or mad). They acted out being sick or mad (Brown 1971: 88).[7] In either role, the little girls embraced the subjectivity I see being constructed in the early empire as *"for them"* (Cohan and Shires 1988: 149). In such ways are self-understandings (re)produced and maintained, as individuals come to imagine and apprehend themselves as particular kinds of subjects, to acquire specifically a consciousness of themselves in such terms. In this scene, for example, the girls posited themselves as poor, empowered by poverty, or as victims of disability in need of cure and care. They come to understand themselves and others as potential members of these specific categories.

This is a book about the creation, in the early Roman empire, of a certain kind of self-apprehension. It is premised upon the belief that textual representations do not just reflect, in some unproblematic way, reality and social institutions, but, rather, help to create and maintain them. My primary point is that the representation in early Christian narratives of a community of sufferers and the persecuted worked not simply to represent a realistic situation so much as to provide a self-definition that enabled the growth of Christianity as an institution. And, moreover, that the same keen attention to the particularities and specificities of the suffering body displayed in Christian narratives (in their representation of the bodies of martyrs, the sick seeking healing, or ascetic practitioners, for example) appears in other discourses in the culture. All these discourses contributed to the creation of a similar self-representation and therefore helped to produce the very subject needed to provide the basis for the institutionalization of Christianity.[8] This new body of knowledge around the suffering body provided a new basis of power and enabled the formation of new institutions incorporating this power.

My study examines writings and their historical effect. This is a book about a cluster of ideas circulating in the thought-world of the early empire. Its focus is on mental constructs rather than "real" events. I emphasize this to head off possible censure that I have gathered textual evidence across a very wide geographical span, and for a different kind of history this would be a proper reproof. But in the study of ideas and their diffusion, when time and chance have already winnowed much of the evidence, a pattern must be discerned from a number of disparate pieces. A past culture is like a puzzle, fitted together from a myriad of these little pieces. By bringing together a number of pieces traditionally kept apart, I have been able, I believe, to offer a clearer glimpse of the picture that is the puzzle of the thought-world of the early Roman empire.

A concern that has bothered me at several points as I wrote this study was that what I was doing would be received simply as a restatement of the obvious. After all, the one thing everyone knows about Christianity is that it centers on suffering in the exemplar of the crucified Christ. In the study of ideologies, of cultural assumptions, however, it is just those points that "everyone knows" that must be examined most carefully. In fact, ideology is itself the construct of all those "ideas and beliefs which seem true or natural as the result of reasonable, common sensible observation" (Cohan and Shires 1988: 133). In this book I want to push the inquiry of early Christianity past the obvious and ask why groups of Christians in the Greco-Roman world chose to foreground their own suffering in their early texts and why they picked the suffering in their founder's life to emulate.[9] It could have been otherwise. Platonists emulated not Socrates' death but his rationale for it and his rationality in accepting it (Droge and Tabor 1992: 17–51). The acceptance of Christian representation as obvious has concealed its effect and the workings-out of its achievement.

The Christian scriptures have not featured in my analysis of Christian discourse, not because I do not feel they would substantiate my argument, but because, lacking a specialist knowledge in New Testament studies, I hesitated to incorporate their witness into my discussions. It will be left to readers to make the often obvious connections between the subjectivity constructed in the Christian discourses I examine and that offered in the New Testament.[10]

A final comment on documentation; I have tried to keep references to a minimum. A number of different topics are treated in this study and I have not attempted to offer a complete bibliography for each, but limited my references to those works that either provided the basis for my argument or were cited in the text.

1

DEATH AS A
HAPPY ENDING

Second-century Christian writings present a world of pain, suffering and death. Graphic detail pictures both the human body and the body social as universally lacerated and harassed. The portrayal in Christian documents of the physical body scraped with claws, pierced with knives, roasted, whipped, strangled and mauled by beasts is a microcosm for a community assailed on every side according to Melito (Eusebius *Historia Ecclesiastica* 4.26.2), Hermas (*Pastor* 3.2.1), and Justin (II *Apologia* 12).[1] If a culture's reality, its sense of the "way things really are," is a product of its systems of representations, the processes and peculiarities used to bring its cultural world to consciousness, the centrality of pain, suffering and death in early Christian representation suggests that Christian "reality" was unrelentingly filled with risk, pain and death.

The traditional explanation for the emphasis on suffering in Christian texts has been that it reflected the desperate situation of a hounded community, but modern scholarship has called this explanation into question. Persecution in the second century appears to have been in T. D. Barnes' words "local, sporadic and random" (Barnes 1968a: 38).[2] Christianity was dangerous to embrace, certainly – a crime punishable by death. But in the early empire there was no concerted state effort to seek out Christians for persecution. The traditional conception of Christians during this period as all in great danger and hiding from authorities is disproved in many contemporary texts both Christian and non-Christian. Lucian, for example, in his depiction of the career of Proteus Peregrinus, a Cynic who killed himself at the Olympian games in A.D. 165, offered a picture of the typical situation. During Peregrinus's Christian period, he somehow had come to official notice and was imprisoned. Peregrinus' arrest, however, did not

15

affect or suspend the public behaviors of other Christians, whom Lucian described as attending Peregrinus, bringing him food and books, even spending the night with him.

Lucian's description emphasized the crowds of Christians coming to the prison to support their leader, and demonstrated that these public actions performed by the Christians did not place the Christian crowd in any danger. Lucian's depiction might be distrusted as part of his satire if his picture was not supported by similar Christian testimony. Ignatius, for example, sentenced to death, traveled from Antioch to Rome; his letters show that all along his route he was visited and supported by representatives of the Christian communities he passed through. Perpetua, imprisoned with a group of martyrs in Carthage, also described the visits of members of her Christian community who like Peregrinus's supporters had bribed the guards to insure better conditions for the imprisoned (ACM 3.7). Such descriptions display the selectivity of persecution in the early period and the relative safety of many Christians even as they publicly acted out their Christian beliefs. Local persecutions did occur; but before the mid-third century, persecutions against Christians arose primarily from local outbreaks of animosity. The situation in this period was as De Ste. Croix has stated, "the ordinary Christian who did not insist on openly parading his confession was most unlikely to become a victim of the persecution at all" (De Ste. Croix 1954: 104).

This is not to say that there were no persecutions. Persecutions did occur and for their victims and witnesses they were horrendous and harrowing. It is in no sense my intention to minimize the heroic witness of Christian martyrs as I question why so much of Christian representation focused on the pain, suffering and death of Christians. But so long as it is uncritically accepted that the emphasis of Christian texts on pain and death resulted from widespread and inclusive persecutions, the extraordinary Christian effort to bring into consciousness a world centered on these topics will go unrecognized. It is my contention that Christian representation in the early Roman empire functioned to offer a particular self-representation to Christians – the Christian as sufferer. The fact that at this point persecutions occurred relatively infrequently gives this representation added significance. For if Christians were not writing texts focused on suffering, and passing these around from community to community to buttress their adherents' resolve to endure systematic and unavoidable persecution, why were they constructing such a subject? And why would the representation of such a subject succeed in attracting adherents in the Greco-Roman world?

These questions are important for understanding one means by which Christianity accomplished its growth. For the so-called "triumph of Christianity" was, as I suggested above, a representational revolution. Through the agency of Christian representation, numbers of persons acquired a changed self-understanding and a changed world-view. Numerous elements likely contributed to this revolution, but a central element in its success was that the Christian representation of pain and death played into a constellation of concerns already manifest in the culture.

Ramsay MacMullen in his *Christianizing the Roman Empire* offered a piece of salutary advice for studying conversion to Christianity in this early period and one that will allow the basis for Christianity's representational success to emerge. MacMullen submitted that any study of conversions must begin from an examination of what Christianity offered its audience: "What *did* Christianity present to its audience? For plainly the process of conversion, that interests me, took place in people's minds on the basis of what they knew, or thought they knew" (MacMullen 1984: 19–20). MacMullen's advice is helpful because it suggests a method to bracket off the great load of assumptions all moderns carry around as heirs of the Christian thought-world. Modern commentators are entangled, wittingly or not, in the shared perspective of centuries of Christianity. Following MacMullen's advice, the focus shifts from modern assumptions about what attracted converts to Christianity to an analysis of what contemporaries focused on or considered significant about this new cult. By examining what contemporaries picked out for notice, Christianity can be located in the context of the surrounding culture's preoccupations and concerns.

MacMullen suggested that before any conversions could take place, inhabitants of the empire would have had to be attracted to the sect on the basis of what they knew or thought they knew about it – that is to say, on the basis of what was generally known, "in the air" so to speak. Tracing out what its audience found noteworthy or provoking should therefore help explain the grounds for Christianity's appeal. MacMullen suggested that Christianity's wonder-working prowess was a major element in its attraction, and at least in part this was most likely true. The early empire was a world full of wonder-workers (see Chapter 5). Christianity would have been viewed as deficient without the capacity to work miracles, and many early Christian documents testified to the cult's superior ability in this regard. But by highlighting wonder-working as the major factor in Christianity's appeal, MacMullen neglected his own advice to concentrate on what Christianity's audience knew, or showed evidence of knowing, about the sect. For the early pagan references to Christianity reflected very little interest in, or knowledge of, Christian wonder-working. Rather, the part of the Christian message that was getting through sufficiently, so that traces of it appeared in the general circulation of knowledge, is very clear. What did inhabitants of the early Roman empire know about Christianity? Notwithstanding the paucity of sources for the period and their elite bias, it is safe to say that one thing contemporaries knew about Christianity (in fact, for some the *only* thing they give any evidence of knowing) is that Christians held death in contempt and were ready to suffer for their beliefs. Robert Wilken (1984) has provided a useful survey of pagan[3] attitudes and knowledge about Christianity and his study established clearly that the earliest pagan references situated Christianity in a context of punishment and pain. In the earliest pagan reference, Christianity's burgeoning growth and wide appeal was already emphasized. About the year A.D. 111, the Roman senator, Pliny, serving as governor of Bithynia and Pontus wrote to the emperor, Trajan, for instructions on dealing with the Christians in his province (Sherwin-White 1966). Part of his reason for approaching the emperor on this topic was the large number of Christians "of every age and status, of both sexes" (*Epistula* 10.96). Pliny wrote to Trajan concerning the proper judicial disposal of cases involving these Christians. His problems were not with confessed Christians – he executed these – but with the lapsed or those who were willing to deny their Christianity in court and offer sacrifice.

The next earliest pagan reference to Christianity appeared in *The Annals* of Tacitus who described how, after the great fire in Rome, Nero picked out as "culprits and punished with the utmost refinements of cruelty a class of men, loathed for their views, whom the crowd called Christian" (15.44). Tacitus said these Christians were convicted, "not so much on the count of arson as for hatred of the human race." Tacitus described their punishment in graphic detail. They were torn to pieces by dogs, fastened to crosses and ignited. The two earliest pagan witnesses to Christianity, thus both referred to its adherents' punishment and death, their anti-social attitudes, and their neighbors' dislike of them. Tacitus spoke of the Christians' hatred of the human race and Pliny of their inflexible stubbornness in court. Such are the impressions of Christianity presented by two members of the Roman upper class in the early second century.

Later in the century, the doctor Galen mentioned Christians more favorably but within similar parameters of interest. In a discussion of the difficulty some people have in following logical arguments, Galen considered the efficacy of using parables for instruction. The mention of parables brought to mind the Christians whom Galen described:

> drawing their faith from parables and miracles, and yet sometimes acting in the same way as those who practice philosophy. For their contempt of death and of its sequel is patent to us every day, and likewise their restraint in cohabitation.
>
> (Walzer 1949: 15)

Galen also noted the Christian self-discipline in food and drink and their sense of justice, and his words suggest a certain familiarity with Christian practice. He displayed a knowledge of their teaching methods, their contempt for death, their abstemious habits and their pursuit of justice. Marcus Aurelius and Epictetus had both less knowledge and less regard for the Christians. A central motif of Marcus Aurelius' *Meditations* was the naturalness of death. The emperor expressed admiration for all those ready at any moment to accept release from life, but he refused to include people like Christians in his admiration. According to the emperor, they embraced death for the wrong reasons:

> But the readiness must spring from a man's inner judgement and not be the result of mere opposition as is the case with Christians. It must be associated with deliberation and dignity and if others are to be convinced, with nothing like stage heroics.
>
> (*Meditations* 11.3)

This explicit reference to Christians is perhaps an interpolation, but in any case, Marcus Aurelius would have included their behavior in his general disapproval for any theatrics of death.[4]

The Stoic philosopher, Epictetus, had also heard of Christian fearlessness in the face of death and danger, but he dismissed this attitude on their part as resulting from "habit," *ethos* (*Discourses* 4.7.6). Epictetus' comment showed that he considered the Christians' contempt for death as so naturally a part of their Christian life to be unreflective.

This rapid survey of early pagan references to Christianity supports one point conclusively: that if Christianity was known at all, it was known for its adherents' attitude toward death and suffering.

The more developed literary reference to Christianity in Lucian's *Proteus Peregrinus* (1936) corroborates this point. Lucian in his satiric attack on Proteus Peregrinus, the Cynic philosopher who incinerated himself at the Olympic games, quoted Peregrinus' reason for his death: "to teach others to despise death and remain strong in misfortunes" (Lucian 1936: 23). Lucian's detailed depiction of Peregrinus' career and death indicates a certain cultural fascination with death seekers during the period. Lucian dismissed Peregrinus on account of his thirst for notoriety and censured the setting and method of his death for its showiness. Just as Marcus Aurelius had discredited theatricality in the face of death, Lucian was put off by Peregrinus' self-dramatization (Francis 1995: 67–77). In Lucian's opinion, Peregrinus should have waited for death in its natural course, or if he chose to die, to have picked a less ostentatious method and setting than leaping onto a burning bier at the Olympic games (Lucian 1936: 21).

Peregrinus is a historical figure mentioned in a number of other sources.[5] Aulius Gellius called him a "serious and steadfast man" (*Noctes Atticae* 8.3). Only Lucian offered evidence for Peregrinus' Christian phase (Edwards 1989). His narrative suggested a pattern in this notorious death-seeker having had an earlier stage as a Christian. Lucian described Peregrinus' instruction in Christianity in Palestine, his quickly acquired status in the cult, becoming "a prophet, a cult leader, head of a synagogue, and everything, all by himself" (11). Eventually Peregrinus was arrested as a Christian. Lucian explained his arrest as another example of his quest for prominence. The Christian community supported Peregrinus in prison. At first they attempted to rescue him, and when this failed they enveloped their leader in constant attention: "from the very break of day aged widows and orphan children could be seen waiting near the prison, while their officials even slept inside with him after bribing the guards" (12). Christians brought Peregrinus elaborate meals and money, coming from all over Asia at their communities' expense to encourage him in his imprisonment. Lucian mocked these Christians for their gullibility, even as he provided testimony for their readiness to donate money in support of their community-member: "so if any charlatan or trickster who can size up the situation comes among them, he quickly acquired sudden wealth by imposing upon simple folk" (18). Lucian's description emphasized both the central role played by the martyr in the Christian community and the connection between the martyr's high standing and the Christians' self-understanding: "The poor wretches have convinced themselves, first and foremost, that they are going to be immortal and live for all time, in consequence of which they despise death and even willingly give themselves into custody most of them" (13). Peregrinus' imprisonment provided a cultural performance of their beliefs for the whole community. Christians clustered around, representatives came from all over to watch Peregrinus act out his contempt for death. Peregrinus performed his Christian faith, just as later he would enact his Cynic convictions in his fiery end after the Olympic festival.

On this occasion, however, the governor of Syria, according to Lucian, refused to play his part in Peregrinus' death drama. He recognized that Peregrinus "would gladly die in order that he might leave behind him a reputation for it, [so] he freed him . . ." (14). Later, Lucian reported, Peregrinus had a falling out with the Christian community and began the trajectory that resulted in his conspicuous final moments.

Lucian's depiction of Peregrinus' release by the governor is supported by other testimony from the period. Several of the *Martyr Acts* depicted judges reluctant to punish Christians and attempting to reason them into a safer course. Tertullian offered actual examples of judges in Africa who released confessed Christians unpunished; he cited the notorious and very likely hyperbolic example from Asia when all the Christians in a community presented themselves before Arrius Antoninus who let most of them go commenting, "wretched men if you wish to die, you have cliffs and ropes to hang yourselves" (*To Scapula* 4, 5). At this point in time Christians appeared to have been more willing to die than Roman officials were to punish them.

In his sketch of Peregrinus, Lucian revealed knowledge of Christianity; he knew about its origin, founder and sacred books. Again, however, the sect's attitude toward death was what had particularly caught his attention, along with the central role played by the martyr in Christian community life. Part of the point of

Lucian's satiric sketch of Peregrinus derived from his play with the idea that one of the period's most notorious death-seekers would have first auditioned for his role as a Christian. Lucian counted on his audience's recognition that Christians were known to have a propensity for dying, "they despise death and even willingly give themselves into custody." Following MacMullen's (1984) advice, it has become evident that what contemporaries knew about Christianity was not so much their miracles as that they experienced pain and death; it was this factor above all others that received explicit contemporary notice and comment.

This testimony exhausts first-hand pagan references to Christianity from the early empire, but a number of pagan statements about Christianity, or what purport to be pagan statements, survive in Christian works from the period. This evidence is consistent with the pagan sources, for again contemporary knowledge about Christianity focuses on the cult's attitude toward death. Justin, for example, described Trypho, his Jewish interlocutor, as rebuking Christians for having "invented a Christ for whom you give up your lives" (*Dialogus cum Tryphone* 8). Similarly, Origen's rebuttal of Celsus made clear that Celsus had accused Christians of "being mad and stirring up for themselves tortures and death" (*Contra Celsum* 8.65). In his *Octavius*, Minucius Felix described a conversion to Christianity of an upper-class pagan, Caecilius, at Ostia, after Octavius had persuasively presented the sect's beliefs. Before he learned better, Caecilius had contempt for Christians, describing them as illiterates who had no place challenging their betters in religious matters. Caecilius was particularly puzzled by Christians' strange attitude toward death: "They despise titles and robes of honour, going themselves half naked, present tortures they despise, yet dread those of an uncertain future; death after death they fear, but death in the present they fear not" (8.5). These views baffled Caecilius; they appeared so illogical. His perplexity matched that of Celsus who Origen quoted as comparing a Christian teacher to a "drunken man who, entering a party of drunkards, should accuse those who are sober of being drunk" (*Contra Celsum* 3.76).

Both actual pagan testimony and the pagans' comments reported in Christian sources make clear that when contemporaries thought of Christians, they thought of them in terms of their attitude toward death and suffering. During the early empire, Christians were particularly recognized for their contempt for death and all the pains associated with it. If, as MacMullen (1984) suggested, the impetus toward conversion must originate from what is generally known, then Christian conversion in the early empire was somehow tied to this perception that Christianity was a sect made up of members ready to experience pain and death.

That contemporaries were so well-acquainted with Christian suffering and dying would be more understandable if during this period Christianity was a harassed and hounded cult under siege on every side, but this was not the case. The testimony examined so far predates any concentrated, general persecution of Christianity (Frend 1965). During this period, the official attitude exemplified by Trajan's reply to Pliny's query about the treatment of Christians in his province seemed to have held sway (Millar 1977: 551–607). Trajan's reply is extant; he informed Pliny that no general rules about the treatment of Christians were possible, but he did provide guidelines for dealing with them:

> These people must not be hunted out; if they are brought before you and the charge against them is proved, they must be punished, but in the case of anyone who denies that he is a Christian, and makes it clear that he is not by offering prayers to our gods, he is to be pardoned as a result of his repentance however suspect his past conduct may be. But the pamphlets circulated anonymously must play no part in any accusation.
>
> (Pliny 1963; *Epistula* 10.97)

Trajan's pronouncements are hardly rabid;[6] Christians were not to be hunted out, nor anonymous accusations entertained. The attitude he enunciated operated to some extent throughout the second century as Lucian's sketch of Christians openly coming and going testified. Contemporaries knew so well that Christians suffered and died not because they witnessed multitudes swept up and executed, but rather because this was how Christians presented themselves. Christian suffering was the message encoded in nearly all of the Christian representation of the period.

It is time to recognize and appreciate the extraordinary Christian effort to produce a particular discursive subject through their representations. The reason pagans knew Christians were willing, even at times eager, to suffer and die – the response of one martyr at hearing his death sentence, "this we long for, this we desire," is typical – was because this was the message Christianity was sending (ACM Justin 4.6). Christian discourse in the early empire worked to construct a particular subject, a particular self-understanding: namely, the Christian as sufferer.

Christian texts of the late first and second centuries almost without exception assiduously project the message that to be a Christian was to suffer and die. The epistle of Barnabas, for example, defined a human as "earth that suffers" (6.9)[7] and quoted Jesus' words "those who will see me and attain to my kingdom must lay hold of me through pain and suffering" (7.11). Irenaeus defined the Christian life, "all those on whom the Spirit of God should rest . . . should suffer persecution and be stoned and slain" (*Adversus Haereses* 2.22). Polycarp counseled the Philippians to be imitators of Christ's suffering, to follow the example of the martyrs and "not to love the present world" (*Epistula ad Philippenses* 9.1). Clement called upon his fellow Christians "to forsake our sojourning in this world and to do the will of him who called" (Lake 1917: II; Clement 5.1). Tertullian describes Christians as "a race ready for death" and a Christian's behavior: "If he is denounced, he glories in it . . . when he is condemned, he renders thanks" (*Apologia* 1.12). Contemporaries knew that Christians belonged to a sect whose members suffered and died because that was how the sect defined and presented itself.

Once it is perceived, the extent of the Christian effort to offer itself as a community of sufferers is impressive. Narratives script reality for readers and Christian texts were inscribing one particular narrative pattern over and over for their readers and listeners. Christian narratives consistently offered a new literary happy ending for readers – death; in particular, the martyr's death. Narratives describing martyrs' deaths were prized during the period and were passed widely between Christian communities. These *Acts of the Martyrs* often took the form of letters. The persecution and death of martyrs in Lyons, for example, was described in a letter from the Christian community in that city to the communities in Asia and Phrygia. Polycarp's martyrdom was described in a letter from the church in Smyrna to the church of Philomelium; a postscript revealed that it passed among other Christian communities. Within fifty years, the letters of Ignatius of Antioch written on his journey to martyrdom in Rome had circulated to Gaul. Obviously texts that described Christian suffering and death were treasured and promulgated; at the same time they worked to offer their Christian audience a particular self-understanding. These martyr texts, all of which end with their heroes' deaths, carefully scripted a narrative path for Christians, a path that without exception ended in premature and welcome death. Lucian's description of Peregrinus as the focus and center of his Christian community embodied the place and role of the martyr in this period. Within the context of Christian representation the martyrs were cultural performers acting out dramatically the community's beliefs that to be a Christian was to suffer and die. Texts recounting such deaths were passed around widely from community to community as Christians internalized how to perform themselves as subjects.

Christian fiction helped to construct this same subjectivity – the Christian as sufferer. The *Apocryphal Acts of the Apostles*, extant examples of Christian fiction, were written in the second and early third centuries and appealed to widely separated groups of Christian readers. Their quick translation into a number of languages and their circulation attest to their popularity. The individual *Acts* differ from one another in doctrine and emphasis, but in certain respects they show a close coincidence of plot and theme (Pervo 1987, 1994). The *Acts of John, Peter, Paul, Andrew* and *Thomas* were likely composed in Greece, Asia Minor and Syria. Each treated the actions of an apostle: his preaching, especially on sexual continence, the problems this preaching caused between women converts and their husbands or lovers, the apostle's persecution by the rejected male, and finally, the death of the apostle.

The *Acts* are so closely related in these aspects of their theme and development that mutual dependency has been suggested (Klign 1962: 22–23), but this similarity may simply reflect the interests of their intended audiences. One need only look to contemporary popular literature to appreciate the demand for and popularity of formula stories.

These *Acts* provide an access into the values and assumptions of ordinary Christians of the second century. For literature, although fictive, is not remote from its readers' social concerns. Rather, in one sense, it can be understood as the "displacement of social problems into an imaginary realm" (White 1980: 366). Popular literature especially helps to uncover the social assumptions of its audience. For it is the medium, modern theorists attest, that "assiduously avoids disappointing its readers' expectations," that strives "to reaffirm the validity of the strategies and conventions that they, as readers, have for making meaning of the world" (Radway 1978: 96).

A reading of the *Apocryphal Acts* indicates that certain Christians made sense of their world by denying traditional social *nexus*. The

Acts were rigorously anti-social, unremittingly opting for the dissolution of social categories and relationships. The goal, death, that
they presented as a transcendence of human society was, in effect,
a repudiation of their contemporary society (Brown 1988: 1–64).
The anti-social bias of the *Acts* emerges from a comparison of their
endings with the typical conclusions of the Greek romances with
which they are contemporary and thematically related (Söder
1932). Greek romances traditionally concluded with a marriage, or
a reunion of a married couple. Chariton introducing the last book
of his romance, anticipated his readers' desires:

> And I think this last chapter will prove very agreeable to its
> readers: it cleanses away the grim events of the earlier ones.
> There will be no more pirates or slavery or lawsuits or fighting
> or suicide or wars or conquests; now there will be lawful love
> and sanctioned marriage.
>
> (8.1.1)[8]

Marriage provided the conventional literary happy ending. The
audience's reaction to this end, "this should be," while sounding
like a moral judgement is, as Northrop Frye points out, a social one
(Frye 1957: 167).[9] Marriage as a resolution pleases audiences
because it displays the protagonists reintegrated into their society;
it is a social judgement reaffirming the worth of human society,
both its present and its anticipated future.

Death, the denouement of each of the *Apocryphal Acts*, also has
social relevance. Especially because the *Acts* insisted that premature
death, rather than to be avoided, provided a longed-for goal. Thomas
explained this to those present at his death: "If I wished not to die,
[you know] that I am able. But this apparent death is not death, but
deliverance . . ." (Hennecke and Schneemelcher 1991: 402).[10]
Divine sanction was given to the martyr's espousal of death, for
example in the *quo vadis* episode that appeared in both the *Acts of
Peter* and *Acts of Paul*. In the *Acts of Peter*, the apostle, warned he is
to be arrested, fled Rome. He encountered Christ entering the city
and asked: "Lord, whither (goes thou) here?" And the Lord said to
him, "I am coming to Rome to be crucified . . ." and Peter came to
himself; and he saw the Lord ascending to heaven; then he returned
to Rome rejoicing and giving praise to the Lord" (314).

Escape from life was presented as a central element in the
Christian teaching presented in the *Acts*. So Andrew was incensed
to learn that his followers had sought his release:

O the great dullness of those instructed by me! O the cloud that overshadows you after so many mysteries. O how much we have spoken to you even till now, and yet have not persuaded our own. What is the great love towards the flesh . . . ?

(150)

Nor was a martyr's death reserved for apostles; Andrew asserted that it was the reward "for all loving, trusting and who confess him [the Lord]" (133).

The apostles' converts in the *Acts* quickly assimilated these teachings. Mygdonia, Thomas' royal convert, was depicted immediately after conversion. "Ashes and sack cloth were spread under her, and she was praying that . . . she depart quickly from life" (392). She voiced her yearning to her nurse: "May the remaining days of my life be cut short for me . . . and may I depart from life, that I may go the more quickly and see the beautiful one whose fame I have heard" (390). An audience of Christians sharing similar transcendent aspirations would presumably have greeted the apostles' death, consummating each of the *Acts* with a satisfied "this should be." And the approbation of this ending, just as it was in the Greek romances, was a social judgement. It disclosed an audience approving their hero's dissociation from human society, his rejection of its immanent worth.

The explanation offered in the *Acts* for the apostles' persecution affirms this social interpretation, for, as is usual in texts bearing social messages, this reiterates the theme of social disruption. The apostles were not persecuted for overtly religious, legal or political reasons, but because their teaching had interrupted the taken-for-granted societal relations between men and women. In each case the apostle's call for sexual continence caused his persecution. The unsettling effect of this teaching is described in the *Acts of Peter*:

And many other women besides fell in love with the doctrine of purity and separated from their husbands, and men too ceased to sleep with their own wives, since they wished to worship God in sobriety and purity. So there was the greatest disquiet in Rome.

(313)

The doctrine of continence was emphasized in all the *Acts*. Paul, for example, preached that there was no resurrection except for the chaste, and he introduced new beatitudes:

27

Blessed are they who have kept the flesh pure, for they
  shall become a temple of God
Blessed are the continent for to them God will speak
Blessed are they who have wives as if they had them not
  for they shall inherit God

(239)

This Christian message offered in the *Acts* was inherently
disruptive to previously accepted relations between husbands
and wives. The characterization of the non-Christian men made it
plain that this denial of sex was, in no sense, a personal matter,
but the consequence of the new Christian social patterns. For the
women converts rejected loving husbands. Affection and a sense
of connubial loss were expressed in Aegeates' plea to his wife:

> Your parents, Maximilla, counting me worthy of living with
> you, . . ." If you were the person you were of old, living
> with me in the manner we know, sleeping with me, having
> intercourse, bearing my children, I would treat you well in
> every way, and yet more, I will set free the stranger whom
> I hold in prison. But if you are not willing, to you indeed I
> would do no harm, nor can I, but through him, whom you
> love especially, more than me, I will torment you.

(144–145)

Andrew insisted that Maximilla reject this human love out of hand,
that she refuse her husband's call to, in Andrew's terms, "a loath-
some and unclean way of life." He knew this advice would result
in his death: "Tomorrow Aegeates will hand me over to be crucified
. . . For Maximilla the handmaid of the Lord will enrage the enemy
in him . . . by not putting her hand to ways that are alien to her"
(146). Through the trope of the marriage union, the *Acts* illustrated
a Christian rejection of contemporary social structure and the
outrage this engendered.[11] That this rejection involved a confrontation of conflicting world-views appears clearly, for example, in the
defense Charisius mounted against Thomas' preaching. He was
dismayed by his wife's response to Thomas' call to abstain from
"[horrid intercourse and the couch of uncleanness] whose outcome
is eternal condemnation" (372). He insisted to his wife that the
apostle's message perverted accepted social mandates: "why wilt
thou not dine with me and perhaps not sleep with me as usual
. . . what nature requires and deity ordains he overthrows" (376).

28

Postulating from his belief system Charisius adamantly insisted right was on his side and he threatened Thomas:

> If you persuade her not [to return] I will both slay these and finally take myself out of life. And if, as thou sayest, after [our release from life here] there is yonder life and death, and also condemnation and victory and a tribunal, I too will go in there to be judged with thee. And if the God whom thou dost preach is just, and awards the punishments justly, I know that I shall obtain justice.
>
> (390)

The disjunction of two belief systems is clearly delineated. What Charisius held as natural and divinely ordained, Thomas rejected as polluted. Nor could Charisius even conceive that Thomas' beliefs would make sense to any just arbitrator. The *Acts* offered a social setting inherently friction-filled, with two world-views coexisting in conflict.

Comparison with the Greek romances again reveals the social ramifications of this view of chastity. Chastity was also a theme in the romances, but sex was not totally prohibited, merely reserved for its legitimized function within marriage. This conception of chastity merely reinforced the social structure, insuring the proper classification of future participants. The treatment of chastity in the *Acts* was antithetical to this; by advocating universal chastity, they implicitly proposed an end to the social structure. Total sexual continence necessarily entails the death of ongoing social life. The depreciation of children in the *Acts* acted as a corollary to this view. John portrayed children as a temptation for sinning: "Do not think if children come to you you can rest in them and do not try for their sakes to rob and swindle" (117). In the *Acts of Thomas* the Lord himself advised Christians to avoid having children. "If you abandon this filthy intercourse you become holy temples, pure and free from afflictions and pains . . . But if you get many children then for their sakes you become robbers and avaricious" (344). Children were depicted as the source of much unhappiness:

> For the majority of children become unprofitable, possessed by demons, . . . lunatic or half withered or crippled or deaf or dumb or paralytic or stupid. Even if they are healthy, again will they be unserviceable; performing useless and abominable deeds.
>
> (344)

Such an attitude reflected a certain disregard for continuing human society. The *Apocryphal Acts*, like the *Martyr Acts,* encoded for Christians a "happy ending" that entailed death that was both personal and social and scripted as ideal for Christians a life centered on death and suffering.

And there is evidence that ordinary Christians identified with this role scripted by their representations. The narrative patterns provided in texts such as the *Martyr Acts* and *The Apocryphal Acts* offered patterns of action which some Christians embraced even without external compulsion. This may explain the examples of "voluntary" or at least "self-assisted" martyrdoms in second-century *Acts* of the martyrs (De Ste. Croix 1963: 21–23). In the persecution motivating Justin's *Second Apology*, for example, three martyrs were involved. One man, Ptolemy, was arrested on the accusation of a husband angered at the conversion of his wife. In court, another Christian, Lucius, brought official attention upon himself by loudly objecting to Ptolemy's death sentence, whereupon he also was sentenced to die (a sentence he received with gratitude, II *Apologia* 2.19). The narrative described another martyr: "a third man also came forward and was sentenced to be punished" (II *Apologia* 2.20). In two of these three martyrdoms, the victims called official attention to themselves.

Other texts of the period also showed Christians seeking to fulfill their role as sufferers. The *Acts of Polycarp* described a Phrygian, Quintus, "who turned cowardly when he saw the animals" (ACM 4). The narrator offered him as an example against voluntary martyrdom, for he was "the one who had given himself up and had forced some others to give themselves up voluntarily" (ACM 4.).[12] Two of the martyrs whose actions won the narrator's special approbation in the *Acts of Lyons and Vienne* had also contributed to their martyrdoms. Vettius Apagathus, like Lucius, rebuked the prefect for his treatment of Christians and was himself then condemned (ACM 1.10). Another Christian, Alexander, was described as standing during the trial "in front of the tribunal and by his attitude urged the Christians to make confession" (ACM 1.49). This so annoyed the crowd that Alexander was also called up, tried and convicted. The example of martyrs motivated others to share their fate. Agathonice in the *Acts of Carpus, Papylus and Agathonice* when she watched Carpus martyred, "suddenly saw the glory of God . . . and taking off her cloak threw herself upon the stake" (ACM: A 42–44). In the *Passion of Perpetua*, it is learned from Perpetua's offhand comment that Saturus, a leader of the Christian group, was also a voluntary martyr. Perpetua, in a dream, saw him climbing a ladder: "and Saturus was the first to go up, he who was later to give himself up of his own accord" (ACM 4.5). Clearly some Christians did understand their membership in the Christian community to entail their seeking death. Not all martyrs were voluntary. But Christian texts with their representation of death as the desired and happy ending obviously had an effect on Christian praxis. Justin felt it necessary to explain why a Christian in support of his beliefs could not just go out and commit suicide (II *Apologia* 4), but Tertullian described a code that facilitated martyrdoms: "If he [a Christian] is denounced, he glories in it, if he is accused, he does not defend himself, when he is questioned, he confesses without any pressure, when he is condemned, he renders thanks" (*Apologia* 1.12). These thanks ring through the *Acts*. *Deo gratias agimus*, the Scillitan martyrs returned at their sentencing (ACM 15). Felicitas's great grief (*magno luctu*) at postponing her opportunity for martyrdom because of pregnancy was as typical as Perpetua's remark that only her non-Christian father "would be unhappy to see me suffer" (ACM 15.2, 5.6).[13] Christian texts were representing a new goal of human desire, namely, death – and a new subjectivity to accompany this – the self as sufferer. And this repeated representation and its enactment had an effect. As pagan testimony showed, pagans equated Christianity with death and pain.

Besides the narratives of the *Martyr Acts* and *Apocryphal Acts*, Christians also represented themselves as sufferers in a different genre. In the second century there were a spate of Christian *Apologies* (Grant 1988). These were formal defenses of Christianity often combined with appeals to those having power (the Senate or emperors) to cease persecuting this innocent community of Christians. Second-century apologies written by Justin, Tertullian, Athenagoras, and Melito are extant, and considerable debate remains over the actual use of these documents. Did they ever reach their designated recipients? Were they really written for their addressees or primarily for internal consumption? Whatever answers are proposed for these questions, one function of these *Apologies* can be clearly glimpsed. They depicted Christians as a persecuted community, a community threatened with suffering and death. At the same time as the writers of apologies made their case for Christianity, they reinforced the image of the church as a persecuted group. The necessity for an apology would seem to presume persecution. An apology did not necessarily, however, imply a widespread persecution, as demonstrated by the occasion of Justin's *Second Apology* (the death of three Christians, two of whom were essentially voluntary). Christian apologies were another means by which Christianity represented itself as a community of the persecuted and suffering.

This survey of pagan and Christian sources demonstrated that early Christian narrative offered a particular self-understanding for Christians – the self as sufferer. The existence of "voluntary" martyrs showed the effect this image had in the actual lives of some community members. The importance and prestige of martyrs and those awaiting martyrdom suggest martyrdom's function as a social ritual in the Christian community. Elaine Pagels noticed how little animosity was directed at persecutors during the period; vehement Christian denunciation was aimed rather at those questioning the worth of martyrdom (Pagels 1980: I.268). Within Christian society, it may be suggested, persecution itself was less threatening than a challenge to martyrdom, the absolute legitimation of the Christian ethos embodied in so much of Christian representation that to be a Christian was to suffer. Rituals are the means by which groups send collective messages to themselves, supporting their social fabric and legitimating their world-view. Clifford Geertz describes them as "models not only of what a people believe, but models for the believing of it" (Geertz 1972: 167). Martyrdom as a ritual fits this description extraordinarily well. Witnessing a martyrdom either in person or by report not only affirmed the Christian world-view that to be a Christian was to suffer, but also added another instance.

In martyrdom, Christians could see vindicated the triumphant worth of suffering. Martyrs were conventionally described in second-century Christian documents as heroic athletes, warriors, victors. Martyrs' struggles were described as being not with persecutors, but with the devil over whom they triumph through pain and suffering. Thus Sanctus, in the *Acts of Lyons*, was depicted: "being all one bruise and wound, stretched and distorted out of any recognizable shape, but Christ suffering in him achieved great glory overwhelming the Adversary" (ACM 1.23.19). Perpetua likewise realized: "it would not be with wild animals I would fight, but with the devil, but I knew I would win the victory" (ACM 10.14). Her victory would, of course, be gained by dying. Christians could see reestablished over and over in the ritual of martyrdom their central beliefs that to be a Christian was to suffer, and that suffering itself was potent.

The recognition of this Christian ethos, and the social necessity that it be established over and over again, permits a clearer understanding of certain elements in second-century Christian society. For example, Ignatius of Antioch has often been dismissed as "abnormal" or "pathological" in Ste. Croix's terms (De Ste. Croix 1963: 23), or as "bordering on mania" in Frend's words (Frend 1965: 197). Within his Christian context, however, a cultural interpretation seems preferable to a psychological one (see Chapter 6).

Ignatius and the voluntary martyrs should be considered as no more abnormal than Plains Indian boys who, on ritual vision quests, inflicted tortures upon themselves. Victor Turner interpreted such behavior: "A normal man acts abnormally because he is obedient to tribal tradition, not out of disobedience to it. He does not evade, but fulfills his duties as a citizen" (Turner 1972: 342). So it is with Ignatius who obviously understood martyrdom as the fulfillment of his Christian duty. His goal was above all to attain to God, and for him this clearly entailed martyrdom. Ignatius begged the Romans:

> suffer me to be eaten by the beasts, through whom I can attain to God. I am God's wheat and I am ground by the teeth of wild beasts that I may be found the pure bread of Christ . . . Then shall I be truly a disciple of Jesus Christ, when the world shall not see my body . . . If I suffer I shall be Jesus Christ's freedman.
>
> (*Ad Romanos* 4.1–3)

For Ignatius, martyrdom was the means of being a perfect Christian.

Should Ignatius' behavior be held deviant in a social context which included Saturninus, who, when the Carthaginian martyrs were discussing their desire for martyrdom and the beasts they would choose to die by, "insisted he wanted to be exposed to all the different beasts that his crown might be all the more glorious" (ACM, *Perpetua and Felicitas* 19.2)? Or Germanicus, described in the *Acts of Polycarp*: "dragging the beast on top of him intending to be freed all the more quickly from this unjust and lawless life" (ACM 3.1). Within the Christian thought-world, none of these men were abnormal; in fact, their aspirations were not only normal but normative.

Martyrdom's ritual nature explains many features described in the *Acts,* such as the ready experience of pain. Painful experiences – circumcisions, nose-piercings, scourgings, various tests – are often associated with initiation rituals. Pain was bearable in these circumstances because it is understood to be a requisite of the initiation experience. That is to say, the initiate's *nomos,* his thought-world, comprehended and made meaningful the pain, and, therefore, made it bearable. Felicitas clearly expressed the difference between nomic and anomic pain in her reply to the guard taunting her during childbirth in the *Acts of Perpetua*:

> "You suffer so much now, what will you do when you are tossed to the beasts?" . . . "What I am suffering now," she replied, "I suffer by myself. But then another will be inside me who will suffer for me as I will be suffering for him."
>
> (ACM 15.5–6)

Other similarities with cross-cultural rituals appear in the acts: trance-like states (Perpetua is depicted in a trance; the martyrs with Polycarp are described removed from their bodies); a sense of bisexuality (Perpetua, in a dream, sees herself transformed into a man); the notion of being ground down and fashioned anew (Ignatius and Irenaeus); the acquisition of special, secret knowledge (Ignatius says his being in chains permitted him to understand heavenly things, the place of angels and principalities, things seen and unseen) (Turner 1969: 341, 343; 1972: 95, 171). Most significantly, the ritual of martyrdom functioned as rituals do cross-culturally, effecting a strengthening of the social fabric. Thus the writer of the *Acts of Lyons* described martyrdoms' effect upon his community (remember that in Christianity's reversed rhetoric "life" in this passage means "death" and thus eternal life):

> Life was what they asked for and he gave it to them and this they shared with their neighbor when they went off completely victorious to God. Peace they always loved and it was peace they commended to us forever. In peace they departed to God, leaving no pain for their mother, no strife, no conflict for their brother, but rather joy, peace, harmony and love.
>
> (ACM 2.7.7–11)

Martyrs affirmed their community's self-understanding that to be a Christian was to suffer. And it was this representation that

Christian documents projected and that, as pagan testimony has shown, was reaching the wider community.

Christian sources insisted that this perception of Christians as sufferers won adherents for them. Modern commentators have doubted the credibility of this testimony (Lane Fox 1987: 441; MacMullen 1984: 29–30). Early Christian sources were, however, emphatic about the power of persecution in attracting converts. Tertullian's testimony is well-known:

> But nothing whatever is accomplished by your cruelties, each more exquisite than the last. It is the bait that wins men to our school. We multiply whenever we are mown down by you; the blood of Christians is seed . . . That very "obstinacy" with which you taunt us, is your teacher. For who that beholds it is not stirred to inquire, what lies within it? Who, on inquiry, does not join us, and joining us does not wish to suffer, that he may purchase for himself the whole grace of God . . . ?
>
> (*Apologia* 50)

The Letter to Diognetus supported Tertullian: "Christians when punished day by day increase more" (6). Justin similarly described the positive benefits of persecution:

> although we are beheaded and crucified, and exposed to wild beasts and chains and flames, and every other means of torture, it is evident that we will not retract our profession of faith; the more we are persecuted, the more do others in ever increasing numbers embrace the faith and become worshipers of God through the name of Jesus.
>
> (*Dialogus cum Tryphone* 110)

Modern commentators' rejection of this testimony seems to beg the question of why this reasoning, which its proponents expressed in graphic terms emphasizing the pains of Christian commitment, appeared legitimate to the Christians of the period. Christian narratives, moreover, testify to a genuine confidence in the efficacy of persecution in attracting members with their repeated representation of their group as a sect of sufferers.

One of the very few actual accounts of an early Christian conversion experience supported contemporary testimony for the seminal role of martyrdoms in inducing conversions. In his *Second Apology*, Justin explained how witnessing the sufferings of martyrs affected his own thinking on the Christian sect:

Indeed, when I myself revelled in the teachings of Plato, and
heard the Christians misrepresented and watched them stand
fearless in the face of death and of every other thing that was
considered dreadful, I realized the impossibility of their living
in sinful pleasure.

(12)[14]

Attracted by his impressions of the suffering Christians, Justin
followed the pattern described by Tertullian; he inquired, and on
inquiry, joined; and joining, eventually suffered himself. In this
passage Justin is quite clear about what it was that affected him –
Christian fearlessness in the face of pain and death. The martyrs'
actions proved to Justin that Christians were not libertine lovers
of pleasure, but, like philosophers, were controlled in the face of
suffering.

Justin's statement located the impetus for his conversion in his
observation of martyrs' actions. There is, however, a complication
that has called Justin's explanation in this passage into question. In
his *Dialogue with Trypho*, Justin gave what has been interpreted as
a different account of his conversion (MacMullen 1984: 30–31;
Skarsaune 1976). In the *Dialogue*, Justin described himself, like so
many young men of the period, going from one philosophical
school to another until he finally ended up undergoing instruction
by an eminent Platonist: "Under him I forged ahead in philosophy
and day by day I improved" (2). In the course of his instruction,
Justin finally reaches the point "that I fully expected immediately
to gaze upon God, for this is the goal of Plato's philosophy" (2).
At this moment, however, Justin encountered an old man in a
secluded seaside retreat, and the two engaged in a philosophical
discussion. The old man led Justin to the recognition that the
Platonic philosophy he cherished did not, in fact, grasp truth. Justin
then asked plaintively: "'If these philosophers,' I asked, 'do not
know the truth, what teacher or method shall one follow?'" (7).
The old man then introduced Justin to the Hebrew prophets:
"They alone knew the truth and communicated it to men, whom
they neither deferred to or feared." (7) After this, the old man
went away, but his effect on Justin was immediate and life-altering:

But my spirit was immediately set on fire, and an affection
for the prophets, and for those who are the friends of Christ,
took hold of me; while pondering on his words, I discovered
that his was the only sure and useful philosophy.

(8)

In this passage Justin traced his conversion to his philosophical discussion with the old man and his affection for the prophets and the "friends of Christ." He made no mention of the influence of martyrs' actions. Justin's two accounts, however, are not necessarily at odds. In the *Dialogue*, Justin explained that his soul was kindled by what he heard about the prophets and the friends of Christ. He left unstated precisely what it was about these men that moved him toward this new "philosophy." Oskar Skarsaune suggested that these "friends of Christ" were the martyrs and the motive for conversion given in *Second Apology* 12 is not completely absent from *Dialogue* 8 (Skarsaune 1976: 58 n. 16). The close juxtaposition of the "friends of Christ" with the prophets in the *Dialogue* makes their identification with the martyrs plausible. Later in the *Dialogue*, Justin explained what the prophet exemplified for him:

> Unless, therefore you . . . apply yourself with such persistence and intelligence to the words of the prophets that you suffer the same indignities from the hands of your people as the prophets did, you cannot derive any benefit from the prophetic writings.
>
> (112)

What Justin took as important in the prophetic writings was a call to suffering. What had set his heart on fire in the *Dialogue* closely resembled what he said had moved him in the example of the martyrs – the prophets' example of testimony in the face of suffering.

In other Christian writings of the period the prophets also stood as emblems of those suffering for their testimony. Irenaeus made the same connection between prophets and suffering in a context similar to Justin's. Irenaeus stated:

> wherefore the Church in every place, because of that love which she cherishes toward God, sends forward throughout all time a multitude of martyrs to the Father. . . . For the Church alone sustains those who suffer all sorts of punishments, and are put to death for the love they bear to God, and the confession of his Son; often weakened indeed, yet immediately increasing her members and becoming whole again. . . . Thus too [she passes through an experience] similar to the ancient prophets as the Lord declares: "For so persecuted they the prophets before you" in as much as she does suffer

persecution in new fashion while the self same spirit rests on her."

(*Adversus Haereses* 4.33.9)

Here, Irenaeus not only offered another example of the contemporary testimony on the efficacy of persecutions for conversions, but he also explicitly linked the martyrs' suffering to the example of the prophets, invoking the Lord's words, "For so persecuted they the prophets who were before you" (Matthew 5.12). Ignatius in his letters also connected the importance of the prophets to their suffering (*Ad Magnesios* 8.2). Justin's two accounts of his motivation for conversion are, after all, not so very different. In the *Second Apology*, he emphasized his observation of martyrs' enduring suffering as a motivation for his conversion. In the *Dialogue* he traced his conversion to his being introduced to the prophets and his desire for them and the "friends of Christ." Like martyrs, the prophets functioned in the Christian context as a "type" for suffering (Schoedel 1985, on *Ad Magnesios* 8.2). In both accounts Justin explained his conversion as based on the examples of suffering provided either by contemporary martyrs or Hebrew prophets. The exact motivations for Justin's conversion may still be obscure, but it seems clear they were somehow related to this example of suffering.

Justin's narrative purported to describe real events and must in some sense grow from his own biography. Even in fictional accounts, however, Christians chose to emphasize the importance of suffering in motivating conversions. Minucius Felix described in his *Octavius* the putative debate between two cultured Romans, Octavius Januarius and Caecilius Natilis, on Christianity. The result is Caecilius' conversion, but a modern reader misses much in the text's exposition of Christianity. As G. W. Clarke has commented: "Scarcely a mention of the Bible, no Christology, nothing of the Word, the Holy Spirit, the Trinity, the redemption (Christ is only mentioned in a paraphrase) no ecclesiology, nothing of the apostles, the ministry, the sacraments" (Clarke 1974: 30). What the *Octavius* did offer, however, is a use for suffering and a hope of immortality. In the *Octavius*, Caecilius mocked Christians, deriding their belief in immortality when their God does not "even protect them in the present life." Caecilius defined the Christian condition in terms of poverty, sickness and pain: "See how some part of you suffer want, toil, hunger; . . . [are] unnerved by danger, parched with fever, racked with pain."

A rebuttal by Octavius ended the debate and obviously secured Caecilius' conversion. Octavius did not reject Caecilius' appraisal of the human condition as precarious and racked by pain. Rather, he showed how within the Christian paradigm suffering functioned for good. For Christians "human and bodily infirmities [*corporis humana vitia*] are not a punishment but a militia, a school of discipline" (36.8). God did love Christians and could have helped them, but used infirmities to explore and test each one. Octavius described the pleasure God had at seeing Christians withstand suffering: "How fair a spectacle for God to see when a Christian stands face to face with pain"(37).

Carlin Barton, in her study *The Sorrow of the Ancient Romans*, has described the fascination in the late republic and early empire with imagery featuring human existence as a battle or gladiatorial contest and humans as soldiers or gladiators. Seneca frequently employed this imagery. Christianity borrowed from the same register to describe all human suffering, not simply that of persecution. In the mid-third century, Cyprian, bishop of Carthage, counseled Christians not to let loss of property, diseases, or the death of wife or children be stumbling blocks for them, but rather battles for "in the battle line the soldier is tested" (*De Mortalitate* 12). Like Minucius Felix, Cyprian called the great suffering caused by the plague training exercises, not deaths (*exercitia ... non funera*). In fact, it was exactly this attitude toward human pain that Cyprian saw as the defining quality of Christians. He explained:

> This finally is the difference between us and the others who do not know God, that they complain and murmur in adversity, while adversity does not turn us from the truth of virtue and faith, but proves us in suffering.
>
> (*De Mortalitate* 13)

Clement of Alexandria made explicit the Christian point of view. "Make your soul strong in the face of disease," he said. "Be of good courage like the man in the arena ... nobly confront toils rendering thanks to God" (*To the Newly Baptized*, in Clement of Alexandria 1919: 377). Christians had a use for adversity, for the sufferings of sickness, loss, or persecution, and could accept these within the context of their belief that to be a Christian was to suffer.

Tertullian, Justin, and Minucius Felix, as well as other Christian writers, gave Christian suffering a privileged position in explaining the impetus behind conversions. It is the privileging of this notion, rather than its validity as an explanation, that is of interest. For such Christian claims show what those making them granted authority to in their own conceptions of what would attract others to their community, and give access to their assumptions about what they thought was effective within their cultural context. That Christians granted authority to the function of suffering in attracting converts implies that suffering held a constitutive position in their own notions of Christianity – just as it did in all the Christian representation examined in this chapter.

⌊This survey of early Christian narrative representation has shown that it functioned to construct Christians as a community of sufferers, that it scripted subjects who embraced death and rejected conventional social life. Christian discourse relentlessly repeated this message and Christian subjects enacted it to the point that in the early centuries even pagan contemporaries who knew almost nothing about Christianity knew that Christians were sufferers. This knowledge marked the point where pagan and Christian cultural preoccupations met in their attention to suffering.⌋

2

MARRIAGES AS
HAPPY ENDINGS

With their projection of death as a happy ending and the social message this ending embodied, early Christian narratives offered a particular social script for inhabitants of the early empire. Around the same period that saw the rise of Christianity, there appeared a new Greek narrative genre, the romance, with very different endings and very different scripts. The appearance of the romance is a suggestive coincidence, [for the emergence of new forms or new subject matters in the aesthetic realm can both respond and contribute to cultural changes](Bender 1987: 7). The precise chronology of this genre's appearance is still not settled, but it is most likely datable to the first centuries B.C./A.D. All extant examples apparently come from the short span between the first and third centuries A.D. (Konstan 1994: 3). Until recently, much of the commentary on the romance has concerned itself with the form's literary genesis and derivation. My interest lies in a different direction; namely, to consider the purpose and effect of the prose romances in the lives of their authors and audiences. For overtly ideological narratives, written from an explicit perspective like the Christian *Acts*, are not the only texts to affect their readers' understanding of themselves and their world. All texts work in this way. As Stephen Greenblatt has said: ["there can be no expression without an origin and an object, a *from* and a *for*"] (Greenblatt 1988: 12). With this in mind, I examine two questions in this chapter, from where, i.e., from what perspective, does the Greek romance proceed and for what end.[1]

My answer to both these questions is closely tied to the centrality of marriage in the genre. Marriage is the conventional social happy ending; it is an affirmation of society and its future. In my reading, the Greek romance, like the lavish civic building programs of the

41

same period, are products of the ebullience of the urban elite of the Greek East. Through their building, their lavish public entertainments, and their romance, the elite in the early Roman period created and projected a sense of their society and their position in it. As Clifford Geertz explained:

> Subjectivity does not properly exist until it is . . . organized, art forms generate and regenerate the very subjectivity they pretend only to display. Quartets, still lifes, and cockfights are not merely reflections of a pre-existing sensibility analogically represented; they are positive agents in the creation and maintenance of such a sensibility.
>
> (Geertz 1973: 451)[2]

In romance we can glimpse one of the means through which the Greek urban elite in the early years of the Roman empire created and maintained their identity.

Only five of the so-called "ideal" Greek romances survive: those with plots focusing on a young couple's falling in love, their separation, travel, trials and tribulations, and their final reunion with its implicit promise of a life together happily ever after. Papyrus fragments testify to the existence of other romances, but how many of these were written and, of these, how many were of the "ideal" type, has not been established with any certainty. What the papyri do show, however, is that the romances had readers in Egypt and were read in the early empire. This is useful information, for antiquity has left little direct testimony on the genre. Egypt alone preserved substantive material evidence for the empire's reading habits, but it is unlikely that its Greek readers' literary tastes were unique. One can thus postulate on the basis of the papyri showing readers for the romances in Egypt that there were also readers for the romance in other parts of the Hellenistic world.

Because the romance appeared too late to be included among the canon of genres discussed by Aristotle or codified by the Alexandrian scholars, in the archaizing climate of the early empire, it was generally ignored by contemporary literary commentators (Bowie 1994: 442). Thus little information survived to show how contemporary readers perceived the romances. What little evidence there is suggests that they were not critically valued. Philostratus in the early third century may be referring to the romance writer when he dismissed a certain Chariton as a nobody whose words would not be remembered (*Epistle* 66). The emperor Julian in the mid-fourth century warned readers to avoid fictions posing as histories with love themes; he may be referring to romances (*Epistle* 63, 301b). The romance's focus on love has been a continuing problem for its critical reception. Many modern commentators have dismissed the genre for its perceived sentimentality and sensationalism and their judgements have influenced their conjectures about an audience for the romance. "Juveniles," "frivolous minded people," and "women" have been suggested as some typical readers.[3] Other commentators, who focused more on the themes of wandering, tribulation, and loving reunion, have suggested an audience composed of the same sorts of people, "attracted to Christianity and the mystery religions" (Hagg 1983: 90). All these suggestions about audiences assumed an audience for the romance that differed appreciably from that for other literary productions in the ancient world – less educated, perhaps, or more adrift.

Recent analyses of the texts, however, have challenged these assumptions. Ewen Bowie, for example, argued that the range of literary allusion and quotations, in both the extant romances and the fragments, pointed to educated authors who wrote for readers with the "ability to pick up the novelists' allusions to earlier literature and to respond to these allusions in the intended direction," that is, an educated audience similar to the audience for other literary works (Bowie 1994: 438). Susan Stephens' examination of the papyrological evidence supported Bowie's conclusions. Stephens noted that Christian manuscripts tended to look different both from the "standard works of high culture" and the writing of the "not-quite literate, or the inexperienced writer" (Stephens 1994: 412). They were written in what has been called "reformed documentary" style. This style bore similarities with that used in ordinary record keeping rather than reflecting either an elite education or professional training as a copyist. According to Stephens, papyrus fragments of the novel looked neither like Christian productions nor like the writings of inexperienced writers. Rather, with a few exceptions that suggested a more expensive or scholarly production, "they appear to have been competent, professionally copied books, indistinguishable from a run-of-the-mill copy of Demosthenes or Plato" (Stephens 1994: 413). The findings of both Bowie and Stephens indicated that romances were produced for very much the same group of people as other literary productions of the period. The people with money to purchase books, and the leisure and education to read them, belonged to the upper educated classes.[4]

A transhistorical examination of the genre further supports the supposition that the ancient romance, like other literary productions of the ancient world, was produced both for and from the perspective of the upper classes. Northrop Frye claimed that romance:

> is the nearest of all literary forms to wish-fulfillment dreams . . . in every age the ruling social or intellectual class tends to project its ideals in some form of romance, where the virtuous heroes and beautiful heroines represent the ideals and the villains the threats to their ascendancy.
>
> (Frye 1957: 186)

This description of the romance genre as an idealizing dream vision of the elite classes has particularly cogency for the ancient romance.[5] These works, focused on the testing and endurance of a social relationship, celebrate the revitalized social identity of the Greek urban elite and offer an ideal representation both of the bonds of contemporary social structures and of the individual's devotion to the social. An examination of the three romances that most straightforwardly reflect the "ideal" form with its restricted plot of love, separation, travel, tribulations, and final reunion – Chariton's *Chaereas and Callirhoe*, Xenophon's *Ephesian Tale*, and Achilles Tatius' *Leucippe and Clitophon* – demonstrates how romances embodied an elite idealized dream of society.[6]

Before turning to the details of the three romances, a brief overview of their action is helpful. Chariton's narrative is a historical romance set in fifth-century Syracuse; his heroine, Callirhoe, is the daughter of the historical general, Hermocrates, the victor over the Athenians (Hagg 1987). Early in the narrative Callirhoe falls in love and marries Chaereas. Her husband, however, tricked into a jealous rage, kicks and apparently kills her. Callirhoe is placed in her tomb, but revived just as tomb robbers enter it. These rough men take her together with the other buried riches and sail for Ionia. Here she is sold to the steward of the governor of Miletus, Dionysius. When Dionysius sees Callirhoe, he immediately falls in love with her. She agrees to marry him because she has discovered she is pregnant with Chaereas' child. Meanwhile Chaereas has learned Callirhoe is alive and has set out to find her. He is attacked and sold into slavery, almost crucified, but finally set free as part of the governor of Caria, Mithridates', attempt to win Callirhoe from Dionysius. The dispute between the two governors goes for settlement before the Great King of Persia, Artaxerxes. The king also immediately falls in love with Callirhoe when he sees her, but a revolt in Egypt distracts him. Chaereas joins the Egyptians and leads them to victory. He eventually captures the Great King's retinue which includes Callirhoe. The couple are reunited and sail back to Syracuse.

Xenophon's narrative is brief and rather simply composed, with little literary ornamentation.[7] The text bears so many similarities to Chariton's romance that dependence has been suggested (Papanikolaou 1964). Again, two young people, Habrocomes and Anthia, fall in love at a festival and are married. They set out on a sea voyage and are attacked by pirates and brought to Tyre. From that point on they run into all sorts of complications. Near the beginning of their tribulations, for example, the pirate chief's daughter, Manto, falls in love with Habrocomes and, when he spurns her, has him imprisoned and tortured. When Manto goes as a bride to Syria, she takes Anthia, who is now her slave, with her and hands her over as a concubine to a goatherd. Many further trials for both hero and heroine ensue in various geographical milieux; more pirates, shipwrecks, crucifixions, and burnings on pyres. Anthia endures a brothel, a rich Indian's caravan, a pit with savage dogs, among other adventures, but in the end the couple finally are reunited and return to Ephesus.

Achilles Tatius' romance is a more self-consciously literary production than either of the other two romances. For this reason it has been dated to a period in the mid-second century coinciding with the heightened interest in style and rhetoric associated with the second-sophistic (Konstan 1994: 4; Anderson 1993: 163). It also has a more overtly licentious focus than the other two romances and in places almost seems to play with the ideal romance conventions (Durham 1938; Fusillo 1988: 28). Nevertheless, Achilles Tatius retained all the conventional elements of romance. Again two young people, Leucippe and Clitophon, fall madly in love, but, in this case, they cannot marry. Clitophon has already been betrothed to someone else. Not letting this stop them, the two arrange to sleep together. Just as they are about to begin the act, however, Leucippe's mother interrupts them. The couple run away, are shipwrecked, and separated in Egypt. Twice in the narrative Leucippe is apparently killed by pirates. After mourning her the second time, Clitophon finally agrees to marry an Ephesian widow, Melite, but refuses to consummate the marriage until the couple have reached Ephesus. There, both Leucippe and Thersander, Melite's husband, turn up alive. Hearing that Leucippe has been murdered again, Clitophon overcome with sorrow and desiring death, confesses that he and Melite have killed her. He is sentenced to death. But Sostratos, Leucippe's father, appears and stops the death sentence. Leucippe and Melite are required to undergo chastity tests; both pass (Melite on a technicality, since she has slept with Clitophon). Finally Leucippe and Clitophon are married and sail back to Tyre, eventually to settle in Byzantium.

These romances filled with travel, adventure, and final union idealize social unity. They offered through their trope of the loving couple a dream of a social union able to endure and overcome every eventuality of fate or fortune. This interpretation of the romance as a celebration of social identity is, however, at odds with another reading of the genre that sees it reflecting the new isolation and quest for individual identity of the inhabitants of the Greek East whose traditional civic identity had been eroded beneath Roman hegemony.[8] This latter reading has cogency only if the centrality of marriage in the genre is ignored. As Brigitte Egger has aptly stated, "marriage is the social backbone of the romances" (Egger 1994: 260). Both Chariton and Xenophon began their narratives with marriage and ended them with a reunion and reconstitution of those marriages. In a structure more typical of later romances, Achilles Tatius concluded his narrative with a marriage; in fact, a double marriage. The romances are explicitly structured around marriage, the archetypal community celebration of social union. Marriage traditionally acts as the social ritual that affirms the basis upon which all other social structures depend. Narratives focused upon marriages show their interest in social structure, its integrity and future.

The emphasis on chastity in the romance, on maintaining a body free from penetration or mingling with anyone other than that particular person society has sanctioned through marriage, also indicates the social agenda for the genre. The goal of chastity, namely, to restrict the body to those socially approved and designated, is society's most overt manifestation of its power over both nature and its members. Chastity is the manifestation of society's power inserted into the very body of its subjects; it acts as the actual embodiment of social control. By focusing on marriage and chastity (even introducing a concern for male chastity), the romance not only reveals, but emphasizes, its concern for the social. The romance narrative focused on the social body at the same time that it focused on the body of the beloved. The discursive attention to bodily chastity in the three romances further indicates that they issued from a society particularly concerned with its social unity and boundaries. As Mary Douglas noted:

> the human body is always treated as an image of society ... Interest in apertures depends on the preoccupation with social exits and entrances ... If there is no concern to preserve social boundaries, I would not expect to find concern with bodily boundaries.
>
> (Douglas 1970 rpt 1980: 70)

Within Douglas's paradigm the romance's attention on bandits and foreigners, and their difference from, and threat to, the protagonists, can be read as defining and affirming social boundaries. That the romances represented these pirates and foreigners as obsessed with penetrating the bodies of the protagonists takes on metaphoric significance (Shaw 1984: 51). The prose romance, the narrative of persons bound together in love, separated, their fidelity proved in hardship, ending with the promise of ongoing harmony, served to manifest in the early empire the Greek elites' idealizing dream of their society and the social structures supporting and surrounding them.

The appearance of the romance coincided with the resurgence and flourishing of the Hellenistic cities under Roman rule. As Douglas Edwards argued in his discussion of Chariton's romance, the ascription of isolation to the inhabitants of the Greek cities in the eastern empire may misrepresent the reality of the period. Edwards drew upon Simon Price's analysis of how successfully Greek cities were able to integrate Roman rule into their own ideological structures. Edwards noted:

> In an important study S. R. F. Price has persuasively argued for an alternative model of life in the ancient Greco-Roman world, especially in the Greek cities of Asia Minor of the first and second centuries C.E. Many individuals during the early imperial period did not "feel adrift in a world they could not comprehend or control." In fact, Greek cities in Asia Minor provided an important locus of political, social, and religious identity for their inhabitants, a process that continued through the end of the third century.
>
> (Edwards 1987: 61; Price 1984: 15)

47

The increased prosperity of the Hellenic cities during this period, as well as their elite citizens' devotion to them, is well-attested (Macro 1980: 682–687). In fact, the lavish civic expenditures of the upper classes was one of the unparalleled features of the period. The wellborn and prominent vied with each other to ornament their cities with the trappings of civic prominence, with temples, theaters and festivals at their own expense. Cities emblazoned their confidence and pride on coins and monuments. In the middle of the second century A.D., Smyrna, for example, proclaimed itself "First in Asia in beauty and greatness: Glory of Ionia" (Macro 1980: 683).

Evidence shows that terms of kinship and affection were used in this period to express the kind of relationship holding between individuals and their cities. Benefactors spoke of giving to their "very dear country land," using the word *glykytatos*, "very sweet or dear," that occured in epitaphic expressions for a beloved spouse, e.g., "my very dear wife." Inscriptions in Lycia made reference to "to her ladyship [*kyria*], my hometown," employing the term *kyria*, that regularly connoted the "mistress" or "lady of the house" (Veyne 1990: 170 n. 122). In a similar fashion Aelius Aristides counseled citizens to become "lovers" of one another (*erastōn allēlois, Orations* 23.72) in the interest of social concord. It is within this context that the image of the married couple became invested with an aura of symbolic resonance. Paul Veyne pointed to a second-century Roman sarcophagus that displayed the three virtues of a Roman: clemency, piety, and concord. *Concordia*, the basis of all social ties, was represented by a marriage scene. This sarcophagus depicted the couple at the moment of their marriage joining hands in the presence of Venus and Cupid. This image was offered as an universalizing emblem for social harmony (Veyne 1987: 165). Putting the picture of his wife on coins proclaiming *concordia*, Marcus Aurelius invoked this same symbolic language. Peter Brown aptly described the symbolic weight of the married couple at this time:

> by the beginning of the late antique period ... the Roman ideal of marital concord had taken on a crystalline hardness: the married couple were presented less as a pair of equal lovers than as a reassuring microcosm of the social order.
>
> (Brown 1988: 16–17)

In the second century the married couple was employed as the image for the type of devotion and harmony holding between all members of a society. The ideal romance, with its narrative focus on the couple, can be read as having a similar subtext – a celebration of the social order as epitomized by the central couple's union preserved through every circumstance.

The narratives of Chariton and Xenophon explicitly marked the symbiotic relationship between the couple and the civic body. In both romances, the high-born couple met at a civic festival, another ritual, like marriage itself, that celebrated social cohesion. Both authors specifically informed their readers that the festival was a national event (*demōtēles* C 1.1.4; *epichōros* X I.2.2).[9] The deities depicted as being honored in the respective festivals also had particular civic significance. In Xenophon's *Ephesiaca*, Anthia and Habrocomes first caught sight of each other at a festival of Artemis. Ephesus was the pre-eminent city of Artemis, and her temple there was among the seven wonders of the world (Rogers 1990). By opening the romance at the festival of this goddess, the author paid homage to both the deity and her city. A festival honoring Aphrodite provided the occasion for the lovers' meeting in Chariton's romance – an appropriate deity to honor in a love story, but one not particularly associated with Syracuse, the setting for this historical novel. As Suzanne Said noted, "the shrine of Aphrodite is far from being the most important temple in a town famous for the temples of Apollo, Athena and Zeus Olympius" (Said 1993: 225). But as Douglas Edwards pointed out, by invoking Aphrodite here, Chariton saluted the goddess of his own city, Aphrodisias, rather than deities more properly associated with the historical setting of his story (Edwards 1987: 25–58). In the sentence that opened his narrative, Chariton had identified himself as a citizen of Aphrodisias. It was the goddess of his own city and her renowned temple that he honored in his narrative.

But while each of the goddesses invoked was relevant to a particular city, the narratives did not particularly stress parochial religious or civic interests. Both of these goddesses, Artemis and Aphrodite, had cults that attracted devotees from all over the Hellenic world. The romances were filled with numerous divinities in various civic manifestations and portrayed their protagonists as being able to find gods to worship wherever they found themselves. This was one of the ways through which the romances conveyed a sense of their protagonists at-homeness in the many Greek cities of the empire, rather than depicting, as some have suggested, individuals isolated in a large and fragmented world. At a certain level the romance reads almost as a genre celebrating geographical space, filled with place names, travel directions, and imbued with a basic cosmopolitanism (Konstan 1994: 228). It seems that these romances delighted in their continual references to changing cities and places (Morgan 1981).

Chariton's and Xenophon's couples met at city-wide festivals in honor of important civic goddesses, and both narratives stressed the support and role of the whole city in bringing about their marriages. Xenophon's narrative indeed framed the couple's meeting within a regular civic and divine concern for the supervision of marriages. The couple first saw each other at the festival when "it was customary to find husbands for the girls and wives for the young men" (X 1.2.3–4). All the girls at the festival towards this end "are dressed as if to receive a lover" (X 1.2.4).

Both narratives also exhibited what Hagg has described as a notable feature of the genre, "the introduction of the observing and commenting collective, such as the people of Ephesus (X 1.2, etc.), of Tyre (X 2.2.4), of Rhodes (X 1.12.1–3), etc." (Hagg 1971: 123). Xenophon showed the city crowds cheering when they saw the extraordinary beauty of Anthia and Habrocomes and shouting for their marriage: "What a marriage Habrocomes and Anthia would make" (1.2.9). They acted as if, as the narrative later did in fact describe Anthia and Habrocomes, they were "children held in common" (*paidōn koinōn* 1.10.5); words that suggest that the couple functioned as the children of the whole city. In Chariton, the civic population also had a crucial role in bringing about the marriage of Chaereas and Callirhoe. After Chaereas has seen Callirhoe and fallen deeply in love with her, he begins to waste away, sick with love. He finally decides to approach his father and explain his situation. But his father can give him little hope for a marriage with Callirhoe. He and Hermocrates, her father, are the two chief men in Syracuse and rivals. The narrative then describes how the city collectivity itself brings about the couple's marriage: "A regular assembly took place at this time. When the people took their seats, their first and only cry was: 'Noble Hermocrates, great general . . . The city pleads for the marriage, today, of a couple worthy of each other!' " (1.1.11).[10] Hermocrates finally consents to the marriage because, as the text explained, he is a lover of his fatherland (*philopatris* 1.1.12). With this phrase, Chariton explicitly links the marriage of Chaereas and Callirhoe to the well-being of the community.

Both romances described the marriages as community-wide celebrations. Xenophon depicted the public rejoicing: "already the revelry filled the city, there were garlands everywhere" (1.7.3); "there were all night celebrations and a feast of sacrifices to the god" (1.8.1). In Chariton's romance, the whole city had a role in the couple's marriage. Once Hermocrates gave his consent to the marriage:

> the whole meeting rushed from the theater; the young men went off to find Chaereas, the council and archons escorted Hermocrates, and the Syracusans' wives too went to his house to attend the bride. The sound of the marriage hymn pervaded the city, the streets were filled with garlands and torches, porches were wet with wine and perfume. The Syracusans celebrated this day even more joyously than the day of their victory.
>
> (1.1.12–13)

By this civic celebration of the marriage, the Syracusans demonstrated their belief that in fact marriage was as essential to the success and continued well-being of their city as had been their victory in battle over the Athenians. From the outset, the two romances represented the central couple's marriage as a concern of the whole population.

Although desire in the romances may initiate the action within them, this is quickly subsumed into a collective context. Marriage and a society's very existence were so intertwined in the discourse of the romance that Achilles Tatius metonymically used "marriages" to refer to a city itself. After Leucippe's mother scared off Clitophon who had entered her daughter's bedroom, she ironically lamented the absence of her husband "fighting for other men's marriages in Byzantium" (2.24.2). The marriages that opened the romances of Xenophon and Chariton, and the civic festivities associated with these, offer little support for reading the genre as appealing to a new sense of individualism and isolation in the period. Rather, both romances opened with an emphasis on the communal celebration of ongoing social unity exemplified in marriage. The couples did indeed fall in love as individuals, but the narratives stressed that, as individuals, they could have done little to further their love. Chaereas had to go to a public assembly for help in forwarding his suit, and Callirhoe played so little a role in achieving her desire that she did not even know whom she was to marry until Chaereas arrived in her chamber (1.1.14). Their fathers acted together to marry Anthia and Habrocomes because an oracle of Apollo had suggested that this was the god's will (1.7.2). In fact, the depictions of love in the two romances suggested that individual love, passion outside of social structures, functioned as a malady.

The representation of love as a sickness had a long history in Greek literature, but the depiction of love sickness in the romance took on a new emphasis according to Peter Toohey: for earlier periods "the dominant reaction to frustrated love in ancient literature was manic and frequently violent" (Toohey 1992: 266). Medea was the archetypal example of the violence of frustrated love. But in the romance, the couple's reaction to love was melancholic and essentially passive; they are shown literally wasting away from their frustrated desire. Habrocomes at first attempted to ward off Eros' assault. But Eros prevailed and Habrocomes' health declined and he moaned and wept until "his whole body had wasted away and his mind had given in" (1.5.5). Anthia similarly suffered: "both, then, lay ill; their condition was critical, and they were expected to die at any moment, unable to confess what was wrong" (1.5.9). The romance made absolutely clear that without the intervention of their fathers, Anthia and Habrocomes literally would have died of their love. In the romance, being separated was offered as either a sickness or a disaster. The cure was to be joined in a socially sanctioned union.[11]

As Xenophon's narrative attested, the day after Habrocomes and Anthia's marriage "they got up much happier, and much more cheerful, after fulfilling the desires they had for each other for so long" (X 1.10.1). The romance with its emphasis on love, brought to fulfillment through the city's or the fathers' actions, should be read as celebrating the saving efficacy of the social order rather than as celebrating the power of individual desire.

The social order celebrated in the romance quite explicitly displays an elite perspective. Providential design itself, the foundation of each of the narratives (indeed of ancient society), already embodied the quintessential elite myth – that things were the way they were meant to be. But the romance legitimated the prevailing social order and the elite's position in it even more directly through its near identification of the wellborn and the divine. Chariton, for example, continually equated Callirhoe, the daughter of the famous Syracusan general, Hermocrates, with Aphrodite or Artemis.[12] He introduced her first by emphasizing her affinity with Aphrodite and its basis – the maiden's extraordinary beauty: "her beauty was more than human it was divine, and it was not the beauty of a Nereid or a mountain nymph, but of the maiden [*parthena*] Aphrodite herself" (1.1.2). The girl's similarity with the goddess provided a constant theme in the narrative. When Dionysius, for example, first saw Callirhoe at the temple of Aphrodite, he mistook her for the goddess and prayed to her. He even chided his servant for addressing the woman as if she were mortal (C 2.3.5). At Callirhoe's marriage to Dionysius, the crowd shouted, "The bride is Aphrodite" (3.2.14). The wife of the Great King of Persia also thought of Aphrodite when she first saw Callirhoe (5.9.1). And her husband who should know – as the narrative informed us, "the barbarians consider him a god on earth" (6.7.12) – recognized the divinity of the girl's beauty: "this woman may indeed be a goddess – her beauty is super-human" (6.3.4–5). The narrative emphasized repeatedly that Callirhoe's beauty was the basis for her identification with the divine.

The same elision between the divine and human occurred in Xenophon. The narrative introduced Habrocomes by comparing him to a god; the city crowds actually prostrated themselves before him and prayed (1.1.3.). Anthia's beauty also caused her to be mistaken for a divinity: "often as they saw her in the sacred enclosure the Ephesians would worship her as Artemis" (1.2.7). In the thought-world of the romance and indeed of the ancient world in general, this beauty, the basis for the protagonists' identification with divinity, simply stood as an outward manifestation of the protagonists' high birth. Dionysius explicitly made this connection between beauty and high birth. And the narrative framed his testimony to give it credence. In the romance, Chariton depicted Dionysius as the epitome of the wellborn, educated, cultured Greek. Brigitte Egger noted that, rather excessively, Chariton referred to Dionysius's excellent *paideia* ten times in the text and called him cultured on three other occasions (Egger 1990: 193). This man steeped in Greek culture was offered as the spokesperson for the correlation between divinity, beauty, and good breeding that was taken as axiomatic in the text. He originally dismissed reports of Callirhoe's beauty on the grounds of her servile position:

> for he was a true aristocrat, pre-eminent in rank and in culture throughout Ionia . . . "Leonas," he said, "a person not free-born cannot be beautiful. Don't you know that the poets say

beautiful people are the children of gods? All the more reason for their human parents to be nobly born [*eugenon*]."

(2.1.5)

Statira, the Persian queen, revealed a related cultural assumption that beauty equaled good character when she thanked Chaereas for having returned her safely to her husband, the Great King: "you have shown a good character, worthy of your beauty" (8.3.14). In Achilles Tatius's narrative, beauty was similarly offered as a mark of high birth; Melite recognized Leucippe's status: "Even in fallen circumstances your beauty proclaims that you are wellborn" (5.17.4). In the society fashioned in these romances, nobility was innate, a factor of birth, and confirmed by the beauty of the well-born. Chariton collapsed all these intertwined concepts of beauty, high birth, and innate right to authority into one simile, comparing Callirhoe to a queen bee. This simile serves to disclose the ordering assumptions of his elite society: "then you could see that royalty is born in people naturally, as is the case of the queen bee in the swarm, for everybody followed Callirhoe spontaneously, as though she had been elected queen for her beauty" (2.3.10). An assumption underlying these romance narratives (*Chaereas and Callirhoe*, *An Ephesian Tale*, and *Leucippe and Clitophon*) was that the elite were born to beauty and privilege. These three Greek romances provide particularly apt illustrations of Frye's description of the genre as a projection of ruling-class ideals.

These romances that exhibited a vision of the affinity of the well-born with the divine and their innate authority functioned as part of the Hellenic elite society's "veil of power." Richard Gordon used this term to describe the social and political functions of ancient religion. According to Gordon, ancient religion modeled the structures of "reciprocity between unequals; providential beneficence; changelessness" and functioned to make the relationship between the elite and others appear normal both to the elites themselves and to everyone else (Gordon 1990: 229). Gordon was careful to point out that the elites did not intentionally use institutions like religion to "mask" the real power relations operating in a society as part of some overt attempt to deceive the other orders. Rather, in societies, ideology in all its various formations creates an "unconscious veil distorting the image of social reality within a class and sublimating its interest basis" even to those benefiting most (Gordon 1990: 192, quoting Merquior 1979: 24–34). The pervasive and

54

casual assumption in the romance narratives of the innate superiority of the wellborn discloses the working of such a "veil of power." The rhetoric of the romance offered the wellborn as just naturally deserving of their place as the focus of the community, and deserving of the community's goods.

A repeated plot element in the romances served to inculcate this sense of the elite's innate right to prosperity and well-being and to veil the material reality affecting most non-elite inhabitants of the early empire. This was the romance projection of what Max Weber has called the "theodicy of good fortune," the contention that the elite deserved to be exactly where they were in society (Gordon 1990: 238). The romances opened with descriptions of the ostentatious riches enjoyed by the protagonists (Schmeling 1980: 30). Most ancient literature depicted the lives of the wealthy, so this is perhaps hardly surprising. What is more interesting is how the romances repeatedly showed their protagonists regaining their riches and status with regular, if astonishing, ease, no matter what disasters struck them. Shipwrecked, cast up on strange lands, captured by pirates, romance heroes and heroines had only a short climb back to a life of luxury. This is an unlikely scenario in any period, but particularly in the ancient world (MacMullen 1988: 77). The romance, by repeatedly representing its wellborn characters almost effortlessly regaining high status and riches, affirmed that those in high places deserve to be precisely where they are, and veiled the harsh realities that kept the majority of people from enjoying a similar existence.

In Chariton's novel, for example, Chaereas and his friend, Polycharmus, having gone in search of Callirhoe, had their ship attacked and destroyed, and were sold as slaves in a chain gang. For a short period of time they suffered deprivation. But at the very moment they were about to be crucified (having been caught up in a slave revolt), Mithridates, the satrap of Caria, discovered that Chaereas was the beloved of Callirhoe with whom he too was madly in love. He immediately interceded and stopped the crucifixion and brought the two men home with him. The narrative depicted him addressing Chaereas as brother and ordering "his servants to take them to the baths and see to their physical well-being, and when they had bathed, to give them luxurious Greek clothes to wear" (4.3.7). A banquet followed. For Chaereas, this was the end of any real material hardship in the story. Later in the narrative, rather as a matter of course, he achieved the rank of general and then admiral when he offered his service to the Egyptians in their revolt against the Great King. The message implied by this plot was those hoary elite aphorisms, "blood will tell" or "rank has its privileges." And it was a good thing, too, for the narrative stressed that Chaereas was not particularly suited to labor: "Digging quickly wore his body out, for many things weighted on him: toil, neglect, his chains, and most of all his love" (4.2.1). Chaereas labored so ineptly in fact that his friend Polycharmus had to arrange a scheme so that he could perform Chaereas's work for him. The narrative explained that Polycharmus gladly took on the extra burden because, unlike Chaereas, he was not a slave to that cruel master, Eros (4.2.3). But the narrative also revealed a likely contributing factor. Later in the narrative, Polycharmus described his relationship to Chaereas: "The other young man was once pre-eminent in Sicily, in honor, wealth and beauty, as for me I am of no consequence [euteles], but I am his companion and friend" (4.3.1). In the context of this elite narrative, Polycharmus's lower rank made him better suited to hard labor than his wellborn friend.

Callirhoe's innate superiority also protected her from the actual experience of material hardship. Although purchased as a slave, she did no work and very quickly regained the trappings of high position. After his first meeting with her, Dionysius instructed his slave, "Now I am entrusting to you the greatest and most precious of my possessions . . . I want her to lack for nothing, I want her to have every luxury. Consider her your mistress; serve her, treat her with respect . . ." (2.6.4–5). In fact, Callirhoe had it in her power to be rich almost beyond imagination. She rejected the overtures of the Great King of Persia whose eunuch had recited the gifts she could anticipate: "Miletus itself as a present, and the whole of Ionia and Sicily, and other nations greater than those" (6.5.7). Chariton's plot made explicitly clear that poverty and work are for drones; queen bees like Callirhoe, although they may feel miserable (2.3.7), just naturally experience the honey in life.

This "theodicy of good fortune" also informed Xenophon's narrative, although Habrocomes undertook more work than other romance heroes – he worked as a fisherman and in a quarry, but only for short periods of time. Rather routinely and almost effortlessly, he, like Chaereas, kept reacquiring material means. Only a short period intervened between his capture by pirates and his being given a position of authority. Initially, Habrocomes suffered torture and imprisonment because the pirate chief's daughter, Manto, had falsely accused him of rape after he rejected her advances (and offers of money). But the pirate chief soon discovered the truth and, not only freed him from punishment, but put him in charge of his whole household and offered him a free-born wife (2.10.2). Habrocomes missed Anthia, however, and abandoned this good situation. The narrator recorded his thoughts: "What use is freedom to me? What is the point of being rich . . . ?" (4.10.3). What point indeed? The narrative had already shown how easily Habrocomes could regain those states of freedom and riches out of the reach of so many in ancient society, and how "naturally" they came to him. Later in the plot, the prefect of Egypt simply had to hear his story to offer him money and load him with gifts (4.4.1). When Habrocomes again found himself without funds in Nuceria, he took on work at a quarry; the narrative recorded the difficulty of his toils: "he found the work arduous, for he had not been used to subjecting himself to hard or physical work" (5.8.3). Nor did he last long; the text explained "he could not bear his labors" (5.10.1). So Habrocomes sailed for Rhodes where he ran across his former slaves who immediately gave him all their goods and took care of him (5.10.12). Their story in fact suggested that even the slaves of the elite had a share in the "theodicy of good fortune." For it turned out that Leucon and Rhode, the slaves, had been purchased by an old man who treated them like his children (2.10.4) and eventually left his large estate to them (5.6.3). This they immediately made over to Habrocomes.

In the world of the romance, wealth was easily acquired and romance heroes were given little opportunity to remain down and out. The "veil of power" that operated in the romance suggested that acquiring wealth and power was no great matter, and that the wellborn, deprived of their material means and unsupported by their institutional power, could easily reacquire their privileged position.

For all her many trials and brushes with real violence and danger, Anthia also seldom suffered from actual material need. When the eirenarch of Cilicia saved her from becoming a human sacrifice, he immediately fell in love and offered her "his considerable fortune" (2.13.7). Even less savory characters, like the Alexandrian slave traders, recognized the girl's value and gave her special handling. A brothel keeper not only dressed her in beautiful clothes and gold, but even after she evaded her brothel duties by feigning sickness, pitied her and provided someone to look after her. (5.8.1). The romance of danger was not the romance of material deprivation. The former was perhaps more imaginable than the latter in the elite perspective that informed these romances.

Achilles Tatius never depicted his hero, Clitophon, in any actual want; his wealth was saved from the initial shipwreck (4.15.6). And he soon acquired the considerable possessions of Melite, the rich, apparently widowed, Ephesian woman he married. Leucippe did experience real hardship in Ephesus, and for a time bore the marks of hard agricultural slave labor: shackles, shaved head, and lash marks on her back (5.17.3–6). But she soon escaped to the protection of Artemis and was reunited with Clitophon and all turned out happily. For that is the subtext of the "theodicy of good fortune" – that all does turn out well in the end and everything is returned to the proper alignment; all are reunited and live happily ever after because that is precisely the way things are meant to be. Those who are rich and privileged are meant to be so; and one proof is how easily they reestablish their wealth and status in the course of their adventures. In such ways the romance manifested the cultural assumptions of the upper classes.

An elite "veil of power" also operates to distort the real situation, or concerns of other groups in a society. It is not in the elite's interest to see too clearly the lives of others (Gordon 1990). Such distortions can be glimpsed in the romance's representation of slaves and workers. Keith Hopkins, commenting on the depiction of slavery in another fictional narrative, noted that slavery in reality was "a cruel and repressive institution" (Hopkins 1993: 5). He cited Tacitus' description of the notorious first-century A.D. case when 400 household slaves in Rome, including women and children, were crucified because one of their number had murdered their master (*Annals* 14.42ff.). This is a horrific example, but more telling are the references Hopkins pointed to cataloging the pervasive almost casual cruelty of slavery. Galen, the physician, for example, mentioned that his mother had bitten her slaves in rage (Kühn 1821–1833: 5.41), that he knew a man who had beaten his slave on the head with the sharp edge of his sword (Kühn 5.17), and that the emperor Hadrian had stabbed a slave in the eye with a pen (Kühn 5.17). Although anecdotal, such references indicate the onerousness of even domestic slavery. The romances did not entirely repress evidence for slaves' mistreatment – this would hardly be possible in any representation of a society so permeated by slaves and slave owners. Leucippe's mother, for example, slapped her daughter's slave companion, angry that she had allowed a man to break into Leucippe's room (AT 2.24.1). The slave girl quickly fled knowing that she would face questioning and the torture that legally accompanied it (2.25.3; DuBois 1991). Leucippe, while a slave in Ephesus, was lashed when she did not submit to her overseer's passion. Chariton gave the clearest evidence for the real hardship of slave existence and slaves' reaction to it in his description of the chain gang's murder of their overseer and their being almost instantaneously, without any hearing, sentenced to crucifixion (4.2.5–6).

More commonly, however, the romances reflected the idealized perspective of slave owners through their repeated depictions of devoted slaves who live only to serve. The devotion of Leucon and Rhode in Xenophon was noted above. Separated from their owners, the pair acquired a kind master, who provided them with every comfort (and later a fortune), "but [they] sorely missed the sight of Anthia and Habrocomes" (2.10.4). After the death of their master, they started home, finally free and wealthy, stopping at Rhodes to erect a pillar to commemorate in gold their former owners. Suddenly Habrocomes appeared, to their great joy, and they immediately made over all their possessions to him. Frye defined the romance as the narrative of wish fulfillment; the characters of Leucon and Rhode seem explicitly drawn in fulfillment of the most profound wishes of a slave-owning class. But Xenophon topped even their devotion in his description of Habrocomes' old slave attendant. As Anthia and Habrocomes sailed away on the pirate ship, leaving behind their companions on a burning vessel, Habrocomes' tutor leapt into the water voicing sentiments that seem ludicrously excessive to a modern reader, but it is in exactly such representations and the ideology they embody that the "veil of power" can be seen to work. The tutor frantically swam after the departing ship, shouting:

"Where are you going, my child," he exclaimed, "without your old paedagogus? Where, Habrocomes? Kill this poor wretch yourself and bury me, for what is life to me without you?" After this plea, despairing of seeing Habrocomes ever again, he finally gave himself up to the waves and died.

(1.14.4–5)

That a slave was dependent materially on his master was a reality; the romance veils this material reality by projecting the dependency onto the emotional plane.

–The romance not only has difficulty seeing the situation of slaves clearly, but that of anyone not belonging to the upper classes. A. M. Scarcella has pointed out how little actual agricultural work Xenophon depicted in his romance, although much of its action took place in the country (Scarcella 1977: 250). Xenophon similarly represented the civic population as an undifferentiated mass acting only in response to external events. They escorted, they admired, they cried out, they wept, they prayed, they exhorted, they provided the crowd for festivals (Scarcella 1977: 262, for citations). What they did not do was stand out as individuals. No individual member of the urban underclass, nor any sign of the social tension historical sources report in the cities, emerged in these narratives (MacMullen 1966: 163–191). Rather, the undifferentiated civic crowd acted as a trope for the unified social body.

Geographical space also has a symbolic function in the romance (Bakhtin 1981: 99–103). Romance represents civic space as the space of the collectivity, the associative – the space of the festival, the public meeting, the marriage, of perfected social unity (Jameson 1981: 66–68). Outside this civic space was danger – bandit or pirate space. Bandits or pirates featured in all three of these romances. Once the cities were left behind, the protagonists became their prey. Bandits were a perennial problem in the Roman empire, and even in narratives less fictitious than romances, they often performed a symbolic role in helping to define and legitimate social power. Brent Shaw has described how the bandit functioned as the archetypal anti-social element, the "outlaw" in the ideology of the Roman empire:

> Whatever their absolute numbers (probably small) bandits were a common phenomenon in the Roman empire and presented the state with a specific problem of integration. Their actions and mere existence are correlated with the very definition and exercise of state power in a way that is reflected not only in legal and other empirical acts, but also in the metaphoric vocabulary in which state power was expressed.
>
> (Shaw 1984: 24)

In the romance the bandits stood as the personification of anti-structural forces (Winkler 1980). Xenophon (3.12.2) and Achilles Tatius (3.9.2) conveyed what happened when people, alone and separated from society, were cast up on a strange beach; they were immediately set upon by bandits! Achilles Tatius gave a graphic description of the Egyptian *boukoloi*, herdsmen/bandits, who attack Clitophon's ship: they are large, black, short-haired, and speak a strange language. They are portrayed as different from the protagonists in every aspect, literally incomprehensible (3.10.2). The romance was one of the few of the ancient genres that incorporated into its plot what must have been a salient reality – that Greek and Latin speakers in the Roman empire were surrounded by populations that both literally and figuratively spoke a different language (Winkler 1982: 104–106). Romance used this reality to emphasize the difference between Greek speakers and those "others." The romance defined this difference as "inhuman" in descriptions of the bandits' savage treatment of the heroines (Winkler 1980). In Xenophon, the bandits displayed their inhumanity and cruelty in their treatment of Anthia. As part of a rite for Ares, for example, they hung the girl from a tree as a target for their javelins (2.13.1–3). Later in the text, she was buried in a pit with two savage dogs (4.6.5), her punishment for killing a would-be bandit rapist. Twice in Achilles Tatius, bandits appeared to kill Leucippe gruesomely. The first time, Clitophon watched as she was disembowelled and her intestines roasted and eaten (3.15.1–5). In another episode the pirates apparently beheaded her and threw the separated parts overboard (5.7.4). In the romance, the bandits, through their inverted social structures – leaders, religious rites, even mock cities (AT 4.13.5), but above all with their violence – provided a foil for the normative structures of elite society. The romance projected upon the bandit a vision of the elites' nightmare of life outside their circle where everyone wanted what they had and took it. The epitome of what they feared can be overheard in the reason Hippothous, a bandit leader at this point, gave to his band for setting out for Cappadocia: "For they tell me that wealthy men live there" (X 2.14.3–4).[13]

The romance was not the genre of realistic particularity, but of ideological cliché. Not only bandits, but cultural "others," such as slaves and foreigners, were the target of frequent negative stereotypes throughout the romances (Scobie 1973: 19–34). In Achilles Tatius, for example, readers learned that slaves are cowardly when frightened (7.10.5), and that Egyptians lacked emotional moderation – either too afraid or too rash (4.14.9). Xenophon defined unreasonable anger as "barbarian" (2.4.5). Chariton's pronouncement on the Great King's eunuch, Artaxates, discloses the point of all such negative references. The narrative portrayed Artaxates as anticipating that it would be an easy task to persuade Callirhoe to submit to the king's overtures; but the narrator articulated the chasm separating this unsavory character's opinions from correct thinking. "He was thinking like a eunuch, a slave, a barbarian. He did not know the spirit [*phronēma*] of a wellborn [*eugenes*] Greek – especially Callirhoe, chaste Callirhoe, the lover of her husband" (6.4.10).[14] In the romance, the function of the bandit, the foreigner, and certain slaves was precisely to define through contrast the ethos of the wellborn Greek. An ethos that was embodied in the romance by the chaste spouse – "chaste Callirhoe, the lover of her husband." Chastity acts as the emblem for the *phronēma*, (a word incorporating connotations of "spirit," "mind," "resolution") of the wellborn Greek.

Throughout the romances, both marriage and chastity bore metaphoric or symbolic weight. Marriage the primary ritual joining non-family members exemplified the social – society. Chastity, the restriction of sex to socially approved arrangements, imaged society's aegis over individuals. As was said earlier, chastity is quite literally the embodiment of social control, or, in Chariton's terms, of a social ethos. The emphasis in the romances on chastity, and in particular their distinctive concern for male chastity, calls into question the interpretation that views the romance as providing evidence for a new cultural focus on personal desire (Reardon 1971). In Chariton, Xenophon, and Achilles Tatius, personal desire played a relatively restricted role. It was the genesis for the couple's love and can be surmised to underlie their attachment to each other. But the emphasis in the three romances' plot was on the almost immediate management of personal attachment by the society at large, specifically, by the city as a collective entity as was seen to happen in the openings of Chariton's and Xenophon's romances. Through the relation established between the couple's attachment for each other and the society at large, marriage comes in the romance to stand as an emblem for social attachments in general. Aristides had told citizens to become lovers of one another in the interests of social concord. The couple became a figure for this social concord, as the romances traced the transformation of their personal desire into a fidelity whose locus is a socially mandated unity – the married couple.[15]

To describe the romance as a narrative of individual desire devalues the importance of marriage and chastity in it. Both Chariton and Xenophon made very clear that without the intervention of city and family, the young couples' love would have been deadly. Individual desire separated from social structure had no future in the romance. It is true that considerable narrative attention is devoted to the separation of the lovers and their separate tribulations, but the romance focus was on the distress of a separated unity not the potency of individual desires. The conventional definition of the contemporary novel as the narrative representation of a society coming to value individuality over community is very likely right. But the romance has a quite different perspective. It is a narrative that at essence still affirmed the traditional model of society where individuals found their meaning in community. While the romance offered a rather broad definition of community (the urban Greek elite), and was less focused on a specific civic entity, its concern was still with society, not individuality. Lukacs's definition of the contemporary novel: "the story of a soul that goes out to find itself, that seeks adventures in order to be proven and tested by them, and by proving itself to find its own essence" (Lukacs 1971: 89) is very far from being a description of the ancient novel. The romance would better be described as the story of two souls that were joined together or wished to be joined together, that underwent adventures to test their commitment and devotion to each other, and by proving their commitment were reunited or united forever in an ongoing social unity. Graham Anderson has aptly caught the essence of the romance in his description of the central couple "as a single organism trying to unite themselves" (Anderson 1984: 62). Rather than being about individuality, the romance was about how individuals are transformed into enduring social unities.

That the romance was concerned with social transformation, from individuality to social unity, helps explicate the emphasis on death that opens all three romances. The association of marriage and death had a long history in Greek thinking, where marriage conventionally was understood as a type of death followed by a rebirth into a new changed state. In Helene Foley's words, "the primary Greek myth of marriage, which played a central role in the ritual life of Greek women, is the story of Persephone's rape by Hades, her stay in the underworld . . ." (Foley 1982: 169). In the conceptual calculus of Greek thinking, the descent into the underworld central to the Persephone myth figured a kind of death for women in marriage. Persephone's reappearance marked women's return to society with a changed status – newly admitted into the social order, insuring its continuity through the production of legitimate children. The

Persephone myth, and the marriage it represented, corresponded to patterns typical, according to van Gennep, of initiation rituals – "the pattern of separation, transition (often including symbolic death), incorporation" (Foley 1982: 170; Gennep 1960). This pattern – separation, transition, incorporation – also displays a striking similarity with the romance plot and suggests that at one level at least the romance also ought to be read as a story of initiation, a story of the individual's initiation into the social order epitomized in marriage.[16]

All three of these ideal romances opened with some form of death, either simulated, threatened, or social. In Chariton's first book, his heroine Callirhoe was kicked by her jealous husband, apparently died and was placed in her tomb, only to revive as tomb robbers entered and carried her off. All the rest of the adventures in the romance followed from this death, until the final reunion of the couple at the end of the story. An ominous oracle precipitated the marriage of Anthia and Habrocomes; it foretold terrible sufferings and toils and tombs for both, before a final and better destiny. A dream of death that graphically illustrates the inherent violence of desire separated from social structure set in motion the action of Achilles Tatius' romance. This romance, the *Leucippe and Clitophon,* alone of the three under consideration did not begin with a marriage, nor treat the separation and adventures of an already married couple. As the story began, Clitophon, in fact, had little hope that he would be able to marry his beloved, his cousin, Leucippe. For his father had already betrothed him to his half-sister, Kalligone. Brigitte Egger has noted that Achilles Tatius' romance underscores this son's complete acquiescence to his father's will (Egger 1990: 215). Clitophon accepted his situation without demurral: "I couldn't marry her: I'm already promised to another" (1.11.2). He recognized his father's authority: "My father is armed with the respect I owe him" (1.11.3). So Clitophon set out to obtain his desire outside the proscribed structures, through seduction. He successfully persuaded Leucippe to admit him to her bedroom. But just as he entered her room to enact his desire, a terrible dream roused Leucippe's mother from a sound sleep: "she saw a bandit with a naked sword seize her daughter, drag her away, throw her down on her back, and slice her in two all the way up from her stomach, making his first insertion at the place of shame" (2.24.5).

Roused by this terrible dream, Pantheia jumped up and ran to her daughter's room and interrupted the seduction before it had begun.

The sexual and anti-social imagery of this dream is unmistakable –the naked sword, the bandit agent. Her dream permitted Pantheia to rescue her daughter from a social death that her words show she considered worse than a physical one. She expressed her horror before Leucippe could reassure her that her virginity was still intact:

> Better you were a wartime atrocity, better raped by a victorious Thracian soldier than this. That would have been a disaster but not a disgrace, if force was used. . . . My dream misled me: the truth was worse than I saw. That incision is much more serious.
>
> (2.24.4)

Pantheia valued social strictures over her daughter's very life. She would have preferred Leucippe's death to her seduction. Pantheia acts here as the spokeswoman for society's position. Nor does the rest of the narrative in any way contest her views; rather the plot proceeds to instill in the protagonists a similar recognition of the importance of chastity. I would be more willing to entertain a reading of the romance as an approbation of individual desire, if Clitophon's seduction had been successful and everyone lived happily ever after. That, however, is not the romance plot. Instead, when the couple, after running away, are reunited for a brief interval, after "shipwrecks, pirates, human sacrifices, ritual murders" (4.1.23), Clitophon suggested that they resume their lovemaking. Leucippe refused. It was now she who had had a dream, in which Artemis had instructed her to remain a virgin until the goddess herself gave her in proper marriage. In fact the couple did not marry until, by fortuitous coincidence, Leucippe's father was present and gave his approval. The narrative can be read as describing the metamorphosis of anti-social desire into a union underwritten by divine and paternal approval. This socially constituted and approved union provided the happy ending. During the course of their adventures, Leucippe and Clitophon had learned to submit their desire to the social order personified in divinity and paternity. The romance traced the transformation of individual desire into marriage and socially sanctioned union. This was the implicit message of all three romances and explains why death and chastity figure so prominently in them. Anthia announced to the tomb robbers, "I am a sacrifice to love and death" (3.8.4–5). Exactly, and so was each of the protagonists in the romance, sacrificing herself or himself to the social covenant exemplified by marriage.

David Konstan in his valuable study, *Sexual Symmetry: Love in the Ancient Novel and Related Genres*, identified the transformation "from an initial infatuation to a relationship of proven commitment" as an essential element of the romance plot. Konstan pointed out the "movement in the Greek novel by which the loyalty appropriate to marriage is distinguished from the spontaneous erotic attraction that brought the couple together in the first place" (Konstan 1994: 11). According to Konstan, the romance showed no "polarization in the nature of love between a transient sexual impulse and the desire for a more abiding relationship" (45). In the course of the narrative, however, "in the face of threats and violence, as well as offers of wealth, prestige, and security in a world fraught with accident and danger" the couple learned "loyalty and commitment" and this "becomes the basis of their association as a wedded couple, recharacterizing the nature of their bond over and against the passionate infatuation that inaugurated their relationship" (46). The essential difference between passion and marriage is enduring commitment. As Konstan argued, "Constancy is the moral center of the Greek novel" (48).

Konstan's discussion of the erotic symmetry between the couple in the romance was impressive. In the course of his analysis he also suggested that the novels offered a new basis for marriage in the changed situation of the Roman empire:

> With the erosion of the city as a discrete social space in the context of the increasingly international or transnational culture of the Roman Empire, marriage came to be perceived, or at least imagined in the novel, as a matter of private attachment rather than a function of civic identity . . . social relations among individuals were apprehended as private affairs, motivated not by traditional civic concerns but by personal desire.
>
> (Konstan 1994: 226)

On this point, I might reverse Konstan's terms. In the transnational culture of the Roman empire, social identity began to be perceived or imagined through the language of personal attachment and marriage. The romance used the trope of marriage to talk about social identity and social structures.

My reading of the openings of Chariton's and Xenophon's novels attempted to show how quickly the couples' personal attachments were appropriated by the civic body and ratified by the social institution of marriage. These romances narrated the testing and survival of the loyalty and commitment holding between a married couple and displayed the durability not simply of a personal attachment, but of a social unity. In Achilles Tatius' narrative the couple must learn not only loyalty and constancy to each other but that their personal attachment must be subordinated to social structure. The marriage bond, the genesis or telos of each plot, informed the romance and transferred its resonance from the personal to the social.

The attention to male chastity in the romance specifically shows how language from the marriage register took on additional emphasis in indicating social commitment in the changed political context of the Roman empire.[17] The valorization in the romance of male chastity usurped the cultural terminology traditionally used to define women's commitment to society and extended it to include males. In the earlier Greek conceptual world, marriage and war had been posited as the opposing poles defining the social roles assigned to the sexes (Vernant 1980: 23). Women fulfilled their duties to society by being married and producing legitimate children; chastity was both the condition and burden of their enacted devotion to the collectivity. In Greek literary representations earlier than the romance, men's chastity was essentially a non-issue. Men's vulnerability in accepting the risks of war signaled their devotion to their society. But in this later Hellenic world, under the Roman aegis, the majority of males no longer had military obligations. A new vocabulary was needed to indicate male adherence to the social. In the romance, a simple appropriation from the female social vocabulary remedied the deficiency. Both male and female submission to the social order could be signified through chastity.

The *Ephesiaca* emphatically foregrounded the chastity of both its male and female protagonists. Habrocomes proposed an oath to Anthia after they were married and about to set out on their voyage: "let us swear to one another, my dearest, that you will remain faithful to me and not submit to any other man and I should never live with another woman" (1.11.4).[18] The rest of the romance, in essence, simply recorded various challenges to, and consequences of, this oath, depicted in different geographical locations. Anthia experienced ten attempts on her virtue in Xenophon's rather short narrative (Egger 1990: 192). As she ennumerated when the two are finally reunited:

I have found you again, after all my wanderings over land and sea, escaping robbers' threats and pirates' plots and pimps' insults, chains, trenches, fetters, poisons and tombs. But I have reached you, Habrocomes, lord of my soul, the same as when I first left you in Tyre for Syria. No one persuaded me to go astray; not Moeris in Syria, Perilaus in Cilicia, Psammis or Polyidus in Egypt, not Anchialus in Ethiopia, not my master in Tarentum. I remain chaste for you having tried every stratagem to preserve my chastity.

(5.14.1–2)

And Habrocomes could answer with the same assurance of his purity:

I swear to you, by this day we have longed for and reached with such difficulty, that I have never considered any girl attractive, nor did the sight of any other woman please me; but you have found Habrocomes as pure as you left him in prison in Tyre.

(5.14.4)

In the *Ephesian Tale* Xenophon represented chastity as an ideal that both hero and heroine made heroic efforts to protect. To this end, for example, Anthia poisoned herself and stabbed a man to death. Habrocomes endured torture (2.6.3–4) and crucifixion (4.2.1). Both did, it is true, experience in their far-flung wanderings moments of doubt and wavering, but in the end each, at great cost, preserved their chastity. Konstan (1994) suggested that Habrocomes' consent to marriage with the horrible Kyno exemplified the relative unimportance of bodily chastity in the novel. This example may, however, indicate only how hard-pressed and exhausted Habrocomes had become from his trials. When he entertained Kyno's proposal, the narrative noted that he did recall his promises to Anthia, but also how much he had already suffered unfairly for his chastity (3.12.4). He was perhaps remembering the imprisonment and torture that followed his rejection of Manto's advances (2.5–6). Nor did Habrocomes in fact compromise his oath. After Kyno killed her husband and approached him, he immediately repudiated her, ran off, and only through divine intervention escaped the crucifixion and the burning to death that her false accusations had earned him (4.2).

Anthia also had moments of wavering in her devotion to chastity. When Perilaus, eirenarch of Cicilia, rescued her from bandits and promised that she would be "all things to him, wife, mistress, children" (2.13. 8), if she would marry him, she alone, and feeling at a loss, agreed. In the end, she took poison in an attempt to avoid the marriage. These moments of doubt seem less a real imputation of chastity than examples of Xenophon's few attempts at characterization in the *Ephesian Tale*.

The more flagrant violations of chastity in the romances were framed to suggest either that the breach served a higher social need or was without social implication. Traditionally, chastity provided a potent signifier for the submission of natural and individual desire to society's interests. In his depiction of Callirhoe's flagrant violation of chastity, her marriage to Dionysius, Chariton emphasized that it fit this same paradigm. When Callirhoe had determined to have Chaereas' child and marry Dionysius and pass the child off as his, the narrative stressed that she chose not what she desired, but what she saw as most beneficial to her family and her city. The text made clear that Callirhoe was acutely aware of the poles of her choice – "chastity or child" (2.10.7). Her choice was a stark one, either to marry Dionysius or abort the child. To help her make her decision, she imagined a debate with all the interested parties present, herself, the child, and Chaereas. She cast her vote first – "I want to die Chaereas' wife and his alone. To know no other husband – that is dearer to me than parents, country or child" (2.11.1). But the narrative made clear that parents, country, and child – that is, society, past, present, and future – had a stronger claim than personal desire. The other two votes overrode her desire for chastity; she dramatized her internal debate:

> And you my child – what is your choice for yourself? To die by poison . . . or to live, and have two fathers – one the first man in Sicily, the other in Ionia? When you grow up, you will easily be recognized by your family . . . and you will sail home in triumph, in a Milesian warship, and Hermocrates will welcome a grandson already fit for command. Your vote is cast against mine . . . Let us ask your father too. No, he has spoken . . . "I entrust our son to you."
>
> (2.11.2–3)

Callirhoe chose against her own wishes and for the continuation of her line. If chastity is construed as the physical manifestation of society's claim upon its subjects, then in these terms Callirhoe has obeyed the spirit if not the letter of its mandate in her marriage to Dionysius. To underline her inherent chastity even after her marriage, the narrative compared the new mother to the two goddesses most vigilant in protecting their chastity:

> First she took her son in her own arms: that formed a beautiful sight, such as no painter has ever yet painted nor sculptor sculpted nor poet recounted, since none of them has represented Artemis or Athena holding a baby in her arms.
>
> (3.8.6)

Even Chaereas recognized the necessity for her choice against chastity. At the end of the narrative, when he finally rendered an account of their adventures to the Syracusan assembly, he explicitly explained that Callirhoe married Dionysius for the Syracusans' benefit:

> when Callirhoe realized she was pregnant by me, she found herself compelled to marry Dionysius, because she wanted to preserve your fellow citizen [*politen*]. . . . Yes, Syracusans! There is growing up in Melitus one who will be a Syracusan, a wealthy one, and reared by a distinguished man – for Dionysius is indeed of distinguished Greek heritage.
>
> (8.7.11)

Callirhoe did violate chastity's claims, but she did so against her own desires and for her society. And as Chaereas's explanation made clear, all that was essential had been salvaged. The institution of chastity exists to insure the lineage and wealth of a society's members. The beneficiary of Callirhoe's violation – a wellborn, wealthy citizen – justified and redeemed her action.

Clitophon also deviated from the mandate for chastity in the romance when he slept with the charming Melite. The narrative showed, however, that his action occurred only after Clitophon had already proven himself a paragon of chastity, sleeping night after night beside Melite but never with her. He only submitted to her appeals after the possibility of any real marriage with her, or real betrayal of Leucippe was past. As Melite insisted, "I no longer ask for length of days and a permanent marriage. . . . A single consummation will be enough . . . you have found Leucippe, and marriage is impossible with any other woman, I willingly concede this" (5.26.3–4). Melite only asked that he sleep with her one time in order to cure her love pangs. In this context, Clitophon agreed to the liaison. He recorded the thinking behind his decision: "I had now recovered Leucippe . . . , and the act could no longer be considered a marital one but was a remedy for an ailing soul" (5.27.2). Later in the narrative he felt enough confidence that his action with Melite had not violated his essential chastity to claim that he had remained chaste during their separation (8.5.2, 8.5.6). Achilles Tatius seems to be playing here with the new romantic emphasis on male chastity. Twice Clitophon referred to the concept with the skeptical phrase "if you can speak of such a thing as male virginity" (8.5.6), suggesting certain doubts as to the possibility for total male chastity. While romance may employ chastity as a new signifier for male dedication to society, Achilles Tatius's narrative, with its ironic perspective, pulled back from totally endorsing its possibility in praxis. This often licentious narrative seemed not quite ready to commit males, even symbolically, to absolute chastity, especially in cases where no possible harm to marriage vows or commitment existed.

As an image of commitment and fidelity, chastity did have a central function in the *Leucippe and Clitophon*. By the end of the text, Leucippe who, at its beginning, had not valued chastity enough, has learned its importance. She proudly declared her virginity which she had retained under the most difficult circumstances as she rejected its last challenger, Thersander. She announced: "Leucippe was a virgin after the boukoloi, a virgin after Chaereas, a virgin even after Sosthenes . . . the greater encomium is 'a virgin after Thersander' " (6.22.2–3). And in a final testimony to her chastity and its importance, she passed a very public chastity test in the grotto of Pan; with the entire populace of Ephesis as witness (8.13.1; Segal 1984). Chastity acted in the romances to figure the subordination of individual desire to social structures. When chastity was abrogated in the romance, its cause was the claim of a higher social good or a suggestion that the particular sexual act had no social relevance. Romance celebrated not so much the achievement of personal attachments as the bonds of social relations. One mark of the romance's idealizing nature was its fiction that these coincided.

The genre's focus on society explains the tragic coloring associated with homosexual relations in the romance. The plots made no distinction on the moral level between heterosexuality and homosexuality. Xenophon had the chastity of both his hero and heroine threatened by pirates–no differentiation was suggested in the moral nature of the threats (1.14.7–15.4). And Achilles included in his narrative a philosophical discussion on the respective merits of the two types of love. The terms of the debate concerned the respective attractions of the love object, not a distinction in the nature of the desire (2.35–37; Konstan 1994: 28). Homosexual love was not disapproved of in the romance; nevertheless, most examples of homosexual relations ended in tragedy and loss.[19] Achilles Tatius, for example, included a vignette describing Kleinias's passion for a boy, Charikles. The narrative related in vivid detail the tragedy of this boy's death riding a horse that Kleinias had given to him. (AT 1.12.5–6). Later in this same romance, Menelaus told the sad story of his tragic love. He accidently killed his beloved in a boar hunt (AT 2.34). In Xenophon, Hippothous had his tragic tale of homosexual relations. After he had rescued his beloved, Hyperanthes, from an older lover, a teacher of rhetoric (3.2.8), the boy drowned in front of his eyes in a shipwreck. Later in the narrative, rich from the death of his wife, Hippothous took up with a wellborn Sicilian, Cleisthenes (5.9.3). The romance showed its approval of their relationship by having them present for the happy reunion concluding the narrative, celebrating the reconstituted society. But the text explicitly noted that Hippothous had adopted the boy as his son (5.15.4). This adoption served to locate the homosexual relationship within the social system that provided the center of the romance. Most of the homosexual relations ended tragically in the romance because they existed outside and apart from this system. They existed only in the domain of personal desire and thus had no function in the society idealized in the romance.

The romance narratives did not focus significantly on the bearing of children. As the recent work of Brigitte Egger and Helen Elsom has demonstrated, the concern with social reproduction operated on a more generic level than the simple production of children (Egger 1990, 1994; Elsom 1992). Egger pointed to the "conservative discourse and nostalgia" at work in the depiction of marriage in the romance. She showed that the romances harked back to marital values and practices more applicable to an earlier period of Greek history; actual marriage arrangements in the Hellenic societies contemporary with the romances were much freer and more open than those represented in the romance narratives (Egger 1994: 266–271). The anachronistic representation of marriage in romance, in Egger's view, was drawn to emphasize the dominant patriarchal orientation of the narratives. Romance provided an idealized depiction of the patriarchal system whose inherent purpose as a social institution was the retention and passing on of male power and privilege. Marriage functions in this system as "'the archetype of exchange' and women are exchange objects . . . *par excellence* whose transfer between groups of men 'provides the means of binding men together'" (Joplin 1991: 41, citing Lévi-Strauss 1969: 480–483). The emphasis on traditional marriage arrangements in the romances exposes the genre's endorsement of patriarchy's concerns.

In her analysis of Chariton's work, Helen Elsom displayed Callirhoe's role as precisely the sort of exchange object necessary for patriarchy to function; the object of desire, a symbol or sign "as something unreal which can be passed around in place of the intangible real – wealth, the phallus or power" (Elsom 1992: 213). Elsom pointed out that the very first sentence of the romance – "Hermocrates, the Syracusan general, who defeated the Athenians, had a daughter" – located the novel within the context of kinship and "traffic" in women (Elsom 1992: 221). Chariton consistently presented Callirhoe's worth and desirability as a factor of her high birth (of which her beauty in Hellenic ideology is a corollary). Throughout the romance, Callirhoe repeatedly defined herself as her father's daughter. After her kidnapping, for example, she lamented: "I, Hermocrates' daughter, your wife, have been sold into slavery" (1.14.10). She identified herself to Dionysius: "I am the daughter of Hermocrates, the Syracusan general" (2.5.10). The basic self-conception of herself that she offered to others was as a daughter of a famous father.

Elsom offered a persuasive analysis of the significance of Chariton's depiction of Callirhoe and Chaereas's return to Syracuse within this patriarchal scheme (8.6–7). Chariton described the ship bearing the couple sailing into the harbor, its deck obscured beneath a tent of Babylonian tapestries. The narrator recorded the crowd's surmise about the contents of the tent – "not people, but rich cargo." Suddenly, the tapestries were drawn back to reveal Callirhoe reclining on a golden couch with Chaereas dressed as a general standing beside her. According to Elsom, the scene embodied the novel's message. Callirhoe reclined, "a passive carrier of value," herself an object of value, while beside her stood her husband, "dressed as a general," his description marking him as a "stand-in" for her father, the famous Syracusan general. In Elsom's words, "Chaereas is revealed as a copy or substitute for Hermocrates in Callirhoe's life" (Elsom 1992: 226).

And once the substitution was made, once Chaereas took his place, as Hermocrates' son-in-law, as Elsom noted, Callirhoe retired to private prayer and her husband proceeded to the public assembly (Elsom 1992: 226). Chaereas both replicated and replaced Hermocrates. In this replication was the sum of the elite-ideal dream projected in the romance – an image of a wealthy and wellborn society continuing changeless over time, as riches and position were passed on, as husbands replaced fathers forever.

The ending of Achilles Tatius' romance inscribed the same conclusion – the eternal replication of society through the perpetual cycle of husbands replacing fathers. Leucippe, as much as Callirhoe, defined herself in terms of her family's high position. She imagined herself addressing Thersander:

> Cease to regard me as a slave. I am the daughter of a Byzantine general, and wife of one of the leading men of Tyre . . . My husband is Clitophon; my country Byzantium; Sostratos is my father and Pantheia my mother.

> (6.16.5–6)

And this romance similarly ended with emphasis on a father (or father-figure) replicated in a husband. Achilles Tatius celebrated double weddings at the conclusion of his narrative – those of Leucippe and Clitophon and of Kallisthenes and Kalligone. For it may be recalled that on the eve of Clitophon's wedding to Kalligone – his half-sister and betrothed (a common situation in marriage arrangements, exhibiting how little real exchange takes place even in this exchange of women) – his wife-to-be was abducted. A certain Kallisthenes from Byzantium had desired to marry Leucippe although he had never seen her, but only had heard of her beauty. Her father refused his suit, so when she went to Tyre, he sailed there to take her by force. But he abducted the wrong girl, Kalligone, whom he mistook for Leucippe. After the abduction, however, Kallisthenes fell in love with Kalligone, and at the conclusion of the narrative, Sostratos described how he had proved himself a worthy husband for her. He did so in fact by turning himself into a double of Sostratos, Kalligone's uncle and Leucippe's father. He proved himself to be wealthy, polite, dedicated, and generous to his city. Sostratos defined Kallisthenes' worthiness in terms that offered him as the replication of his beloved's male relatives, the epitome of the wellborn elite male. Sostratos described the young man's metamorphosis:

He became very attentive to my needs, called me "Father" ... he became a superior soldier, strong and talented. He also donated a good deal of money to the city. They elected him a general along with me, after which he was even more considerate to me, making himself my subject in all matters.

(8.17.8–10)

Sostratos again described the patriarchical pattern, the passing of power from one father to his duplicate. The society that the devotion and fidelity of the principal couple imaged in microcosm in the romance was the traditional elite patriarchal society passing, essentially unchanged, from one generation to another. The couple's love featured in the romance should not be mistaken for a new valorization in the ancient world of personal attachments. Rather, it was a romanticized emblem of the long tradition in antiquity of the individual's submission to, and embrace of, the social order. The wedding or reunion of the wedded couple that ended the romance celebrated the burgeoning elite societies of the early Roman empire. The couple's love and fidelity were a type for the concord and harmony idealized as providing the basis for this society. The romance, the narrative embodiment of an elite wish-fulfillment dream, projected a society going on forever the same. It incorporated a dream of changeless permanence. Bakhtin correctly identified the essentially static heart of the romance:

No changes of any consequences occur, internal or external, as a result of the events recounted in the novel. At the end of the novel that initial equilibrium that has been destroyed by chance is restored once again ... The hammering of events shatters nothing and forges nothing – it merely tries the durability of an already finished product. And the product passes the test. Thus is constituted the artistic and ideological meaning of the Greek romance.

(Bakhtin 1981: 106–107)

Konstan rightly objected that Bakhtin overlooked the transformation, in the course of the novel, of the couple's initial passion into proven constancy. But even this transformation belongs to the romance's resistence to change; constancy, the "moral center of the Greek novel" (Konstan 1994: 48), is a valorization of duration through time, of endurance, of changelessness in the face of events. This is the essential utopian core of the romance – that the hammering of events is without effect. The protagonists pass through all their tribulations and troubles and emerge, as Bakhtin saw, the same; they passed through suffering but bore no mark that they had experienced it. The final reunion celebrates the reintegration of a society in which pain and adversity have no place. As Frye pointed out, the happy ending of the romance was reserved only for those who made it to the celebration at the end (Frye 1976: 135). In the society of the early Roman empire, relatively few belonged to the charmed circle idealized in the Greek romance.

3

PAIN WITHOUT EFFECT

The central "subject" of romance, the character who passes through suffering but is unmarked by the experience, is not an anomaly in the representation of the early centuries A.D. That this was a cultural subject, a so-called "subjectivity," a particular historical self-understanding, is evidenced by its representation at different points in the culture. The generation of a new genre, the romance, to display this "subject" in action, suggests its importance.[1] In this chapter I will show that both Stoic philosophical texts and romantic texts, for all their difference in tone and surface detail, essentially construct the same subject – a self that is exempt from the experience of pain and suffering. This is not to suggest that the authors of either set of texts necessarily were familiar with each other's works, but to demonstrate that this subject was circulating in the ideological environment of the period.

Stoicism was, as Brent Shaw has testified, "*the* idea system associated with most of the high period of the ancient classical world"; it achieved its greatest point of influence in the early empire (Shaw 1985: 17). Stoicism provided a sort of philosophic *koine* in the period, as James Francis has pointed out; its tenets were widely known in at least a general sort of way (Francis 1995: 1).[2] Stoicism had appeared around 300 B.C.; by the early empire, its writings, such as those of Seneca (4 B.C.–A.D. 65) and Epictetus (*c.* A.D. 55–135) emphasized its ethical teachings as a practical guide to life. Epictetus provides a text particularly valuable for disclosing the kind of cultural script available in the period. For the *Discourses* purported to be actual lectures that were transcribed by his student, Arrian, just as he had heard them delivered. They should therefore correspond to readers' experiences of the material standard for such lectures, even if they are not in fact verbatim transcripts.[3]

Epictetus' text thus offers a valuable entrance into the thought-world of second-century culture, for it is common that educational structures do play a primary role in a culture's communication of its messages.

Epictetus was born a slave and became a follower of the Roman Stoic Musonius Rufus. He was exiled from Rome with the rest of the philosophers by Domitian, probably in A.D. 92–93. He resumed his teaching in Nicopolis in northwest Greece where Arrian became his student around the year A.D. 108 (Millar 1965). The *Discourses* provide evidence that Epictetus' students were from the wealthier strata, not necessarily training to become professional philosophers, but expecting to assume the normal social duties of the Greek urban elite (Brunt 1977: 23, 26). One can assume on the model of Arrian, himself from Bithynia and destined for both imperial service and literary accomplishment, that the *Discourses* addressed young men not too dissimilar from the heroes of the romances or even, perhaps, their authors.[4] Epictetus' text provides an example of the kind of self-understanding offered to such young men as they trained to assume their privileged place in their society.

To digress for a moment: Stoic texts also make explicit the analogy between marriage and society that I suggested was operating implicitly in the romance texts (Schofield 1991). Cicero, following the Stoic Panaetius, had defined the primary bond in society as the marriage bond leading to children and a household, providing, in his words, "the foundation for the city and as it were the seed bed of the state" (*De Officiis* 1.54). In the second century A.D., the Stoic Hierocles offered an image of all the members of the human community enclosed by a series of concentric circles around the self. He drew the first circle around the individual's body, with the mind at its center. The next circle contained wife, children, parents, and siblings. The third enclosed more distant relations, aunts, uncles, cousins, until the whole human race was included, encompassed in ringed circles. (Long and Sedley 1987: 57G = Stobaeus 4.671,7–673,11). Hierocles recommended that persons ought to survey the circles and keep transferring people from outlying circles to circles closer in, i.e., to think of one kind of social relationship in terms of another. His statements displayed how natural it was during the period of the romances' production to compare other social bonds to that holding between a married couple.[5] Other romance themes also appeared in the Stoic texts. Both Seneca and Musonius Rufus

(Epictetus' teacher) enjoined chastity on both husbands and wives (*Epistulae* 94.26; Lutz 1947: X11, 92); and a tantalizing fragment from Zeno, the founder of the school, connected eros with the harmony of cities (Schofield 1991: 2–56). In his *Deipnosophists*, Athenaeus comments that:

> Zeno of Citium took Eros to be a God who brings friendship and freedom and concord, but nothing else. That is why in the *Republic* he said that Love is a god, and there as a helper in furthering the safety of the city.
>
> (13.561C)[6]

Zeno very likely was referring to the eros between males in this passage, but nevertheless Athenaeus' remark revealed a tradition of linking eros to the bonds of friendship and concord uniting a city. In celebrating the enduring love between a couple as the emblem of social unity, the authors of the romance had extended a tradition already constructed in other contemporary texts.

A central tenet of Stoicism was the control of emotions; Stoics projected as the goal of the virtuous person, the Stoic wise man (*sapiens*), a life without passions (defined as violent movements of the soul).[7] Such a state became possible through an individual's recognition that virtue alone was the only good, and vice the only evil. Everything else in life was indifferent. Virtue was defined as living life in accordance with nature; by this, Stoics meant bringing one's life into conformity with the actual course of events. As Epictetus had succinctly expressed it: "do not seek to have events happen as you want them to, but instead want them to happen as they do and your life will go well" (*Handbook* 8).[8] Stoic discourse constructed subjects who directed their most concerted efforts at exercising control over what was in their power; as Epictetus says, controlling what was "up to us" (*eph' hēmin*) and not changing outside circumstances. Epictetus had provided a list of precisely what was within an individual's control:

> our opinions are up to us, and our impulses, desires, aversions, in short, whatever is our own doing. Our bodies are not up to us, nor are our possessions, our reputations or our public offices, or, that is, whatever is not our own doing.
>
> (*Handbook* 1)

Virtue was a matter of self-mastery; it was achieved by the self's control of its own attitudes and desires.

The emphasis on self-mastery appeared in the two words Epictetus used, according to Aulus Gellius, to sum up the foundation of the good life; these are often translated "bear" and "forbear," but would perhaps be better rendered "endure" and "refrain."[99] Gellius reported on Epictetus' understanding of the worst vices: "a lack of endurance [*intolerantiam*] and a lack of self-control [*incontinentiam*], when we do not endure or bear the injuries which we have to bear or do not refrain from [forbear] those matters and pleasures we ought to refrain from" (17.19). Virtue for Epictetus was enduring without complaint exterior circumstances however harsh they might be and refraining from transgressions no matter how enticing they appeared. The virtuous person bears and forbears, endures and refrains.

If two verbs were needed to summarize the plot of the three ideal romances considered in the previous chapter, the two chosen by Epictetus to describe virtuous behavior, "endure" and "refrain", might well be selected. That the philosophical texts and the romances represent a similar subject is indicated by how precisely these Stoic watchwords function as a synopsis for the action of romance. The phrase "endure and refrain" captures the very essence of the romances of Chariton, Xenophon, and Achilles Tatius. These romances developed around the protagonists' endurance of hardship piled on hardship, shipwreck, capture by pirates, slavery, war, service in a brothel, chastity trials, and their repeated forbearance of actions that, although tempting, were violations of chastity, e.g., Anthia's rejection of Perilaus and Hippothous, or Clitophon's refusal of Melite's riches, or Callirhoe's rebuff of the Great King of Persia's offers. And in each case the couple's endurance and forbearance allowed them to reach their goal; not only reach it, but, as Bakhtin noted, reach it virtually unchanged, unscathed by "the hammering of events." The couples were reunited and reassumed their former positions in their society, seemingly untouched by their trials. The romances constructed a subject for whom, in the end, pain did not matter.

Epictetus inscribed this same subject in his discourse – a "self" unaffected by pain or suffering. Only virtue and vice mattered; pain belonged to that large category of things outside a person's control and was therefore an indifferent. Robert Dobbin described the sense of self in Epictetus as having two components: *prohairesis,* a subjective self, the "I," the interior ordering faculty; and *prosōpon* or *persona*, an objective self, the "me," that others saw (Dobbin

1989: 131). *Prohairesis*, deliberate or moral choice or purpose, was Epictetus' key term in his definition of the self. Epictetus defined, for example, the essential task of education:

> as learning what is under our control and what is not, and the only thing under our control is *prohairesis* and all the works of *prohairesis*, but not under our control are the body, the parts of the body, possessions, parents, brothers, children, country.
>
> (1.22.10)

It is through *prohairesis* that people were able to make the correct judgements about external events – to determine whether they were under our control or indifferent. In this scheme, persons were held responsible only for what was under their control, and how they exercised that control manifested their real self. Epictetus made this point repeatedly: "You are not flesh, nor hair, but *prohairesis*" (3.1.40). Again, "a person cannot be pointed out with a finger like a rock or a piece of wood, but when one points to a person's judgements [*dogmata*] one shows the person" (3.2.12). Dobbin explained: "The premise is that the self is that which is unconditionally under our control. Hence his incessant harking after things in our power [*ta eph' hēmin*] is really Epictetus' way of searching for the core of man, the inalienable self" (Dobbin 1989: 122). Kahn explained Epictetus' notion: the *prohairesis* is "the true self, the inner man, the 'I' of personal identity" (Kahn 1988: 253).

One of the points in the *Discourses* that Epictetus was most intent to convey to his students about this core, this self, was that it is untouched by pain or any hardship. No one, for example, should be concerned by violence; Epictetus chided someone expressing fear: "'What if someone should attack me when I am alone and murder me?' 'Fool, not murder you, but your paltry body'" (3.13.17). Nor could disease or handicaps affect the real you:

> disease is an impediment to the body, but not to the moral purpose [*prohairesis*] unless that wills. Lameness is an impediment to the leg, but not to the moral purpose. Say this at whatever befalls; for you will find the thing to be an impediment to something else but not to yourself.
>
> (*Handbook* 9)

Epictetus advised his students to exercise their *prohairesis* in order to train themselves to recognize correctly the indifference of external things. He modeled the exercise:

a certain man's son is dead. Answer, "That lies outside the sphere of moral purpose, it is not an evil" ... Now if we acquire this habit, we shall make progress ... His son is dead. What happened? His son is dead. Nothing else? Not a thing. His ship is lost. What happened. His ship is lost ... But that "he fared badly," each person adds on his own.

(3.8.5)

Epictetus emphasized that humans have no control over what happens outside themselves, over death or shipwreck, for example. They do have control over their attitudes toward these external events, and it is these attitudes that they must master to live a virtuous life. Death is an external event; it is indifferent. The judgement that death was an adverse event was internal; it is also evil because it does not conform to the way things are, i.e., to nature.

Epictetus repeated this lesson over and over again in his *Discourses*. He insisted that his students should go out at dawn and practice making judgements on what things were good and what were indifferent. Those that did not fall within the control of moral purpose were of no concern.

What did you see? A man in grief over his child? Apply your rule. Death lies outside the control of moral purpose. Get rid of it. Did a Consul meet you? Apply your rule. What is a consulship? Outside the control of moral purpose or inside? Outside. Get rid of it, it does not meet the test. Throw it away, it does not concern you.

(3.3.15)

His students must train themselves to recognize that high position and wealth are not goods, nor pain and poverty evils. He reports that they have, unfortunately, not yet learned this lesson. They see a consul and think "lucky man." Or they see people grief-stricken, exiled or poor and think "how wretched they are"; but these thoughts, as Epictetus specifies, are exactly the attitudes that are supposed to be thrown away:

This is the subject upon which we should exert ourselves. What is weeping and lamenting? A judgement. What is misfortune? A judgement ... outside of moral purpose [*aprohairesis*], those being of good and evil. Let a person transfer his judgements to things that lie within moral

82

purpose [*prohairesis*], and I guarantee that he will be steadfast, whatever happens around him.

(3.3.18–19)

Epictetus maintained that humans have the interior resources to be happy in any eventuality. They therefore have no cause to complain no matter what befalls them (3.8.6). No one should ever allow his or her interior state to be affected by any external cause. Epictetus imagined the serene interior monologue of someone trained in philosophy: "now nothing bad can befall me, for me there is no such thing as a pirate, for me, no earthquake, everything is full of peace, everything is full of tranquillity" (3.13.13). Epictetus described his ideal: "show me someone who though sick is happy, though in danger is happy, though dying is happy . . ." (2.19.24). Physical states have no effect on the real "self" and are of no concern. Disease is not a bad thing – "I shall shine in it, I will be firm, I will be serene" (3.20.14). "My leg has become lame. Because of one little leg do you blame the universe?" (1.12.24). Hunger even to starvation is not an evil: "Yes, but what if he [god] does not provide food? Why, what else but that as a good general he has sounded the recall? I obey, I follow, I shout assent to my leader" (3.26.29). Death is nothing to be feared; it involves simply a return to the constitutive elements – "what there was of fire in you shall pass into fire, what there was of earth into earth, what there was of breath [*pneuma*] into breath" (3.13.15). This last comment reminds us that when Epictetus talks of "god" and the "recall," he speaks figuratively. Terms such as "god" or "Zeus" refer to the "divine reason," the "designing fire," "nature" that permeate all existence, not to a personal deity, in the Christian or pagan sense (Kahn 1988: 258).

Epictetus made his point repeatedly – no good or evil inhered in external events, but only in an individual's judgements about these that they were good or bad. He insisted that it was no sign of god's disfavor if certain people should suffer poverty, sickness, exile or prison, but merely a sign that god wished to use them as witnesses, in Greek, "martyrs," that nothing outside of moral purpose could cause harm (3.24.112–114). Pain, poverty, exile, prison, loss of status were all indifferent and could not affect the real self. Epictetus' text constructed a subject very similar to the one appearing in the romance; subjects that passed through suffering unaffected and unchanged by the experience. As there were no

83

pirates or earthquakes for the *sapiens* (3.13.13), by the end of the
romances, it was as if the pirates and terrors had never been.

All externals may be indifferent, but how each individual reacted
to them was crucial. Epictetus' emphasis was on controlling one's
attitudes, in bringing these into conformity with what is given.
This is the realm of virtue. He repeatedly compared humans to
actors playing parts. The role was indifferent; it was how it was
played that counted.

> Remember that you are an actor in a play; the sort of play
> is whatever the playwright wishes: short, if he wants it short,
> long if he wants it long. If he wants you to play a beggar,
> play even this part skillfully, or a cripple, or a civic leader,
> or a private citizen. For this is your business, to play the given
> role well. To choose the role is another's.
>
> (*Handbook* 17)

The duty of each individual was to perform well in any circumstance. Just as it was of no import for actors which role they were
assigned – Epictetus had pointed out that an actor does not act
Oedipus the King with any finer voice or pleasure than Oedipus
at Colonus, the outcast and beggar[10] – it shouldn't matter to
individuals what role they were assigned, only how they handled
their assignment mattered. Epictetus held that "although life is a
matter of indifference the use you make of it is not a matter of
indifference" (2.6.1). There are no bad roles. People, like actors,
can shine whether they are cast as cripples or leaders. They shine
by exhibiting their equanimity and tranquillity in the face of
external circumstance.

It is easy to see that tenets such as these held by Epictetus might
well prove a valuable addition to the veil of power described in
the preceding chapter: the ideological veil that functions in societies
to mask, both from the elites themselves and others, the facts
of social reality. Stoicism's traditional emphasis on fate and
providential design already favored an elite perspective. As Stoic
attention shifted more to ethics in the early empire, this tendency
to confirm prevailing social structures intensified. In James Francis's
words: "Stoicism turned the maintenance of the prevailing social
and political order into a command of reason and nature hallowed
by the dictates of philosophy" (Francis 1995: 19).[11] Epictetus'
emphasis on the internal, on self-mastery, and self-formation, as
well as his denial of the importance of externals, would have served

to divert the attention of his students and others like them away from attending to social or material conditions. [His teaching supported the status quo, and any affirmation of the status quo acts to affirm an elite's position. Stoic insistence that poverty and social position did not matter fitted into an elite agenda better than into an underprivileged one: as does the corresponding counsel that what did, in fact, matter was how well you did at being poor, imprisoned, or politically unpopular. ["Well" was defined as how little you allowed the conditions to upset or disturb you.] This teaching, along with emphasis on control directed at the interior self, had significant relevance for the social body; it would work to restrain social as well as personal disturbances. James Francis, in his *Subversive Virtue*, demonstrates that Stoic philosophy acted as a bulwark in supporting the operating social structures of the early empire.

A regular effect of a "veil of power" is to distort the concerns of the non-elites in a society and to obscure their real situation. And since a culture's ideology entangles to some extent every member in its perspective, it is not anomalous to find such distortions even in Epictetus, although he was himself born a slave – his teaching, for example, that poverty shouldn't be feared because it was conducive to living longer than normal appears to reflect such distortion:

Did you ever easily see a beggar who was not an old man? Wasn't he extremely old? But though they are cold night and day and cast down on the ground, and have to eat only what is necessary, they reach a state where it is almost impossible to die.

(3.26.6)

His statement hardly seems to fit with what we surmise must have been the reality of the effects of the life he described on those experiencing it. Perhaps Epictetus needed to consider that such a miserable existence might well make anyone *appear* old, or perhaps he just needed to look more closely. For in another statement, he suggested that people's normal response was to avert their eyes from beggars (3.22.89). Most likely he simply displayed here the ideological lens that affected his vision, for as Slavoj Žižek explained, ["an ideology really succeeds when even the facts which at first sight contradict it start to function as arguments in its favor"] (Žižek 1988: 49). An axiom in the *Handbook* showed a similar

85

depreciation of the harsh reality of experiencing want: "For it is better to die of hunger, being without grief and fear, than to live troubled in abundance" (*Handbook* 12). This type of statement also reflects an elite bias; for it could only seem reasonable to those in no danger of starving (and famine was not unknown in Epictetus' period [MacMullen 1966: 250]).

The "veil of power" also appears in elite claims of the inherent difficulties associated with power or luxurious living. It is conventional in cultures to legitimate elite lives by insisting that they are exposed to more burdens than the less privileged are. In Shakespeare's phrase: "uneasy lies the head that wears the crown" (*Henry IV – Part II*: Act 3, scene i). Epictetus endorsed this elite myth (that anxiety and tragedy belong particularly to the lives of the powerful) when he comforted those finding themselves left destitute and sleeping upon the ground: "do so with good courage, snoring and remembering that tragedies find a place among the rich and kings and tyrants, but no poor man fills a tragic role except in the chorus" (1.24.15). Epictetus confused being excluded from a central role in cultural representations with actually escaping tragedy and anxiety themselves. The poor have tragedies, but their tragedies remain hidden from the cultural gaze. Both Epictetus' text and the ideal romances constructed a subject that was untouched by pain or sorrow, and both functioned to reflect an elite perspective making the status quo appear fixed and natural, while at the same time, veiling the realities and concerns of the non-elite.

Xenophon concluded his romance with a prophesy of future joy and happiness for the reunited couple: "the rest of their life together was one long festival" (5.15.4). Epictetus believed that this same designation "festival" or "holiday" was the appropriate term for all of human existence (3.5.10, 4.1.108–9, 4.4.24). He meant that once humans truly recognized that life followed a divine plan and nothing external could cause them harm, they would enjoy and welcome whatever happened. Since no pain could touch or disturb the real self, there was never an appropriate cause for sorrow. Epictetus gave short shrift to complainers. He rebuked, for example, a man distressed about the loss of his wife and children.

> Will you not yield to your superior? – Why did he bring me in such circumstances? If they do not suit you, leave; he has no need of a fault-finding spectator. He needs those joining

in the holiday and the dance, that applaud, and glorify and sing praise about the festival.

(4.1.108–109)

Humans existed to find joy in the universal order, and Epictetus wasted little sympathy on those who would not find this joy. Epictetus' emphasis was on the will, the *prohairesis*. It was up to each person to control, to master, himself or herself so as to acknowledge that nothing external could affect inner joy and tranquillity. If his teachings were assimilated, Epictetus insisted, people would no longer need someone to comfort or encourage them, for they would recognize that nothing adverse could actually befall them (3.3.116). If bad things only happened because individuals mistakenly judged that they had happened, there is no requirement for sympathy. It was up to each person, rather, to make life a festival, by naming and recognizing it as one, whatever external hardships it brings.

Already in antiquity, according to Seneca, the Stoics' lack of sympathy had won them a reputation for harshness. Seneca wrote his *De Clementia* in part to disprove this characterization; his proof rested on the distinction between pity (*misericordia*) and mercy (*clementia*). Seneca saw their essential difference as one of detachment. Seneca disapproved of pity because it identified too emotionally with its object. He explained:

> pity is near to misery because it is partly composed of it and partly derived from it . . . pity is a fault of minds too disturbed by misery, and if anyone requires it from a wise man, that is very much like requiring him to lament and groan at the funerals of strangers.

> (*De Clementia* 2.6)

People do not cry at strangers' funerals because they are not emotionally engaged; they do not cry because they do not feel strongly about strangers. The presence or lack of emotion defined the difference between pity and mercy. "Pity is the sorrow [*aegritudo*] of the mind brought about by the sight of the distress of others . . . But no sorrow befalls the wise man; his mind is serene" (*De Clementia* 2.5).[12] The *sapiens* did not allow himself to become disturbed by others' pain. Seneca indicated that this did not mean that he was unmerciful, only that he was in control of his emotions. Mercy, unlike pity, was rational (*De Clementia* 2.5). The primary responsibility of persons was to protect their own serenity – and this could not be compromised by feeling too keenly another's pain. As Epictetus specified, "another's grief is no concern of mine, my own grief is." Within the context of his teaching this was not a selfish statement, but a central tenet – nothing external is under my control.

Seneca maintained that the *sapiens* would perform precisely the same actions as someone feeling pity, and would simply do so while controlling his feelings, with a tranquil mind, without causing himself misery: "he will bring relief to another's tears, he will not add his own" (*De Clementia* 2.6). In fact, according to Seneca, the wise man acted more correctly than those who wished to be thought of as having pity "who fling their coins and feel disgust for those they help" (2.6).

> He will not avert his face or his mind from anyone because of a crippled leg, or wrinkled face, or old age supported by a staff, but he will aid all the worthy and in the manner of the gods looking graciously upon the unfortunate.
>
> (2.6)

Seneca advocated charity, but a detached charity. He scripted a subject who, like the gods, was remote from human suffering and observed it from afar, but who did not allow himself to share the sufferer's experience.[13]

Epictetus valorized this same subject who protected his or her own serenity in the face of another's sorrow. He warned that people should not be carried away when they saw someone weeping and immediately believe that something bad had happened. They should remember, rather, that nothing bad can happen, but only a mistaken judgement that it had. Epictetus had reiterated repeatedly that the real "self" cannot suffer from any external cause. Therefore, there was no reason for anyone to grieve. Epictetus advised his students, if they should happen to observe someone in grief, to pretend but not feel the pain of sympathy, "Do not hesitate, however, to sympathize verbally, and even to groan with him if the occasion arises; but be careful not to groan inwardly" (*Handbook* 16). Epictetus' text offered an inner self untouched by pain, its own or another's.

In essence, Epictetus' text was about control. He instructed his students in techniques for mastering and controlling their attitudes and feelings to insure that their equanimity could never be disturbed. He taught them to construct a self immune from desire, pain, grief, or fright. The basis of his teaching was a detachment from everything outside the control of the mind (Rist 1978a). This included the body. The Stoics, materialists, were not dualists, but as A. A. Long has explained, their tradition did to a certain extent perceive the body as a tool of the mind:

> But the soul's activities as mind – perceiving, judging, desiring, etc. – though dependent on the soul's relationship with the body, are not reducible or equivalent to that relationship. Psychologically and morally speaking, persons for the Stoics are states of rational consciousness, or more literally and accurately, "intelligent warm breaths" which inhabit flesh and bone bodies, and use them as instruments for their own life.
>
> (Long 1982: 53)

At several points Epictetus reflected attitudes very much like scorn for the body: "the paltry body, which is not mine, which is a corpse by nature" (3.10.15); "this [body] is not yours but is clay ingeniously mixed" (1.1.2); "the body is nothing to me; the parts of it are nothing to me" (3.22.21). This denigration of the body was a consequence of Epictetus' efforts to discount its effects, as he discounted everything outside the control of moral purpose. For central to his scheme of self-mastery was the belief that nothing outside of a subject's judgements and attitudes could affect the real self. Epictetus' text issued from a didactic setting and its purpose was to instruct individuals how to master an interior self, how to recognize the self's area of oversight and its limitations. According to Epictetus, the self must learn to limit itself to what "is in its power" – its attitudes and opinions.

A society's subjects come to understand themselves through all the self-representations their society offered them. But writings like Epictetus' had the overt purpose of teaching people how to conduct themselves properly. They were explicitly designed to help people to reform and refashion themselves to conform to a particular cultural ideal. What ideal for emulation did Epictetus hold out to his students? At least in part he constructed a "self" for whom pain, grief, and hardship had no effect. Epictetus' text was written and was circulating among readers in a period that very likely overlapped with that of Xenophon's and Achilles Tatius' romances and was perhaps not too much later than that of Chariton. These writings all fabricate a particular cultural subject – a subject for whom pain essentially doesn't matter. The romances' heroes and heroines embodied this subject. The romances showed their protagonists undergoing nearly all of their culture's most dreaded experiences. Hero and heroine encountered the very stuff of nightmares – burials alive, shipwreck, capture by pirates, purchase as slaves – one disaster on top of another, only to emerge unscathed, unchanged, ready to reenter their society once again just as if nothing had happened to them. The implicit message of romance is clear, and it is the same as that Epictetus offered; pain and hardship did not matter. And Epictetus might add that pity was unnecessary. In the early empire, from a number of discursive points, a particular subjectivity was being offered to inhabitants as a model for self-understanding – a self immune to the effects of pain and suffering.

The recognition that the romances generated a particular subjectivity, based upon a particular set of cultural assumptions, may help to explain why the romance subject, especially the hero, has offended modern critics, who operate within a different perspective. Until recently the Greek-ideal romance found few admirers; one of the genre's perceived flaws was its heroes' characterization. Commentators faulted the heroes for being weak, passive, and overly prone to threaten or seek suicide.[14] The romance protagonists did not conform, it appears, to contemporary expectations of behavior proper for the male lead. But notions of proper behavior change over time; people learn how to act from the representations their culture offers them. Rather than dismiss the romance hero, his representation can be useful for revealing the cultural subject being offered to elite inhabitants of the early empire as a model for their own self-conceptions.

Innate cultural assumptions and connections are frequently difficult to penetrate for those outside the culture, either geographically or chronologically or both. Cultural assumptions are so taken-for-granted by those within the culture that they are seldom articulated. It is fortunate that Achilles Tatius, with his rather arch stance toward the conventions of romance (Reardon 1994), did articulate the similarity between the romance hero and the philosophic rendition of the same subject. He did so in an episode that critics have identified as a notorious example of the romance hero's weakness and passivity – Clitophon's failure to respond to a violent physical attack.

When Thersander, Melite's long-lost husband, suddenly returned home to discover Clitophon in his house, he immediately attacked him, punching him and beating his head on the ground. Clitophon said that he could feel the anger (*thumos*) in Thersander's blows (5.23.5), but he made no attempt to either strike back or protect himself although he claimed he was capable of doing so (5.23.6). At last the attack ended; Clitophon explained, "finally we grew tired; he of beating me and I of philosophizing." By describing his lack of action with the word *philosophōn*, Clitophon related his "passivity" to a philosophic context where his refusal to become angry and retaliate made perfect sense. Clitophon's passivity in this episode ought to be interpreted as simply a narrative display of the behavior constructed and valorized in philosophic exhortations of the period.

Epictetus directed a great deal of attention in his *Discourses* to instructing his students on how to control their responses to external circumstances. Like Achilles Tatius in this representation of Clitophon, Epictetus constructed subjects who did not respond to angry acts with angry reactions. Epictetus approved the following sort of interior monologue for someone wronged by another: "Am I to harm the man who has harmed me? . . . Since this one has injured himself by harming me, shall I not harm myself by doing him some wrong" (*Discourses* 2.10.24–27). According to Epictetus, individuals' efforts toward achieving virtue should be directed at controlling their reactions to outward events, just as Achilles Tatius depicted Clitophon doing, tiring himself "living rationally" (*philosophōn*) and not responding to Thersander's blows. Clitophon's behavior was not a character flaw, as critics have held, but a virtuous action in the discursive context of the early empire. In fact, Seneca explicitly valorized an action identical with Clitophon's restraint: "The mark of true greatness is not to notice you have received a blow . . . The man who does not get angry stands firm, unshaken by injury; he who gets angry is overthrown" (*De Ira* 3.25.4). Control of the emotions was the essential goal for Stoics, and a text preserved from the first century A.D. described the inherent gentleness of the Stoic *sapiens* and his rejection of anger: "he is always gentle [*praos*, a word carrying connotations of meekness, mildness], his gentleness being a tenor by which he is gently disposed in always acting appropriately and in not being moved to anger against anyone" (Long 1987: 65W = Stobaeus 2.155.5–17). Even as it has been in the modern period, in antiquity such mildness could be misconstrued as cowardliness. Diogenes Laertius recounted that Cleanthes, an earlier Stoic (331–232 B.C.), had once been reproached for cowardly behavior, but he replied "that is why I seldom sin" (*hamartanō* 7.171). Clitophon's lack of response to Thersander's attack was not cowardliness, but rather, a narrative example of a subject of the sort valorized in Stoicism – "not being moved to anger against anyone."

Epictetus advised his students to direct their most concerted efforts to controlling their attitudes. For, in his view, these were the only things under individuals' control, the only things "up to us." As he affirmed, "our opinions are up to us, our impulses, desires and aversions . . . our bodies are not up to us" (*Handbook* 1). The *prohairesis*, moral purpose, was the real self, not the body. Habrocomes' internal monologue, as he attempted to avoid falling in love with Anthia, showed Epictetus' self in action, even as it failed its goal. "The girl is beautiful, but what of it? To your eyes, Habrocomes, Anthia is beautiful, but not to you, if you will it" (X 1.4.3). Habrocomes' words show that in his sense of "self," he made the same distinctions between his body (his eyes) and his faculty for choice ("not to *you*, if you will") as Epictetus did. Many episodes in the romances depicted characters displaying this same self-understanding. They distinguished between their body and their inner faculty of choice, their moral purpose, that called by Epictetus *prohairesis*. Epictetus had advised his students to always have before them two general principles:

> no one is the master of another's *prohairesis*; and: in this sphere alone are to be found one's good or evil. No one is therefore a master to give good to me or involve me in evil. I myself alone have authority over myself in these matters.
>
> (4.12.7–9)

Many episodes in the romances read almost as narrative enactments of Epictetus' points in this passage.

When, for example, Manto the daughter of the pirate chief made overtures to Habrocomes, he rejected her out of hand.

> I am a slave, but I know how to keep vows. They have power over my body, but I have a free soul [*psyche*]. Now let Manto threaten me if she pleases – with swords, the noose, fire and everything that the body of a slave can be made to bear, for she could never persuade me to do wrong against Anthia willingly.
>
> (X 2.4.4)

Habrocomes was ready to die; Manto's control extended only to his body and his soul was still free to make the correct choice. In

Epictetus' terms, Manto's power extended only to Habrocomes' limbs and hair, not his real "self," his *prohairesis*. Callirhoe exhibited this same attitude when she is told a foreign general is in love with her: "I will not submit to marriage. I pray rather for death. They can goad me, burn me; I will not get up from here. This place will be my tomb" (C 7.6.8). And when Thersander threatened Leucippe, she withstood him, holding to the inviolability of her will.

> I am unarmed, alone, a woman. My one weapon is my freedom, which cannot be shredded by lashes, dismembered by sharp blades or burned away by fire. It is the one thing I shall never part with. If you try to set it on fire, you will not find fire hot enough.
>
> (6.22.4)

These statements show that their speakers assumed that they possessed an essential self, exempt from any outside control and distinct from their body. Epictetus represented this same self. He described the answer appropriate for someone being menaced with threats: "'But I will fetter you.' What is that you say, man? Me? My leg you will fetter, but my *prohairesis* not even Zeus himself has power to conquer. 'I will throw you into prison.' My paltry body rather" (1.1.23–24). Epictetus' text, along with the romances, projected a self-understanding that defined the "self" as the agency controlling moral choices. It is this self that existed free and unfettered from any control except its own, and equally this self that each individual must work to master and control. Throughout his *Discourses*, Epictetus reiterated these points – persons must learn to control their attitudes, emotions, and desires to bring them into accord with nature, and, if it proves impossible to live rationally, then they had the option to depart from this life.

In the self-understanding offered by Epictetus, control was primary. The importance of control can also be seen in the romance emphasis on suicide.[15] Epictetus with other Stoics held that anything outside the self's control was indifferent. Death, along with pain, was among these indifferents. Therefore, it was not unreasonable to choose death if a life in accord with nature became impossible. Cicero summarized a Stoic position: "When a man has a preponderance of things in accordance with nature, it is his proper function to remain alive; when he has or foresees a preponderance of their opposites, it is his proper function to depart from life" (Long and Sedley 1987: 66G = *On Ends* 3.60–61).[16] Epictetus had defined the aims of the Stoic good life: serenity, *euroun*, a good flow, and *apatheia*, freedom from disturbances (*Discourses* 1.4.1). Seneca similarly described the good life as one having "peacefulness and tranquillity" (*securitas et perpetua tranquillitas,* *Epistulae* 92.3). Epictetus made clear throughout the *Discourses* that when individuals could no longer preserve their serenity in the face of circumstances, rather than err by misjudging their situation (i.e., thinking it bad rather than indifferent), they should depart. He compared life to a game that should be continued only as long as it could be played pleasurably (1.25.8). When that was no longer possible, his advice was to pick up and go:

> only do nothing as one burdened, or afflicted or thinking yourself to be in evils; for no one forces you to do this. Has someone made smoke in the house? If he has made moderate smoke I shall stay; if too much I go outside. For one ought to hold fast to this, that the door stands open.
>
> (1.25.17–18)

Epictetus had this to say about the person who could not control his sorrow about the loss of a city or a woman; "why does he who is at liberty to leave the banquet, and to play the game no longer keep on annoying himself by staying. Does he not stay like children only as long as he is entertained?" (2.16.35–37).[17] According to Epictetus, it was up to each individual to determine the circumstances under which life could be lived. It is in this context of self-evaluation that the frequent attempts at suicide in the romances become comprehensible.

Chariton's narrative repeatedly showed Chaereas choosing death as the cure for the misery he found himself in after losing Callirhoe. Carrying her tomb offerings to her, he decided on his own death as the only "remedy for his sadness" (C 3.3.1). Later when he discovered that Callirhoe had married Dionysius, he again attempted suicide. Kissing the noose, he addressed it: "You are my relief, my advocate. I am the victor, thanks to you; you show more affection to me than Callirhoe" (C 5.10.9). His words reveal that he shares Epictetus' assumption that in certain situations death was the only way to relieve the pain of intolerable circumstances. In Achilles Tatius' narrative, similar reasons motivated Clitophon's suicide attempts. Believing Leucippe had been disemboweled, killed, and eaten, he decided to kill himself in sorrow over her gruesome death. When his friends tried to stop him, he explained that death was the only possible "medicine" for the evils he had seen (AT 3.17.3). Later, when Leucippe had apparently died, Clitophon once more sought in death a "medicine" for misfortune (7.9.2). In each of these cases the narrative offered death as a cure for intolerable misery; the same function Epictetus had claimed for death. Epictetus explicitly recommended death to those who were not strong enough to stand being separated from their loved ones. He included a dialogue addressed to one who complained that death might take his family:

> yes, but I want my little children and my wife to be with
> me: — Are they yours? Do not they belong to him who gave
> them? To him who made you . . . Why, then, did he bring
> me into the world on these conditions? — And if they do not
> suit you, leave.
>
> (4.1.107–108)

Epictetus' words make clear that he believed that death was preferable to complaint or prolonged sorrow, although acceptance of whatever life brings is best. Epictetus picked out Heracles for praise because he could abandon his children without groaning or yearning for them (3.24.14) and censured Homer's depiction of Odysseus sitting upon a rock and weeping for his wife (3.24.18). The good man will bring his desire into accord with what happens and be happy, but if this is impossible, he will depart.

[In Epictetus' terms, death offered a person freedom from living life as an unhappy spectator of the divine order.] When Chaereas censured his friend Polycharmus for saving him from suicide, his words showed this same understanding of death: "You are my worst enemy under the cloak of friendship. If you were my friend you would not begrudge me my freedom . . . how many times have you destroyed my chance for happiness?" (6.2.8–9). In the texts of the early empire opting for the freedom provided by death was not construed as weakness, but as a reasonable choice. Seneca's advice has been held to be excessive, but its clarity is indisputable:

> we shall show that in any kind of servitude the way lies open
> to freedom. If the soul is sick and because of its own imper-
> fection unhappy, a man may end its sorrows and at the same
> time himself . . . In whatever direction you may turn your
> eye, there lies the means to end your woes. You see that
> precipice? Down that is the way to freedom. You see that sea,

that river, that well? Freedom sits at the bottom. You see that
tree, stunted, blighted and barren? Yet from it hangs freedom
. . . You ask the route to freedom? Any vein in your body.

(*De Ira* 3.15)

For Seneca, death offered the ultimate freedom; as he says, "I shall
not endure myself on that day I find anything unendurable"
(*Epistulae* 96.1).

Epictetus was more conservative in his approval of suicide than
Seneca, and set limits for its choice (Droge and Tabor 1992:
34–37). Recognizing that the Stoic teaching on voluntary death
might entice his students, he included a scenario to show when
voluntary death was appropriate. In this he depicted students
coming to him and giving their reasons for wanting to commit
suicide:

Is not death no evil? And are we not related in a manner to
God, and have we not come from him? Allow us to go back
from where we came; allow us to be freed at last from these
fetters [of the body] . . . Here are pirates, robbers and law
courts and those called tyrants. They think they have power
over us because of our bodies and its possessions. Permit us
to show they have power over no one.

(1.9.13–16)

Notice that Epictetus' list included some of the same factors,
pirates and robbers, that influenced the romantic hero's choice for
death. In this case, Epictetus advised the students against suicide.
In the tradition of Socrates and Zeno, he told them to remain
where they had been stationed until they received a signal and not
to depart from life irrationally (1.9.16–17).[18] They must wait for
their recall.

But how is one, in fact, to recognize the signal and know that
a life in accordance with nature had become impossible? The *sapiens*
may have no difficulty, but what of the vast majority still only on
the way to true wisdom? Here the Stoic notions of appropriate acts
(*kathēkonta*)[19] and role (*persona* or *prosōpon*) become important.
The chapter entitled "How it is possible to discover appropriate
actions [*kathēkonta*] from names" (2.10) begins with the imperative
"Examine who you are." Epictetus explains that it is from such a
self-examination that persons could determine what actions were
appropriate for them. This self-examination proceeded, according

to Epictetus, not from scrutiny of some inner self, but from a review of the conventional social roles one assumed in the course of life. The self was conceived explicitly in terms of "names" or social designations – human, citizen, father, son, brother, town councillor. Each title entailed particular appropriate acts, or duties. Philip De Lacy explained the connection between roles and appropriate actions:

> The Stoics do not explain individualization in terms of some unique essence or substance, but rather in terms of a unique set of relations . . . [Epictetus] speaks of our relations to other persons and the deity. Some of these relations are natural, others are acquired. Examples are pious, son, father, brother, citizen, husband, wife, neighbor, companion, ruler, ruled. The good man is true to his relations, and his duties are measured by them. The moral agent is thus characterized by his collection of relations.
>
> (De Lacy 1977: 171)

In another *Discourse*, Epictetus explained the importance such roles played in helping individuals determine whether they should continue to live or not. He offered the example of an athlete, who chose to die rather than have his genitals amputated. When someone asked Epictetus "if he had done this as an athlete or a philosopher," he answered, "as a man, a man who had been proclaimed at the Olympic games" (1.2.26). For this athlete, with his understanding of his role as an Olympic victor, Epictetus suggested, death was appropriate. Although he pointed out that another man, holding lower standards for himself, might have chosen to have his neck cut off if he could only have lived without a neck (1.2.29). Epictetus held, according to De Lacy, "two determinates of what is reasonable in any particular situation: one's *prosōpon* and the value one places on external things" (De Lacy 1977: 167). In this same *Discourse*, Epictetus offered a rather odd example of how far one ought to go to maintain a role. He explained that as a philosopher he would have to choose to die before he allowed his beard to be shaven off (1.2.29). Was Epictetus implying here that his role as philosopher entailed his retaining a beard? But could he not continue to philosophize beardless?[20] His statement rather underlined the social nature of the *prosōpon*; as a category that was explicitly a social construct. The *prosōpon* or *persona* is the "me" perceived by others (Dobbin

1989: 111). Other people recognized a philosopher by his beard. They expected philosophers to be bearded. Epictetus' example demonstrated how important such social expectations are in defining an individual's *prosōpon.* Being a philosopher, or anything else for that matter, inhered in maintaining the socially established standards for that role.

Epictetus' *Discourses* offered an understanding of the self comprised from two interrelated strands; in one, the self was the various roles and sets of relations one found oneself in in the course of life, and in the other, the self was the moral choices one made on the basis of these roles. Epictetus explicitly set off both aspects of this "self" from the body. He repeatedly drew the distinction between the moral purpose and the things of the body: "you are not flesh or hair, but moral purpose" (3.1.40). He made this same distinction between the body and an individual's roles:

> in the case of humans, it is not material that must be honored, bits of flesh, but principal things. What are these? To be a citizen, to marry, to beget children, to honor God, to give heed to parents . . . the proper performance of each of these acts, and that is, in accordance with our nature.
>
> (3.7.26)

In Epictetus' text, it appeared that a "life in accordance with nature," one in which a person was expected to remain alive, was a life where one could appropriately fulfill his or her roles. If central aspects of the role became impossible, one might, like the athlete and the philosopher, choose to depart.

A similar notion of role, *persona,* functioned in characters' choices for suicide in the romances. The heroes and heroines chose death when they believed their roles as husband and wife had come to an end and they were dissuaded from death by having their duties toward their spouses invoked. Polycharmus, for example, stopped Chaereas' attempted suicide by recalling duties he still owed his wife. "Traitor to the dead, will you not even wait to bury Callirhoe. Will you trust her body to another. Now is the time to provide her with rich funeral offerings" (C 1.6.1). When Anthia was being forced into an unwanted marriage, she tried to procure a poison and promised Habrocomes that she would remain his bride even to death (X 3.5.4). Habrocomes determined to die when he heard that Anthia was dead and her tomb robbed, but he remained alive to perform his proper duties to find and bury her (X 3.10.2). Later in the robbers' cave

Anthia warded off advances; her role as wife sustained her. "I pray that I may remain the wife of Habrocomes, even if I have to die, or suffer still more than I have already" (X 4.5.6). Anthia endured to live because Habrocomes remained her husband. "If you are still alive, then my plight is nothing; for some day perhaps we will be together; but if you are already dead, it is vain that I struggle to live" (4.6.7). Clitophon also determined to die and falsely accused himself of murdering Leucippe when he believed she had died. Kleinias defended him in court by explaining that his desire for death resulted from a belief that his wife was dead. Kleinias referred to Leucippe with the word *gyne*, "woman," used for "wife" in Greek, just as Clitophon had referred to her in his self-accusation (7.7.4). Their commitment, tested by separation and hardship, was by this point a marriage for Clitophon. In each of these episodes, the narratives displayed characters' opting for death because of their sorrow at the ending of a defining relationship.

The importance of "roles" in a person's assessment of the value of continued life helps to explain some rather curious suicides or suicide attempts in the romances. Xenophon's romance shows both Habrocomes' and Anthia's parents, when they hear no news from the couple, losing heart because of their old age and ending their lives (5.6.2–3). These characters seemed to share the self-understanding outlined in Epictetus' text. The couples determined that they no longer were living "a life with a preponderance of things in accord with nature." Old, with their children lost and those duties completed, they chose to end their lives. The death of Habrocomes' tutor was portrayed similarly, and again an aged person is involved. "Venerable, but pitiful in his old age," the tutor leapt into the sea to follow Habrocomes, carried off in the pirate ship. The narrative depicted the scene and commented on the reason for the death; the tutor called to Habrocomes: "'kill this poor wretch yourself and bury me, for what is life to me without you?' After this plea, despairing of seeing Habrocomes ever again, he finally gave himself up to the waves and died" (1.14.5). Like the parents, the aged tutor interpreted the ending of his role as a "recall."[21]

Epictetus' text, with its emphasis on the significance of roles and duties, provides a context for understanding one of Chaereas' suicide attempts that commentators have found particularly odd. As Chaereas embarked on his journey in search of Callirhoe, his parents pleaded with him not to leave them. His mother exposed her breasts to him and begged him to stay; she used the same words Hecuba had used to implore Hector to remain in Troy: "respect these breasts and pity me." Chaereas was so overcome that he flung himself into the sea, as the narrative explained, "wishing to die, to flee one of the two alternatives, either not to seek Callirhoe or to pain his parents" (3.5.6). His sailors rescued him, and the journey continued.

David Konstan has pointed out that this scene with its Homeric quotation is modeled on the twenty-second book of the *Iliad*, and Konstan noted the differences between the two heroes' actions:

> Hector, of course, chooses the path of honor, against the wishes of his parents. Chaereas, whose love for Callirhoe cannot be in doubt, nevertheless fails to put his desire to recover her above the claims of filial duty. Rather, he is paralyzed by the conflicting demands and seeks a way out in suicide. The contrast with Hector underscores the anomalousness of his response.
>
> (Konstan 1994: 17)[22]

But Chaereas was not paralyzed; he acted; he jumped from the boat to kill himself. The romance showed a man who refused to choose an action that would violate the duties of his *persona*. Unfortunately, as the narrative emphasized, he was faced with a choice that entailed failure in the demands of either one role or another. So, to avoid transgressing the duties of either son or husband, Chaereas chose to die. This is neither paralysis nor passivity, but the action of the very subject constructed in Epictetus' text. If virtue is the only good, and death a matter of indifference, one is expected to choose death over vice. In this episode Chaereas was placed in precisely the situation Epictetus had described as a prompt for suicide. In a discussion of how people must hold and fulfill their assigned roles, Epictetus set out an acceptable reason for abandoning one's station: "If you send me to a place where humans have no means of living in accord with nature, I shall depart, not disobedient to you, but as though you were sounding the recall" (3.24.101).[23] In the context provided by Epictetus' contemporary commentary, Chaereas' suicide is an appropriate response to his situation. He found himself placed in a position where he had to violate either his role as dutiful husband or pious son. To avoid either violation, he chose to exercise his only control – over himself and his own actions.

That this episode has cultural currency is underlined by its invocation of Homer. As Konstan noted, Hector, unlike Chaereas, had chosen to disregard his parents' claim upon him. How is the reader to interpret the force of this comparison? Again Epictetus supplies the context. Repeatedly in the *Discourses*, Epictetus offered epic and tragic heroes as anti-models. He characterized tragedies as either the portrayed sufferings of those who had chosen to admire "external things" (1.4.26), or the portrayal of actions that were the result of false sense impressions (1.28.32). Epictetus explicitly claimed that the tragic action in both the *Iliad* and the *Odyssey* resulted from an individual's neglect of the behavior appropriate to his role. In the course of demonstrating that "great things" resided not in "wars and deaths and the destruction of cities" (1.28.14), but in each person's preserving "self respect, faithfulness and intelligence" (1.28.21), Epictetus cited the examples of Alexander (Paris) and Achilles. He imagined someone asking him if Alexander hadn't in fact experienced a "great fall" when his city had been devastated and all his brothers were dying. Epictetus' response was unequivocal: "No; no one falls because of someone else's actions" (1.28.23). Epictetus explained that Alexander fell, rather, when "he lost his self respect, his faithfulness, his respect for guest-friendship, his good behavior," that is, in Sparta when he neglected the role of a good guest, and carried off his host's wife (1.28.23). Similarly, according to Epictetus, Achilles' downfall came not when Patroclus died, but when "Achilles was enraged, crying over a girl, when he forgot that he was there, not to procure lovers, but to make war" (1.28.24–25). In other words, when he forgot the duties entailed by his role as warrior. In both examples, Epictetus underlined that the epic hero's fall had begun when he incorrectly chose to disregard the duties of the role in which he found himself. Epictetus' point in these examples from epic was the one he made so often throughout the *Discourses*. Great events only happened internally; they happened within the realm of moral purpose where persons chose to act appropriately and rationally in whatever roles and conditions they found themselves. In Epictetus' estimation, tragedies and epics represented the actions of those who had not properly controlled themselves.

Epictetus might well have described Chaereas' suicidal leap, as this man's attempt to retain his "self respect, his faithfulness, his good behavior" even at the cost of his life. Just as Epictetus' text did throughout, Chariton's romance offered in this episode a subject who found his primary meaning and blueprint for action in his given roles and put all his attention on controlling his own behavior, bringing himself into tune with what was appropriate. Finding his duties to his wife and his parents in conflict, he "forbears" from compromising either of his roles. He retained his "good behavior" by throwing himself overboard and avoiding wrong action. Fortunately for the plot, his sailors rescued him; he retained his morality and his life.

Moderns appear to find the extroverted drive of the epic and tragic hero more appealing, but both the romance and the philosophic texts generated a different subject, namely, one intent on refraining from wrong, rather than performing grand actions.[24] The romance hero was a very different subject from the epic hero and he was intended to be so, as the implicit comparisons built into Chariton's narrative imply. Epictetus' motto for virtuous behavior, "bear and forbear," had it been followed, would have denied posterity epic and tragedy, but it provided romance with its plot. The heroes and heroines of romance "endure and refrain"; and the constancy, defined as the moral center of the genre, ensues from their endurance and abstinence. The subject constructed in the romances and philosophic texts is a passive subject, if passivity means directing control inward instead of out into the world. Romance subjects, like their philosophic counterparts, were intent on mastering themselves and enduring whatever circumstances brought. Both texts reflected an innate conservatism, constructing subjects intent not on changing their world, but on enduring and controlling themselves in whatever world they found themselves.

The most salient point about suicide in the romance is perhaps that so few of the threatened suicides or actual attempts are successful. The couples all endured to the end where their reunion or marriage affirmed the reintegration and survival of their society. Unlike the *Apocryphal Acts* and the *Martyr Acts*, where the death providing the happy ending tokened a rejection of the surrounding social world, the marriage concluding the romance affirmed that world. Even the suicide threats and the actual suicides in the romance acted to affirm the significance of the surrounding social world. The characters chose to die to avoid violating social rules, such as chastity, or out of sorrow for the loss of a spouse and the end of the significant social relation that entailed, or when their social roles were concluded. It is significant that the successful suicides in the three romances all involved old people who saw that their social roles, either as parent or teacher, had come to an end. Suicides functioned in the genre to underscore the primacy of social relationships and to reinforce the reading of romance as a celebration of the communal strength and meaning found in the social community that is idealized in this genre.

4

SUFFERING AND POWER

Written reports of martyr *Acts* were cherished Christian documents from the earliest times. The earliest martyr texts exist in the form of letters shared between Christian communities. Such Christian texts passed among Christian communities, in my estimation, need to be seen as more than reports of events; they need to be considered as key documents in early Christian self-fashioning.[1] The early martyr *Acts* not only narrate events, but they work to create and project a new "mental set toward the world," a new system for understanding human existence at the same time as they work to challenge the surrounding ideology of the early Roman Empire.[2]

Because the representational revolution abetted by the martyr *Acts* prevailed, it is often difficult now, removed by time and caught up in the effects of that revolution, to recoup their initially subversive agenda. But a reading of the *Passion of Perpetua* will demonstrate how an early Christian text, by locating new sources and avenues of power, functioned to subvert the hierarchical structures holding sway in the early Empire (Shaw 1993). The narrative world constructed in the *Passion* poses an explicit challenge to that of the Greek romances, with their celebration of elite patriarchal society.

The *Passion of Perpetua and Felicitas* recounts the imprisonment and martyrdom in Carthage of Vibia Perpetua, a 21-year-old wellborn matron with a nursing baby, and a pregnant slave woman, Felicitas. This text is an extraordinary document, for the narrator, by including Perpetua's first-person record of her imprisonment, preserves for us the clearest woman's voice (except, perhaps, Sappho's) to speak from the ancient world. Guaranteeing their legitimacy, the narrator introduces Perpetua's words: "Now from this point on the entire account of her ordeal is her own, according to her own ideas and in the way that she herself wrote it down" (2.3).[3] "What

Perpetua's "own ideas" offer is a self-representation of a woman subverting and transcending her society's strictures, buttressed by a growing sense of her empowerment through suffering.

Perpetua opens her account by describing a confrontation with her father.[4] He comes to beg her to recant, but, pointing to a vase, Perpetua insists that she can no more stop being called a Christian than it can cease being named a vase. Christianity now subsumes her existence. Her answer so infuriates her father, she says, that, "He moved toward me as though he would pluck my eyes out" (3.3). He does not, in fact, attack Perpetua but departs "vanquished," as Perpetua says, "along with his diabolical arguments" (3.3). "Vanquished" (*victus*), Perpetua's new identity, as a Christian, allows her to begin her narration by presenting herself as overcoming her father, the *pater familias*, the pivot of legitimate authority in the Roman system. As W. K. Lacey has observed, the *patria potestas* "was the fundamental institution underlying Roman institutions" (Lacey 1986: 123). Perpetua's narrative opens, however, with a rejection of both her father's authority and the institution supporting it as, in essence, evil and diabolical. From the outset, Perpetua presents herself as an unruly woman, a woman who refuses to bow to society's expectations. The unruly woman is a trope often employed in texts "to rehearse a hierarchical revolution" (Stallybrass 1989: 54). Usually by the text's closure, however, the woman has been put back in her place and the gendered hierarchical system safely affirmed. But in this text, at the end, as a result of redefinitions of pain and death, even with Perpetua dead, society's power is not affirmed, but radically reinterpreted instead. Perpetua's place turns out to be very different from that assigned to her by society.

After her father's departure, Perpetua is baptized and, directed by the Holy Spirit, asks only for "the perseverance of the flesh" (*sufferentium carnis* 3.5). Her wish is soon put to the test; her group of Christians is arrested and moved to the prison to await trial. In short staccato sentences she describes her terror, the dark, the overcrowding, and heat, "and to crown all, I was tortured with worry for my baby there." Soon the martyrs' situation is improved; bribed by the deacons, the soldiers move them to a more comfortable section of the prison and Perpetua receives permission to keep her baby. Her words reflect her joy: "At once I recovered my health, relieved as I was of my worry and anxiety over the child. My prison had become a palace, so that I wanted to be there rather than anywhere else" (3.9).

At this point Perpetua's brother addresses her, "Mistress Sister [*Domina Soror*] you are greatly privileged" (4.1) and begs her to seek a vision to ascertain if they will be freed or condemned. Perpetua agrees, assenting to his high estimation of her: "For I knew that I could speak with the Lord, whose great blessings I had come to experience" (4.2). The dream that follows affirms her power. Perpetua sees an enormous ladder stretching into the sky; from it hang all sorts of sharp weapons – swords, spears, hooks, daggers, spikes – "so that if anyone tried to climb up carelessly . . . he would be mangled and his flesh would adhere to the weapons" (4.3). An enormous dragon guards the ladder. In her dream she sees Saturus climb up first. Later, he gave himself up of his own accord.

According to her, "He had been the builder of our strength, although he was not present when we were arrested" (4.5). In the dream, he warns her to beware of the dragon, but this dragon causes Perpetua no problems: "Slowly, as though he were afraid of me, the dragon struck his head out . . . Then, using it as my first step, I trod on his head and went up" (*et quasi primum gradum calcarem, calcavi illi caput et ascendi* 4.7). With her double repetition in Latin, *calcarem, calcavi*, Perpetua underlines her treading on the dragon's head and begins a pattern emphasizing the priority of the lower half of the body over the upper that continues through her narrative. Like the unruly woman persona, this emphasis rehearses a subversion of hierarchical structures, metaphorically portending a reversed world when what is below will be on the top (Stallybrass 1989: 45).[5]

Perpetua climbs the ladder to a garden where she is welcomed by a white-haired shepherd milking sheep. He calls her "child," and gives her a taste of the cheese he is milking. She wakes with "the taste of something sweet in her mouth" and tells her brother, "We would have to suffer, and that from now on we would no longer have any hope in this life" (4.10). This dream featuring a welcoming father figure recalls Perpetua's last rancorous interview with her father; the ladder, as Peter Dronke suggests, besides recalling Jacob's ladder, instances the common folkloristic and initiatory motif of "the difficult way" of ascent; in particular, here, the ascent to heaven (Dronke 1984: 7). Perpetua's dream manifests her resolve to move beyond the present world to what she sees as a better, more nurturing existence. She is resolved, but the dream betrays her unease about the process of dying. The weapons hanging on the ladder are gladiators' weapons and their presence exposes Perpetua's fear of having her flesh torn, lacerated by such tools (Mertens 1986: 23). In her dream she confronts and surmounts this dread, recognizing that only through this initiation of pain will she reach the garden. Martyrs often allude to the deaths they particularly fear. Later in the *Passion*, Saturus expresses his fear of the bears and hopes he will be finished off by one bite of a leopard (21.2). His concern is probably well-founded. Names of some of the bears are recorded: *Homicida, Crudelis, Phobos* (Robert 1982: 247). Perpetua's first dream reflects her internal effort to prepare herself for the coming ordeal, to accept her death, and detach herself from this life.

After this dream, Perpetua describes another visit from her father. He comes begging her to have pity on his grey head, reminding her that her actions will affect the well-being of the whole family. He begs her, "Give up your pride! You will destroy all of us!" (5.4). Perpetua describes his kissing her hands, throwing himself at her feet and she states, "He no longer addressed me as daughter but as mistress" (*dominam* 5.5). Jan Den Boeft and Jan Bremmer have testified to the scandal inherent in this appellation (Den Boeft and Bremmer 1982: 389). This entire scene is presented in terms of a radically reversed hierarchy – a father at a daughter's feet, calling her mistress. Moreover, Perpetua suggests that her actions result from a revised notion of human power. She explains to her father that "we are no longer regulated by our own power but God's" (*scito enim nos in nostra esse potestate constitutos, sed in Dei* 5.6).

In the next episode, Perpetua carries her unruliness to a higher level. The group is taken before the governor; again Perpetua's father intervenes: holding her baby, he drags her down from the step and begs her to perform the sacrifice for the emperor and have pity on the infant. She refuses and the governor, Hilarianus, orders him to be thrown to the ground and beaten; again a father is subordinated because of a daughter's actions. Perpetua continues to defy both patriarchal and state authority; she is sentenced to the beasts and she and her fellow martyrs "[return] to the prison laughing" (6.6). The martyrs' joy seems real; later in the *Passion* they are again depicted "stressing the joy they would have in their suffering" (17.1). Perpetua does have one sorrow; her father, as is his right, has taken her baby and refuses to return the child. She appears reconciled: "But as God willed, the baby had no further desire for the breast, nor did I suffer any inflammation; and so I was relieved of any anxiety for my child and of any discomfort in my breasts" (7.8).

But a second dream suggests her continued concern at this premature weaning and the loss of her baby. Perpetua writes that, a few days later, while praying, she suddenly said the name "Dinocrates." She adds:

> I was surprised; for the name had not entered my mind until that moment ... at once I realized I was worthy [*dignam esse*] to pray for him ... That very night I had the following vision. I saw Dinocrates coming out of a dark hole, where there were many others with him, very hot and thirsty, pale and dirty. On his face was the wound he had when he died. Now Dinocrates had been my brother according to the flesh; but he had died horribly of cancer of the face when he was seven years old, and his death was a source of loathing to everyone.
>
> (7.1–5)

Perpetua describes Dinocrates, like Tantalus, as unable to drink in the underworld. She wakes and realizes that her brother is suffering (*laborare*), but she is confident that she can help him (7.9). She recognizes and relies on the power gained through her own sufferings. Perpetua prays day and night and is rewarded with a third vision: "I saw the same spot ..., but there was Dinocrates all clean, well dressed and refreshed. I saw a scar where the wound had been" (8.1). Soon Perpetua saw Dinocrates able to drink and going off to play. Then she said, "I awoke, and I realized that he had been delivered from his sufferings" (8.4).

This dream at one level displays, as E. R. Dodds has noted, Perpetua's sorrow at the loss of her child (Dodds 1965: 53). She comforts herself by experiencing her ability to aid another child in pain. At another level, however, this dream displays Perpetua's recognition of a difference between pagan and Christian suffering. Dinocrates' plight in the afterlife is offered in terms resembling Perpetua's experiences in prison. Both endure heat, dirt, and darkness. But unlike Dinocrates, Perpetua can make use of her suffering; she is confident she can help her brother. She believes her suffering in prison has earned her favor and influence with the deity. But poor Dinocrates, who suffered grievously on earth (Perpetua says his death was hateful to all), gained nothing for his pain. Christianity offers Perpetua a use for her pain; her dream shows clearly, however, that this opportunity is limited to Christians. Dinocrates' suffering merited him nothing, while

Perpetua's imprisonment and acceptance of death, coupled with her prayers, wins him release from pain. Christianity offered converts a useful function for pain and a structure for understanding human suffering. Within this paradigm, Perpetua is able to place her own coming death and her maternal concern for the loss of her baby. She sees her suffering as powerful and redemptive.

The text suggests that others also recognized the power that the martyrs gained through their suffering. Immediately following her recitation of these two dreams, Perpetua describes how the prison official Pudens, in her words, "began to show us great honour, realizing that we possessed some great power within us" (9.1). What power? Perpetua does not specify the cause of Pudens' change of heart, and clearly *post hoc* cannot equal *propter hoc* here, but the collocation of the episodes is suggestive. Could the power that Pudens recognized have been the one earned by Christians' acceptance of pain and death, the ability to use their suffering to obtain favors and power? Later in the text, converts seem swayed by similar claims. For example, on the day before their death, the martyrs had a great effect on the crowd coming to watch them eat their last meal: "They spoke to the crowd with the same steadfastness, warned them of God's judgement, stressing the joy they would have in their suffering . . . Then everyone would depart from the prison in amazement, and many of them began to believe" (17.1). Here the narrative plainly links Christians' acceptance of pain and its reward at the last judgement to conversions. Pudens' change of heart may show a similar motivation. Perhaps hearing of Perpetua's ability to rescue her brother from pain in the afterlife, he comes to recognize the power inherent in the Christians' endurance.

Perpetua's father, worn out, visits for a last time, and her description once more underscores the reversed hierarchical world her conversion has brought into being. Yet again he throws himself on the ground face down, first plucking the hairs from his beard and throwing them to the ground (9.2). This body imagery, enacting the downthrow of what is above, continues, in a visual rendition, the challenge that Perpetua's continued disobedience to her father's authority constitutes.

Her final dream brings Perpetua to a full recognition of her power and her rejection of the subordinate female role decreed by the norms of a male-dominated hierarchy. She sees herself hurrying to the arena, where, instead of the beasts she expected, she is opposed by a foul Egyptian. Handsome seconds attend her. In preparation for the fight, they strip her and rub her with oil; she is surprised to look down and discover that she is a man (Meeks 1974). The Egyptian, in his preparations, rolls in the dust (prefigured as a man already brought low?). Also present is a marvelously tall official holding the prize – a green branch with golden apples. He announces the rules: "If this Egyptian defeats her he will slay her with a sword. But if she defeats him, she will receive the branch" (10.9).

The description of their fight continues the emphasis on the supremacy of the lower half of the body over the top, another dramatization of the subversion of hierarchy:

> My opponent tried to get hold of my feet, but I kept striking him in the face with my heels. Then I was raised up into the air and I began to pummel him without as it were treading on the ground. Then . . . I put my two hands together linking the fingers of one hand with those of the other and thus I got hold of his head. He fell flat on his face and I stepped on his head.
>
> (10.10–11)

Perpetua kicks her opponent's head; her feet float upward; the Egyptian's face is on the ground; she steps on his head. Each detail of the contest affirms the dominance of the lower half of the body. This Christian victory is explicitly offered in terms that emphasize the subversion of the top by the bottom, metaphorically conveying a subversive social message. Perpetua accepts her prize, walking from the arena through the victors' gate in triumph (*in gloria*). Then she awakes and concludes her narrative:

> I realized that it was not with wild animals that I would fight but with the devil, but I knew that I would win the victory. So much for what I did up until the eve of the contest. About what happened at the contest itself, let him write who will.
>
> (10.14)

What Perpetua calls her victory will, of course, be her death; she reveals a Christian logic as reversed as the imagery surrounding it.

This last dream of Perpetua's has been extensively analyzed and interpreted. The Egyptian is the devil; the official stands for the Lord; the nudity and oil recall, perhaps, Perpetua's rite of baptism. Louis Robert has offered what seems the definitive explanation of

110

the details of the contest – from the official's dress, shoes, the prize – to the type of contest. These reflect Pythian games held recently in Carthage (Robert 1982). In her final vision, Perpetua rejects a conception of herself as a victim, an object supplied to the beasts. Throughout her narrative she has become increasingly aware of her power. She withstands her father and the governor, receives vision communications through which she releases her brother from his sufferings; she has been empowered by her experience of pain. Her presentation of herself as an athletic contestant continues this self-understanding. Traditionally the games conferred prestige and renown on participants, but not without cost. Athletics, especially the pankration, the wrestling and boxing event that Perpetua envisions herself in, have been described as "always tough and bloody" (Pleket 1975: 53).

The diction and imagery of the games occur in all the early *Acts*. Polycarp, burnt and stabbed, is described, for example, "now crowned with the garland of immortality, and the winner of the incontestable prize" (17.1). The martyrs are never portrayed as victims, but their ordeals are incorporated into the universal and traditional ideology of the athletic games. H. W. Pleket has suggested that key words for summing up the athlete's code in the ancient world are "courage," "toil," and "endurance" and he explains:

> a special feature of the endurance is that the athlete who "endures" wants *either to win or to die* . . . A 2nd century A.D. Olympic boxer prayed to Zeus for "either the wreath or death." We know from his epitaph that the poor unfortunate died.
> (Pleket 1975: 176–177; Brophy and Brophy 1985)

Perpetua's narrative has explicitly conveyed her courage, toil, endurance; the martyr *Acts* depict martyrs rejecting the victim's role by their subtle collapsing of the athlete's code. They hold that to die *is* to win; the wreath *is* death. Death itself becomes in Christian terms the victory (Barton 1994).

Although Perpetua ends her narrative, the narrator continues to depict her as a challenge to societal, especially patriarchal, structures. His description of her and her companions' proud entrance into the arena embodies her defiance:

> The day of their victory dawned [*illuxit*], and they marched from the prison to the amphitheater joyfully . . . Perpetua went along with shining face and quiet poise, as the beloved

111

of God [*Dei delicata*], as a wife of Christ [*Matrona Christi*], beating back the gaze of the crowd with the power of her eyes.

(18.1–2)[6]

To the end Perpetua is represented refusing objectification, refusing to be a spectacle for the crowd's gaze. In the course of her experiences and her narration of them, she has fashioned an understanding of herself as powerful, empowered by her sufferings. Beating back the crowd's gaze (*vigore oculorum deicens omnium conspectum*), she repeats once more her resistance to the normative gender-based hierarchy. In Western patriarchal culture, woman's role has been to be the object of the male gaze; looking at women is a male's privilege. Even for women themselves, being looked at defines their place; in the Greek romances contemporary with the *Passion*, women are represented as essentially passive, objects existing for the male gaze (Egger 1990: 355–358). Perpetua defies this cultural objectification; empowered by her new self-definition as Christian, she is represented as looking back. If her fate were not already set, this action would seal it. In Western mythology, Medusa illustrates the woman who looks back. Medusa's threat, as the story implies, inheres in the recognition of someone else's look, the recognition that the other sees and thus resists being objectified (Newman 1990: 1031). Medusa's punishment is death and so is Perpetua's. But in the reversed world that Perpetua and the martyrs have constructed, death is no punishment; it is a victory. By not recognizing her punishment, by not naming it, Perpetua embodies a transcendence of both the punishment and the hierarchical structures it purports to support.

Until the very end, Perpetua is represented as an active agent even appointing her own death:

> She screamed as she was struck on the bone; then she took the trembling hand of the young gladiator and guided it to her throat. It was as though so great a woman, feared as she was by the unclean spirit, could not be dispatched unless she herself were willing.
>
> (21.9)

The "unruly woman" is in control until the end. The *Passion* is, at least in part, a narrative of Christian self-realization. Through her dreams, Perpetua fashions a powerful conception of herself. She climbs to heaven; she cures others' pain; she vanquishes a strong and evil male opponent in a triumphal contest. This self-conception empowers her daily life where she consistently defies the patriarchal authority of her father and the state. This reversal of the normative hierarchy is stressed throughout by images of the subordination of the top to the bottom. Perpetua, a "real" woman, fashions herself into an icon of the "unruly woman," employing narrative representation that displays the potentiality that Christian empowerment offered for turning the social and political body of the Roman empire upside down.

Nor is this *Passion* the only one of the early martyr *Acts* insisting that those below could be raised up, empowered through suffering. The *Acts of Lyons and Vienne*, in their representation of a savage persecution, explicitly link suffering with empowerment. This persecution seems to have begun as a near riot in these two Gallic cities:

> In the first place, they heroically endured all that the people *en masse* heaped on them: abuse, blows, dragging, despoiling, stoning, imprisonment, and all that an enraged mob is likely to inflict on their most hated enemies.
>
> (1.7)[7]

The text focuses particularly on the heroic endurance of a few of the martyrs, especially Blandina, a slave woman. The depiction of this character manifests the Christian inversion of societal categories:

> Blandina, through whom Christ proved that the things humans think cheap, ugly and contemptuous are deemed worthy of glory before God, by reason of her love for him which was not merely vaunted in appearance but demonstrated in achievement.
>
> (1.17)

The text stresses that although Blandina may appear contemptible within the operating hierarchy, within the Christian context her suffering ennobles her. In fact in her final depiction, Blandina is explicitly likened to a noble mother: "The blessed Blandina was last of all: like a noble mother encouraging her children, she sent them all . . . to the king" (1.55). This Christian discourse, like the *Passion of Perpetua*, projects a subversion of the contemporary hierarchy through the power acquired by suffering. A second time, in socially loaded language, the text repeats the message embodied by Blandina to underline it: "And tiny, weak and insignificant as she was she would give inspiration to her brothers, for she had put on Christ, that mighty and invincible athlete" (1.42). The text also projects the equality of all classes before pain. Blandina's power is explicitly contrasted with her mistress's worry about lacking the strength to endure: "Yet Blandina was filled with such power that even those who were taking turns to torture her . . . admitted they were beaten" (1.18).

This description of Blandina interprets the ability to endure suffering as power; the narrative almost insists on the curative power of pain. A certain Sanctus, for example, endures extensive tortures until finally red-hot bronze plates are applied to the tenderest parts of his body (1.21). Although he is completely bruised, no torture affects him, for as the text says, he shows there is "nothing painful where we find Christ's glory" (1.23). A few days later, Sanctus, his body horribly swollen, is brought back for further tortures:

> He could not even bear the touch of a hand . . . but . . . his body unbent and became straight under the subsequent tortures; he recovered his former appearance and the use of his limbs. Indeed, the second trial by the grace of Christ proved to be not a torture but rather a cure.
>
> (1.24)

If not always a cure, the endurance of pain is consistently represented as empowering in the early martyr *Acts*. It is, perhaps, to make this point more explicit that these *Acts* seem to focus particularly on society's most vulnerable members. Blandina is a slave woman; her companion in death is a 15-year-old boy. Perpetua is a nursing mother; the slave, Felicitas, rises from her childbed to die. The texts underline the physical infirmity of even those martyrs with high status in the Christian community. Pothinus, the Bishop of Lyons, is described as "ninety years of age and physically quite infirm" (1.29). He only holds onto life, the text explains, so "Christ might triumph in him." Polycarp is also old, eighty-six when arrested. He might have escaped, but he refused and his captors "were surprised at his old age, and why there should have been such concern to capture such an elderly man" (7.2).

This focus on women and the infirm serves to emphasize the martyr *Acts*' position that the endurance of pain is empowering even for the those without power in their contemporary society. All can share in the victory and triumph of death. For just as Perpetua's is, all martyrs' deaths are depicted as victories, defeats of the opposing powers. All the early *Acts* share the view of the *Acts* of Polycarp where it is maintained that Polycarp, through his endurance, i.e., death, "overcame the unjust proconsul" (19.2). Enduring and dying in every case is interpreted as domination. As anyone with good sense should recognize, so the *Acts of Lyons* assumes that the pagans "were not humiliated by their defeat, because they lacked human comprehension" (1.58). In the discourse of the martyr *Acts*, Christian empowerment is evidenced by Christians dying, a reversal underscored in the case of Perpetua by images of gender reversal and the trampling of her persecutors' heads beneath her feet.

Traditionally injuring other people, killing them, provided a method of establishing dominance, of establishing in explicit terms a winner and a loser (Scarry 1985: 137). Bruises, wounds, broken bodies, provided unassailable, palpable evidence of realized power. But Christian discourse reverses this equation and thus redefines some of the most basic signifiers in any culture – the body, pain, and death. Moreover, these radical redefinitions function to create politically subversive texts. The representation of Blandina, Perpetua, Polycarp, and the other martyrs triumphing over Roman proconsuls and governors plays out a drama that explicitly calls into question Roman authority. A Christian proponent in Minucius Felix's *Octavius* makes this point clearly as he articulates what we have already seen dramatized in the martyr *Acts*: "Nay, our boys and tender women are so inspired to sufferance of pain that they laugh to scorn crosses and tortures, wild beasts and all the paraphernalia of punishment" (37.5). What these boys and women scorn are, of course, the most severe punishments of the Roman state: what they laugh at is the manifestation of Roman power.

Christian discourse challenged the discourse of power being constructed in other texts of the period. Consider the approbation of Roman power by Aelius Aristides, a citizen of Smyrna, writing at about the same time the *Acts of Polycarp* were written. His words praise the unparalleled peace provided by Rome and show the close connection between the religious and the political in the prevailing ideology.

> But that when you [Rome] took charge; the confusion and faction ceased and there entered in a universal order and a glorious light in life and government and the laws came to the fore and the altars of the Gods were believed in.
>
> (Behr 1986: 2.26.103)[8]

115

Aristides testifies to the universal hope for the empire's endurance: "the whole inhabited world speaks in greater harmony than a chorus, praying that this empire last for all time" (2.26.29). At another point, reflecting his culture's biases, he suggests the basis for the Roman success: "you have made citizens all those who are more accomplished, noble and powerful people . . . while the remainder you have made subjects and the governed" (2.26.59). In Aristides' view Roman rule has provided a harmonious, well-ordered existence. In fact, the second century is almost notorious for its harmony. Gibbon's estimation has often been cited: "If a man were called to fix the period in the history of the world during which the condition of the human race was most happy and prosperous, he would, without hesitation, name that which elapsed from the death of Domitian to the accession of Commodus," that is, from A.D. 96 to 180 (Gibbon 1946: 1.2.61). Even Irenaeus, a likely author for the *Acts of Lyons*, offers testimony for the sense of security provided by Roman rule: "the world has peace thanks to the Romans, even we Christians can walk without fear on the roads and travel whithersoever we please" (*Adversus Haereses* 4.30.3). Irenaeus's comment reminds us that, in the second century, Christians were not subjects of continuous persecutions, and martyr *Acts* did more than reflect a surrounding reality; they worked to construct a particular world-view centered on the empowerment of pain and death. The tone and outlook of the selections from Aristides' oration show their position was quite at odds with the dominant discourse of the period. And the contemporary Greek romances offer a very different narrative world, where not only do pain and suffering have no real effect, but they have no place in the reconstituted society celebrated in the romances' endings. But in the martyr *Acts*, we perhaps overhear the voices of those who resisted being "made subjects and the governed." The martyr *Acts* are seminal documents in a struggle between two competing systems for investing meaning in human action. And, like all such world-constructing documents, they suppress in their narrative the justification for the other side just as they mask, to a certain extent, their own interests.

The emphasis on violence in the martyr *Acts* is indicative of this discursive struggle, and Nancy Armstrong and Leonard Tennenhouse's point is germane:

> violent events are not simply so but are called violent because they bring together different concepts of social order. To

regard certain practices as violent is never to see them just as they are. It is always to take up a position for or against them.

(Armstrong and Tennenhouse 1989: 9)

But from what possible viewpoint could the actions described in the martyr *Acts* – scourgings, beheadings, burnings alive, being devoured by beasts – not appear violent? Their neighbors would likely answer: when they are viewed as justice. In the Roman empire, sovereignty, the social order reified, was manifested to a large extent through display, the public showing-forth of the emperor's might and magnanimity. The tortures and death of martyrs had a role in this display (Coleman 1990). Recall that Perpetua and her companion martyrs suffered as part of the official military games held to honor the birthday of Geta, the son of emperor Septimius Severus. In Lyons also, the martyrdoms were part of official, state exhibitions.

Such shows held throughout the empire functioned to manifest the power of the state before gathered-together civic populations. Torture, it ought to be remembered, although experienced as pain, is always intended to be interpreted as power (Hopkins 1983: 14, 29). In the large civic events staged at public expense in Lyons and Carthage, the torture and death of martyrs and other criminals showed forth for all to see the vanquishing and destruction of those who refused to conform in the society. To quote Randall McGowen commenting on another chronological period: "The violence of punishment was a language employed by authority to write the message of justice. . . . The broken body of the condemned represented the restored order of the body politic" (McGowen 1989: 143). But just as Perpetua, the represented "unruly woman," refused to be put in "her place" by society's forces, or even recognize "this age" as having a place for her, so the language of the broken body speaks in another register in Christian discourse. The martyr *Acts* refuse to read the martyrs' broken bodies as defeat, but reverse the reading, insisting on interpreting them as symbols of victory over society's power. This difference at the level of explanation between the discourse of the martyr *Acts* and the inscribed spectacles of public punishment displays the nature of this conflict between social orders.

By rejecting that they experienced pain or defeat, Christians rejected the power structures surrounding them, and rejected the social order these supported. Their neighbors' fury shows their

117

recognition and reaction to this Christian rejection. Popular support for the martyrs' punishment is quite clear from the martyrs' *Acts* themselves. In the *Acts of Lyons*, the populace's rage at the Christians continued even after their deaths:

> some men raged and ground their teeth at the bodies as though they were trying to take some further special revenge on them. Others laughed and mocked them, at the same time exalting their own idols, attributing their punishment to them.
>
> (1.60)

These actions of residents of Lyons ratify the Christian's punishment and see it as the vindication of their own belief system.

The situation in Smyrna is similar. News of Polycarp's arrest is greeted with shouts of approval; the crowd shouts again "in uncontrollable rage" naming Polycarp "the teacher of atheism" (12.2).[9] General hostility toward the Christians must also be behind the Carthaginian crowd's demand that the martyrs be brought back into the arena and be killed before their eyes (*oculos suos* 21.7).

The treatment given to Christian bodies in Lyons indicates that their neighbors knew about Christian rejection of the prevailing social order before they enacted it in the arena. Guards were assigned to watch over the unburied mangled and burnt bodies of the martyrs, many in pieces, for six days until they were finally burnt up, reduced to ashes, and thrown into the River Rhône. The narrator quotes the explanation provided for these actions:

> And they did this as though they could overcome God and deprive the martyrs of their restoration, in order, as they themselves said, that they might have no hope in the resurrection in which they put their trust when they introduce this strange new cult among us and despise the torments, walking readily and joyfully to their death. Now let us see whether they will rise again, and whether their god can help them and rescue them from our hands.
>
> (1.63)

The residents of Lyons were well-acquainted, it seems, with doctrine of the resurrection and the attitude to earthly life it engendered: "walking readily and joyfully to their death." Christian discourse supports their interpretation. Tertullian clearly articulated a rejection of the contemporary social order: "nothing matters to

us in this age but to escape from it with all speed" (*Apologia* 41.5).
Justin reflects similar views: "But because we do not place our hope
in the present, we do not mind when men murder us, since death
is inevitable anyway" (*Apologia* 11). Likewise Athenagoras: "we shall
suffer no great evil even should our lives be taken from us
. . .'(*Legatio* 12)

Christian discourse not only changed the rules for empowerment,
it extended the stage for exercising power. The different spheres of
insult leveled by each side provides evidence. Participants in social
conflicts often attempt to nullify the other side by subsuming them
into something perceived as alien or abhorrent (Greenblatt 1981: 9).
Such categorization allows "the other" to be treated violently with
impunity. So the Christians were routinely accused of cannibalism
and incest: crimes which by their nature betray a misunderstanding
of human society and its basic rules, and so make those guilty of
them deserving of expulsion or destruction.[10] These charges also
demonstrate that the pagans understood their conflict to be a social
one. Christians were accused of violating primary social categories.

The Christians, however, relocate the conflict outside the natural
world. Those who challenge Christians are depicted as either
demons, devils, or their dupes. Perpetua understood her contest
with the Roman authorities as a contest with the devil. The martyrs
at Lyons are depicted fighting with the archetypal "opponent"
(1.23) or "the Beast" (1.57). The gaolers are not described as men
performing their set duties but as those "inflicting all sorts of other
indignities, which gaolers when aroused and filled with the devil
are accustomed to inflict upon prisoners" (1.27). Justin similarly
describes judges sentencing Christians as the "slaves and worshipers
of wicked demons, like rulers under demonical influence" (II
Apologia 1). By such labeling, the Christian texts banish their
enemies beyond the natural world itself, and display the scope
of the drama martyrs see themselves enacting in their theater of
martyrdom. They look for power and vindication, not in this
world, but in the transcendent world to come.

Martyrs' deaths, portrayed as so joyfully and exuberantly embraced
in Christian discourse, display not the power of the Roman state but
rather the power of the Christian community's reordered beliefs
about pain and death. The broken bodies of Christians gave
testimony not to the "restored order of the body public" but rather
to a new understanding of the social body extended beyond life's
natural limits. As Minucius Felix's Octavius says; "Poor fools, you

119

do not see that without reason no one would voluntarily submit to punishment or without God's help endure the tortures" (37.6). "But the soldier of God is not forsaken in his pain nor does death end all" (37.3).

One thing death did not end for many was the body's existence. The body seen lacerated, torn to pieces, burnt in the early Christian *Acts*, had its analogue in the body reformed and resurrected that featured so prominently in other Christian discourse of the period. For it is precisely in the period of the early martyr *Acts* that a shift in emphasis occurred in the discourse on the resurrection. What had been a belief in the resurrection of the body became more and more an affirmation of the resurrection of the flesh (Davies 1972). Paul's teaching on a transformed risen body loses ground to a concerted insistence on the resurrection of the fleshy body; resurrection becomes not a transformation but literally a reanimation of the earthly body (Davies 1972: 450–452).

Christian apologists refute objections such as those that likely prompted the treatment of the martyrs' bodies in Lyons. Tatian, for example, insists:

> Even though fire destroy all traces of my flesh, the world receives the vaporized matter; and though dispersed through rivers and seas and torn to pieces by wild beasts, I am laid up in the storehouses of a wealthy God . . . He will restore the substance that is visible to him alone to its pristine condition.
>
> (*Oratio ad Graecos* 6)[11]

To modern ears, the elaborate and extended defense of this doctrine in the Christian discourse of the second century seems almost obsessive, but it indicates the doctrine's centrality. Recall that while Tatian, Minucius Felix, Theophilus, and Athenagoras in their apologies for Christianity all manage without mentioning Christ or his birth, death, and resurrection, they all refer to the resurrection of the body (Bernard 1976: 11). Elaborate rebuttals were mounted against any challenges to this doctrine.

Athenagoras, for example, displays the most up-to-date medical knowledge on the digestive system to buttress his lengthy defense of the resurrection of flesh (Bernard 1976: 13). Opponents had apparently suggested that in certain circumstances it might be impossible to separate out the flesh of two human bodies for the reconstitution of the resurrected body. They apparently proposed for an example the situation when animals eat human flesh and then in turn are themselves consumed by humans (*De Resurrectione* 4–8). Athenagoras objected to this argument, basing his rebuttal on the nature of the digestive system. Different foods are suitable for different animals. Humans are not naturally nourished by human flesh and so their bodies would never combine with bodies like themselves – they would vomit or void nutriment from human bodies. It is not difficult to image the possibilities for excretory comment such very material arguments gave opponents. Tertullian, in his *Resurrection of the Flesh*, mentions that out of respect for his pen (*pro stili pudore*) he has cleaned up his summary of the arguments non-Christians made against the resurrection, but they could be heard uncensored in public discussions (4.25). Tertullian also provides evidence that Athenagoras's concern with humans consuming animals who have consumed humans may not be as remote as it seems. In his *Apology* he describes man-eating animals from the arena being sought for meat – "the bellies of the very bears are sought, full of raw and undigested flesh" (9.11).

Christians proposed arguments focused on such pronounced physicality to convey the extent of their commitment to a radically material understanding of their existence after death. Death was seen as merely a slight interruption in the material existence of the body. But, as John Gager has noted, doctrines that focus on the body are "especially concerned with social relationships . . . the human body is never seen as a body without at the same time being treated as an image of society" (Gager 1982: 347). The Christian community's emphasis on a resurrected body materially identical to the present body suggests not only its rejection of the contemporary social order but its belief in a new social order, restructured for Christian empowerment. This is Perpetua's reversed body writ large. The reason for the emphatic insistence on the fleshy body is clear, not only so Christians can physically be present to rule during the millennium – the influence of millenarian expectations on a belief in fleshy resurrection seems established, and Justin, Tertullian, and Irenaeus (the latter two putative authors of the *Passion of Perpetua* and *Acts of Lyons*, respectively) were convinced millenarians – but to insure a complete judgement after death, to reverse the unjust allocations of this life. So Tertullian requires that the whole man must be produced in the divine court: "It is not sufficient for the soul without the flesh to be comforted or tormented for works which belong to the flesh" (*De Resurrectione* 17.24–26). It is this very material understanding that underlies the martyrs' actions. And if pain inflicted is

121

to be construed as power, power is what the martyrs look forward to. The martyrs are quite clear about this in the *Acts*; just as they refuse to recognize the power of the State's torture, they insist on their own coming power won by their suffering. On the day before they die, for example, the martyrs at Carthage speak to those who have come to watch them eat their last meal:

> They . . . warned them of God's judgement, stressing the joy they would have in their suffering, and ridiculing the curiosity of those that came to see them. Saturus said: "Will not tomorrow be enough for you? Why are you so eager to see something you dislike . . . But take careful note of what we look like so you will recognize us on that day."
>
> (17.1–2)

The martyrs with their reference here to "that day" (*illo die*) refer not to the next day of their execution, but to the day of judgement when their roles will be reversed. Saturus and the martyrs make this point clearly as they enter the arena: "then when they came within sight of Hilarianus, [the governor] they suggested by their motions and gestures: 'you have condemned us, but God will condemn you' was what they were saying," (18.7–8). Needless to say, this enraged the spectators who demanded their scourging. At this the martyrs only rejoiced the more, having "obtained a share in the Lord's suffering" (18.9).

Polycarp, also rejecting the victim's role, displayed similar defiance. Urged to recant by the proconsul in the amphitheater and say "away with the atheists," he looks up at the crowd, shakes his fist and says "away with the atheists" (9.2). Polycarp also looked to a future judgement for retribution. He answers the proconsul's threats to burn him alive with his own threats: "The fire you threaten me with burns merely for a time and is soon extinguished. It is clear you are ignorant of the fire of everlasting punishment and of the judgement that is to come that awaits the impious" (11.2). Christians do not reject power, merely, as one of the Scillitan martyrs says, "the power [*imperium*] of this world" (6). They rejected their contemporary social order for another where the power would be theirs, a reversed world in which, as Justin says, even the emperor will be judged (I *Apologia* 68), where those whom we have witnessed in the early martyr *Acts* resisting "being made subjects and governed," as did Perpetua, will at last triumph. The discourse of the martyr *Acts*, representing pain as empowering and death a victory, helped to construct a new understanding of human existence, a new "mental set" toward the world that would have far-reaching consequences. This discourse created a new paradigm for understanding suffering and death and, consequently, the experiential world they supposedly authenticated. Things that had universally been thought bad and contemptible, such as pain and death, were suddenly seen as valuable, just as Blandina thought "cheap, unsightly and easy to despise" was recognized as noble in her courageous endurance. This empowerment, together with the emphasis on the resurrected body, displays the subversive underpinnings of this discourse. To project a material body just like this material body is to suggest a social body just like this social body, only with a different hierarchy based on new rules of empowerment. The early martyr *Acts* provided a discourse that enacted a subversion of deference and hierarchy that history would fulfill. If power is to impose one's version of key cultural terms upon the world, then the early martyr *Acts* are extraordinarily powerful discourses.

5

HEALING AND POWER
The *Acts of Peter*

Societies are characterized by competing relations of power, but, distanced by history, cultures often appear univocal. Either only the discourse produced by the dominant culture is left or, dulled by time, our ears are not keen enough to overhear the competing strains. Such a situation adversely affects the understanding and tracing of social change over time. It is by good fortune, therefore, that, from the social body known as the Roman empire, narratives remain that embody the voices – the values and passions – of alienated groups at the brink of momentous change.

I maintain that in the so-called *Apocryphal Acts of the Apostles* signs and strategies of an emerging representational and social challenge are preserved. These texts, the *Acts of John, Peter, Paul, Andrew*, and *Thomas* were composed over a range of geographical locations – Greece, Asia Minor, Syria – in the second and early third centuries. Each exhibits a similar plot line, tracing the adventures, preaching, and death of a particular apostle (Pervo 1994).[1] Their content may well reflect oral material circulating widely among early Christian communities; their form, as has been noted, recalls the ancient novel, for the prose narratives of both the *Acts* and the novel share an emphasis on adventures and trials, on travel, on the marvelous (Söder 1932). The connection may be more substantive than these coincidences of plot. Studies of the ancient novel have explained the emergence and popularity of these fictive prose narratives by pointing to new and changed social needs (Reardon 1971); in Chapter 3, the romances were discussed as affirmations and celebrations of the elite societies of the Greek East. Recently, Averil Cameron has discussed the *Apocryphal Acts* in related terms as group structure-building and structure-maintaining narratives (Cameron 1991: 116). The fictive prose narrative was

124

the genre of choice in the early empire for groups to construct and define both their being and their being within the world.

The Apocryphal Acts, like the ancient romance, ought to provide evidence for the mental categories and sense-making efforts of communities in the early empire. But, until recently, the *Acts* have been largely ignored: by religious scholars because of their fictiveness and purported heresy, in some cases; and by literary historians because of their Christian content (Kaestli 1981). It is now time to integrate their testimony into a less artificially partitioned picture of the early empire. Their witness becomes increasingly important as the recognition grows that the ancient novel was not, as earlier scholars had claimed, written by and for the unsophisticated. *The Apocryphal Acts* preserve rare access to examples of a popular narrative voice.

This examination will concentrate on the *Acts of Peter*, a text most likely written in Asia Minor in the late second century. The *Acts* is extant in a third- or fourth-century Latin translation and Greek versions of a final section depicting the apostle's martyrdom, as well as a Coptic fragment.[2] The Latin translation shows a close correspondence with the Greek portions; moreover, the language and style of both the Greek and Latin versions display quite clearly that these texts were directed to a non-elite audience. In fact, C. H. Turner has labeled the Latin style "rough" (Turner 1931). The plot of this narrative is simple. The apostle Paul departs from Rome, leaving his flock vulnerable to his rival, Simon, who calls himself "the great power of God" (48.22).[3] Nearly the whole congregation apostatizes; only a few believers and the housebound sick remain true (49.16). Finally Peter arrives, promising to reclaim the converts through his "deeds and marvelous powers" (54.26–27). Peter challenges Simon to a contest in raising the dead. Peter wins the contest and quickly gains converts, and the text concludes with his condemnation by officials who are annoyed by his teaching on continence, his crucifixion, burial, and return in two dream visitations.

The *Acts* is not simply a religious text focused on Christian morality, hopes for immortality, or some other such homiletic orthodoxy, but rather a narrative with an implicit social agenda. The narrative emphases of the *Acts* establish the superior healing prowess of the Christian community, affirms suffering as profitable, and contests the power and routes to power inhering in the surrounding culture. In her *Authoritarian Fictions*, Susan Suleiman

(1983) offered a taxonomy for studying the genre of the ideological novel, the *roman à thèse*. She suggested that redundancies were the mark of such novels. According to Suleiman, ideological novels, namely those intent on conveying particular meanings, repeatedly enact and reenact their meanings. Although the *Acts of Peter* is not quite a "novel" in the modern sense, Suleiman's taxonomy suggested an interesting approach to reading this overtly ideological narrative, namely to be attentive to the narrative's repetitions as signals of its "message."

Suleiman's model was premised on realistic fiction, but this is not necessarily a problem in considering this narrative focused on the marvelous. The *Acts* is full of prodigies – talking dogs, flying men, dreams, and apparitions. But as Ramsay MacMullen has cautioned, it would be the *not* believing in miracles and wonders that would be irrational and unrealistic in the context of the early empire, and his point is equally valid for visions (MacMullen 1984: 22). It is instructive here to recall that, on the evidence of what he calls reliable witnesses, Tacitus testified that the emperor Vespasian miraculously cured blindness and a crippled arm (*Historiae* 81.1–3). Near the same period as the *Acts of Peter* were written, Irenaeus listed the duties of clerics as healing, exorcising and raising the dead (*Adversus Haereses* 2.32.4), and Galen's father chose his son's career as a result of a dream vision (*On Prognosis* 2.12). [Realism is a socially constructed category.]

According to Suleiman, ideological novels feature only two plot types, either an apprenticeship plot or a confrontational plot. The confrontational plot is based on a dualistic system of values. Its principal characters are unequivocally characterized as "good" or "bad." It is this confrontation plot that underlies many types of modern popular fiction, such as the war novel, detective fiction, and Westerns. The plot of the *Acts of Peter* conforms closely with this pattern. The first four-fifths of the narrative depicts Simon Magus blowing into town in a cloud of dust (*pulvis in caelum*), rustling away many of Paul's converts (only the homebound sick remain faithful), until he is challenged by Peter and defeated in front of the whole city in a contest likened by commentators to a Western "shoot-out."

The *Acts* is quite explicitly a narrative about competing power structures. Its central episode is a contest to prove whose god is more powerful, Simon's or Peter's. Stands are erected and a fee charged as all of Rome turns out to witness this contest in raising the dead (62.32, 70.28). Interruptions repeatedly break up the narrative of this contest, which begins when the prefect Agrippa instructs Simon to kill one of his retainers. Simon kills the man by whispering in his ear. Agrippa then challenges Peter to restore the servant's life. Only the first half of this process has occurred when a widow intrudes and begs Peter to raise her dead son. The dead boy is sent for, and thirty young men, first checking to see that he is "fully dead," carry him to Peter "so that he may revive him" (73.28). But Peter first must attend to Agrippa's man. He brings him back to life and then raises the widow's son. Both resurrections generate faith in the onlookers; they shout, "Thou art God the Savior, thou, the God of Peter, the invisible God, the Savior" (74.14–15).

At this point, the mother of a senator approaches Peter and asks that her dead son be restored to light. Peter uses this opportunity to challenge Simon to another contest: "Let him revive the body which lies here; . . . but if he cannot then I shall call upon my God; . . . and you [shall] believe that this is a sorcerer and a cheat" (75.19–22). Stooping down three times and standing up three times over the body, Simon does act like a sorcerer as he manages to create some movement in the body: "[the dead man] had raised his head and was moving, opening his eyes and bowing toward Simon" (76.1–2). Peter mocks these feeble movements and insists that Simon move away from the body; this causes the man to fall back into death. The sorcerer's effect depends on close proximity to its object. Simon's trick so angers the crowd that they wish to kill him until Peter chides them, "We have learned to love our enemies" (77.1). Peter then calls on Christ, touches Nicostratus, the senator, who stands up, unties his jaw, asks for his clothes, and recounts his dream. Peter exults, "this is how the dead are restored to life" (77.28).

This scenario exemplifies Suleiman's point that redundancy is the sign of the ideological narrative. Instead of one resurrection, there are three; instead of one contest, two. The point is brought home repeatedly that Peter, the Christian champion, is a superlative healer (reviving the dead is the ultimate healing act), and the narrator underscores this when he describes the effect of the resurrections on the crowd: "from that same hour they venerated him as a god, and laid at his feet such sick people as they had at home, so that he might heal them" (78.5–7). Throughout the text, even before this contest, Peter is first and foremost a healer. On Peter's visit to the senator Marcellus' house, for example, his healing prowess is emphasized. He cures a blind widow when he enters and another group of blind women when he leaves (66.27–28, 68.25–30).

The *Acts* stresses Peter's healing powers, emphasizing vividly the real physicality of the diseases he heals:

> and they brought the sick people also to him on the Sabbath, entreating him that they might be cured of their diseases. And many paralytics were healed, and many sufferers from dropsy and from two-and-four-day fever, and they were cured of every bodily disease, such as believed in the name of Jesus Christ.
>
> (80.15–21)

But the *Acts* also locates healing more widely, in Christ and the Christian community. To this end, Peter is depicted twice sharing Christ's healing power with others. Peter did not in fact raise Agrippa's retainer; Agrippa himself did. Peter first prays: "and now in the sight of them all, O Lord, in thy power raise up through my voice the man whom Simon killed . . . ," and then he instructs Agrippa, "come, take up his right hand, . . . and Agrippa the prefect ran and came to the boy and taking his hand restored him to life" (73.30–35). In the episode of the broken statue, it is Marcellus, instructed by Peter, who actually sprinkles the statue with water and restores it. The text focuses not on Peter as a miracle worker so much as on Peter, Christ's intermediary in healing. Peter repeatedly ascribes his power to Christ, and his actions demonstrate that anyone, even a Roman prefect, can heal with Christ's help.[4]

The *Acts* also emphasizes and reemphasizes that those outside the community are pseudo-healers. After the contest, Peter follows Simon, exposing his false cures until Simon finally announces he is going to fly back to his father. Peter realizes that a successful flight would win many converts for Simon so he prays, "make haste, Lord, with thy grace; and let him fall down from [this] height, and be crippled, and not die; but let him be disabled and break his leg in three places" (82.18–26). Peter's prayer is answered. Simon does fall, break his leg, and, abandoned by his followers, dies of a bungled operation: "But Simon in his misfortune found [some] helpers who carried him on a stretcher . . . to a man named Castor . . . there he underwent an operation; and thus Simon, the angel of the devil, ended his life" (84.5–10). In this narrative focused on healing, it is not surprising to find divine justice manifested in a mishandled operation. Nor is the emphatic emphasis on the physical novel; earlier in the narrative a sacrilegious woman had been paralyzed from her head to her toenails (46.25–26). Both descriptions belong to the narrative's repeated attention to Christianity's concern for the body and its health. The *Acts* shows that Peter, the Christian spokesman, is a superlative healer and that he can share his healing power. Simon, his rival, is able neither to heal nor be healed. He dies abandoned to the care of a sorcerer. The narrative functions to offer the Christian community as a community of healers and the healed.

One of the central aims of the *Acts of Peter* was not a call to Christian virtue or way of life, or even the allure of immortality, but, rather, to demonstrate the Christian community's powerful concern with sickness, health, and human suffering. Health was a major religious concern in the period, by far the benefit people most prayed for (MacMullen 1981: 49–51). Christianity offered itself as a healing cult in these early centuries and repeatedly employed the metaphor of medicine to embody its message (Harnack 1892). Ignatius began a hymn, "there is one physician who is flesh and spirit" (*Ad Ephesios* 7.2). Much of Clement of Alexandria's *Paedagogus* rests on the simile of Christ as physician, the Christian message as medicine, and salvation as eternal health. The *Acts of Peter*, a narrative that opened with the injunction to Paul, "Arise and be a physician to Spain," connects these medical metaphors with the attention to health and the body so prevalent during this period. The *Acts of Peter* repeatedly illustrates that Christianity's stance as a superior healing cult would have attracted proselytes (48.3–25, 62.26–30, 73.35–36).

This reading of the *Acts*, as a narrative intent on showing the superiority of Christianity, as a healing religion, would work better if the narrative ended with Simon's death. But the *Acts*, as so many other Christian narratives, ends instead with Peter's martyrdom. How can we account for this death in a narrative about healing? This ending identifies another element central to Christianity's message in these early centuries. The *Acts of Peter* not only shows a community deeply committed to Christianity's superior healing potential, but it displays a community with a structure ready for understanding suffering if healing should fail. Suffering, the narrative emphasized, can be profitable in itself.

The narrative repeatedly makes the point that infirmity is part of God's plan and can even be beneficial. The Coptic fragment of the *Acts* showed a crowd rebuking Peter for healing other people while he ignores his own paralyzed daughter. So, to prove that "God is not weak or powerless," he heals the paralyzed girl. But as soon as he has demonstrated God's power, Peter instructs his daughter: "go to your place, lie down and return to your infirmity, for this is profitable for you and for me" (*Papyrus Berolinensis* 8502 140).[5] The narrative explains that the girl's paralysis has saved her from a life of lust. At the end of the episode, Peter reiterates God's compassion notwithstanding human pain, saying "God cares for his own and prepares good for every one of them, although we think God has forgotten us" (*Papyrus Berolinensis* 8502 140).

The same message is repeated in a very similar episode preserved in a later text. Peter prays that his gardener's daughter receive what is best for her soul, and she immediately falls dead. When Peter gives in to her father's pleas that she be returned to life, she soon falls into a life of sin (Pseudo-Titus *De dispositione sanctimonii* 83–84). The moral of the scene is that the girl's death was best for her and God does at times inflict human suffering, not necessarily for chastisement, but because suffering is best. The *Acts'* description of Peter's experience at Christ's transfiguration conveys this same theme. Peter is lifted from suffering by accepting it. Overcome by Christ's radiance, he falls down believing himself blinded: "'perhaps my Lord willed to bring me here to deprive me of my sight.' And I said, 'if this be thy will, Lord, I do not gainsay it'" (67.16–17). At these words, Christ gives Peter his hand and lifts him up.

The often imitated *Quo vadis* scene dramatically enacted the message of the divine affirmation of suffering. Fleeing persecution in Rome, Peter meets Christ who is entering the city and asks him where he is going. Christ's answer, "I am coming to Rome to be crucified," amazes Peter. "Lord, art thou being crucified again?" Christ answers, "yes," and ascends (88.5–12). Peter comes to himself and returns to Rome, rejoicing in his recognition that, through his martyrdom, he will become "another Christ."

It is within this context that Peter makes his response to the crowd that attempts to rescue him from crucifixion: "... soldiers of Christ ... remember the signs and wonders which you saw through me, remember the compassion of God, how many healings he has performed for you" (90.11–14). Peter reminds the crowd that God is powerful and compassionate and could rescue him if this were best. But Christ has shown him that it is otherwise. Peter insists on God's compassion even as he permits human suffering. The final statement of the place of suffering in the narrative occurs in Peter's last speech from the cross. His advice to his listeners is:

> come to the cross of Christ. . . . The spirit says "for what is Christ but the word, the sound of God? So the word is the upright tree on which I am crucified; but the sound is the cross-piece, the nature of man; and the nail that holds the cross-piece to the upright in the middle is the conversion [*epistrophe*] and repentance [*metanoia*] of man."
>
> (96.6–11)

Peter explains conversion as the human acceptance of and union with the suffering Christ. The reified image of conversion is the nail, and it is at this point, in the nail, in suffering, that Christ's human nature meets his divine nature, and where humanity is joined to both. The *Acts of Peter* represents pain and death as divinely affirmed.

Christianity's ability to cure sickness and death or to provide a profitable function for them is patent throughout the *Acts*. This healing ability is read as tangible evidence of Christianity's superior power. The text is openly focused on power. One of Simon's followers, for example, comments after Simon has fallen and broken his leg: "Simon, if the power of God is broken, shall not the God himself, whose power you are, be proved an illusion?" This focus extends beyond what one of the Roman crowd calls "a contest between two Jews on worshipping God" (70.1). Even as the *Acts* affirms the superior healing prowess of the Christian community and shows suffering as profitable, it challenges the power and routes to power inhering in the surrounding culture. In the early empire, religion and politics often shared the same discourse (Price 1984: 235).

Readers of the *Acts* live in an upside-down world – a world of reversed values and forms (Smith 1969–1970). Peter's explanation of his desire for an upside-down crucifixion defines this world. He wishes to die upside down because Adam's birth:

> established the whole of this cosmic system . . . and changed the signs of their nature, so as to consider fair those things that were not fair, and take those that were really evil to be good. Concerning this, the Lord says is a mystery, "Unless you make what is on the right hand as what is on the left

> ... and what is above as what is below and what is behind
> as what is before, you will not recognize the kingdom."
>
> (94.5–15)

This is a message with obvious radical social overtones if taken in a "this world" sense; other textual elements suggest that taking it so in this text would not be misreading.

The *Acts* plainly represents that the wrong leaders are on top in this world. In a work so emphatically centered on mercy and multiple forgiveness, Nero is portrayed quite harshly.[6] Early in the text, Nero is called, on good authority, a voice from heaven, a "godless and wicked man" (46.9). He exposes his wicked nature again after Peter's martyrdom when he is angry because "he would have liked to punish him [Peter] more cruelly and with extra severity" (100.17–18). But Nero is no match for Peter perfected by death. The apostle appears to the emperor in a dream, scourges him and says: "Nero, you cannot now persecute or destroy the servants of Christ. Keep your hands from them!" (102.2–3). This dream embodies a powerfully subversive image – the emperor enduring a servile punishment as well as an inversion of reality: martyrs on occasion were tortured and put to death at imperial festivals.[7] Peter's triumph over the emperor could not be clearer: "And so Nero being greatly alarmed because of this vision, kept away from the disciples from the time that Peter departed this life" (102.4–6).

In this way, Peter decisively removed Nero as a threat to his community. It is a bold move. The person of the emperor and the imperial cult were critical in articulating power relations in the Greek East. And yet even earlier than this in the *Acts*, a statue of the emperor is destroyed, kicked to pieces by a demon exorcised by Peter. Marcellus, a senator and owner of the statue, is terrified and with good reason. There is evidence that a citizen was executed merely for urinating near an imperial statue; Dio of Prusa was harassed for supposedly burying his wife and son in the courtyard of a building that contained an imperial statue.[8] In the *Acts*, Peter calms Marcellus, telling him that if he really believes in Christ he can restore the statue by sprinkling it with water. "And Marcellus did not doubt," the narrator says, "but believed with his whole heart" and so successfully reformed the statue averting harm from himself" (59.19). Simon Price has demonstrated how the imperial cult reinforced the charisma of the emperor and his government

(Price 1984: 191–206). Yet the action of this scene deflates the constitutive power surrounding the cult; it displays that with belief in the Lord and trust in his leaders, the imperial statue is in reality just "stones" (*lapides istos* 59.23).

Moreover, a complex of images in both these scenes hints at what is understood to be deficient in the imperial power. Marcellus' hands are repeatedly referred to throughout the statue scene: "Marcellus was uplifted in spirit, because this first miracle was done by his hands" (59.39). Throughout the text, the healing or helping hand of the Christian community is emphasized. When Peter meets a blind widow he gives her his hand and tells her, "Jesus gives you his right hand . . . and he says to you through me, 'Open your eyes and see and walk on your own.' And at once the widow saw Peter laying his hand on her" (66.18–25). Peter himself has experienced this helping hand; when he was struck down and blinded at the Transfiguration, the Lord gave him his hand and lifted him up (*et dans mihi manum elevavit me* 67.16–17). This complex of images woven throughout the *Acts* suggests that its readers were looking for a helping, healing hand. That help was not seen to be provided by the hostile hands of the emperor or the rule he embodied. In its depiction of the emperor, the *Acts* projects one aspect of the world that is upside down (what is above that should not be) and at the same time strikes out at two central supports of any political culture – deference to superior authority and the state religion.

The fiction of the *Acts* allows its audience to imagine the function of the senatorial class in its community – not a very likely scenario at this period (Jones 1963: 17). Once again, what is above should not be. The high birth of Marcellus, the Christian senator, makes it harder rather than easier for him to help his community. Save that his conversion and reconversion affect many dependents, Marcellus is not an untypical convert. First he was converted by Paul, only to be seduced away by Simon; then, like others, he was reconverted by Peter's signs and wonders, in his case a talking dog sent by the apostle to castigate Simon.[9] But the text underlines an inherent weakness in the senator (Stoops 1986: 98). On the night before Peter's decisive contest with Simon, Marcellus has a dream. In this dream he sees Peter and before him:

a woman, all black, . . . dancing with an iron collar around her neck and chains on her hands and feet. When you saw her you said aloud to me, "Marcellus, the whole power of

Simon and of his god is in this dancer; take off her head!"
But I said to you, "Brother Peter, I am a senator of noble
family, and I have never stained my hands nor killed even a
sparrow at any time."

(70.9–15)

A likeness of Peter has to do the deed. The *Acts* clearly locates
Marcellus' weakness and his inability to protect the community
from Satan in his class consciousness. Marcellus errs again later in
the narrative and, again, it is his status that betrays him. After
Peter dies, Marcellus takes him down from the cross:

> he washed him in milk and wine; and he ground up seven
> pounds of mastic, and also fifty pounds of myrrh and aloe
> and spice and embalmed his body, and filled a trough of
> stone of great value with Attic honey and laid in his own
> burial vault.

(100.1–5)

Yet Marcellus gets no praise for his devotion and expense. Instead
Peter returns from the beyond to reprimand him: "Marcellus, you
heard the Lord saying, 'Let the dead be buried by the dead?'"
(100.6–7). He rejects Marcellus' actions; actions, it should be
noted, that include the most typical of his class, namely the ostentatious display of his wealth.[10] Peter reminds us that the Lord's
words now direct Marcellus even with respect to how he spends
this wealth. The source of Marcellus' error is clearly articulated: he
acted without "taking anyone's advice, since it was not allowed"
(98.16). The text repeats its basic point that the requisites of
Marcellus' high position disabled him and prevented his acquiring
the knowledge he needed to act correctly.

The same message about the detriment of high birth reappears
in the characterization of another high-born character, Agrippa.
Before his crucifixion, Peter begs his followers not to be angry at
Agrippa "for he is the servant of his father's influence." Vouaux
thought this phrase (*patrikes energeias*) referred to Satan, but the
Latin translator who explains *traditionis illius* understood it better.
Agrippa is constrained from seeing his error by his lineage, his
tradition. Through Marcellus, who cannot act to kill Satan and
Agrippa (who acts badly in killing Peter), the *Acts* reveals leaders
who must be rejected for the very reason that the surrounding pagan
political culture admires them. The phrase "like his ancestors" can

be found in numerous honorific inscriptions throughout the Greek East (MacMullen 1974: 101). In the surrounding culture, as the themes of the Greek romances attest, high birth helped to insure leadership.

The dream reproach Peter issues to Marcellus, his assumption that Marcellus' actions (even his expenditures) are under the control of the Lord's word, has important implications, especially as it is linked in the *Acts* to a more radical redirection of patronage. In feudal societies, it has been suggested, power functioned essentially through signs and levies (Foucault 1984: 66). In the early Roman empire, power functioned through signs (such as the rites and ceremonies of the imperial cult) and through the public patronage of the upper classes. Individuals spent lavishly in their quest for *philotimia*, i.e., for honor and prestige. The importance of this kind of expenditure cannot be overstated. Cities prospered through the expenditures of the wealthy; money, buildings, entertainment, supplies and services were all donated by wealthy individuals. Cities responded with public testimonials of thanks. Such patronage is, as Oswyn Murray has noted, at basis a sign of an unequal distribution of power – "I give because you cannot" (Veyne 1990: xiv). When a group consistently displayed its superiority by such means, it acted as a political class. Patronage should be recognized as a political act. Veyne shows how the numerous honors voted by cities to their benefactors (in the empire, most conspicuously the emperor, the governor, and other notables) proclaimed for all to see what the established order was (Veyne 1990: 125). Patronage was one of the means by which those on top manifested their power and dominance, and it is in this context that the repetitious emphasis on patronage in the *Acts* needs to be considered.

Robert Stoops (1986, 1991) has examined the operation and importance of patronage in the *Acts*, and noted the repeated occasions of patronage shown in the narrative. Both the resurrected senator and his mother, for example, are patrons:

> She came to Marcellus' house bringing Peter two thousand pieces of gold and saying to Peter, "Divide these among the virgins of Christ who serve him." But when the boy who had risen from the dead saw that he had given nothing to anyone, he went home and opened his chest and himself brought four thousand gold pieces.
>
> (79.8–13)

Such large amounts of money, in fact, may not be so inflated for a cure. Galen received the very substantial sum of 40,000 sesterces for his cure of Boethus' wife and there is evidence that a doctor "would have been rich for life if he had made a particularly successful cure."[11] Eubula also acts as a patron after her stolen goods are restored: "But Eubula having recovered all her property gave it for the care of the poor . . . and despising and renouncing the world she gave [alms] to the widows and orphans and clothed the poor" (65.19–23). Peter even accepts the donation of a notoriously rich and adulterous woman, Chryse, and he rejects the advice that he not accept such money:

> But Peter, when he heard this, laughed and said to the brethren, I do not know what this woman is as regards her usual way of life; in taking her money I did not take it without reason, for she was bringing it as a debtor to Christ, and is giving it to Christ's servants; for he himself has provided for them.

> (80.10–14)

Patronage is an important theme in the *Acts*, where Christ is offered as the ultimate source of all blessings. No longer are wealthy human patrons honored for their largess. This narrative enterprise, depriving patrons of their honor, ought to be understood as a political act, just as bestowing honors on benefactors was. If, as Veyne maintains, the honors shown benefactors publicly project the established order, redirecting such recognition to another entity not only destabilizes the established order, but erects a competing order in its place. The characterization of patronage in the *Acts* supports the narrative's critique of the surrounding political culture.

In this way, the *Acts* replaces prevailing pagan social institutions with a Christian community. When "the only person explicitly called a patron in the *Acts*," Marcellus, buried Peter, he acted as a typical member of his class (*Acts* 100.1–5; Stoops 1986). He demonstrated his wealth by his display of his riches. The narrative's specificity (seven pounds of mastic, fifty pounds of myrrh) reflects the culture's avid interest in accounting such details. It surprises us at first that Marcellus' action, seemingly harmless and done out of love, is serious enough to warrant Peter's return from the beyond. That it does, alerts us to the importance of the apostle's message: wealth is no longer in the control of the wealthy, but susceptible to Christ's word and control. Stoops interprets this scene as showing that "the wealth of believers is to be used to benefit others. The honor it brings belongs to Christ" (Stoops 1986: 98). In the Roman world, honor shows power, and our text is quite explicit about what sort of being this Christ is who receives honor. Peter experienced Christ at the Transfiguration and describes him – he, "who is both great and little, beautiful and ugly, young and old, . . . beauteous [*speciosum*], yet appearing among us poor and ugly [*humilem*]" (68.18–19). Similarly, the widows see the Lord in many forms (*quomodo alias et alias dominum viderint*).[12]

These descriptions suggest that the "polymorphic" Christ embodies in himself a utopian community, a mingling of classes diverging almost totally from the reality of the second century where status was being increasingly delineated in law, and contempt for the common people [*vulgus*] by the wellborn was nearly universal.[13]

Some of the vocabulary used to describe Christ, in fact, belongs to the socially stratifying vocabulary of the period (MacMullen 1974: 109; Garnsey 1970: 221–233). One can almost hear in the depiction of Christ as both *speciosum* and *humilem* the defiance and desire for recognition of those who, like this Christ, may appear low and base to those on top in this world of reversed values, but who value themselves as somehow beautiful – *speciosum*. By presenting this Christ, who is a hypostatized and utopian image of the community, the *Acts* betrays its sense that the community itself, as well as its Lord, deserves power/honor.

The text's repeated financial references also suggest that the *Acts* issued from a community interested in constructing an alternative social structure. Attention to finances seems almost obsessive in the *Acts*; few scenes have no financial references. Some of these perform a narrative function. In the Coptic fragment, for example, Ptolemy saved from his lust by the fortuitous paralysis of Peter's daughter, leaves her a bequest. This scene serves to depict Peter, a church leader, as a good money manager and trusty dispenser of charity:

> He bequeathed a piece of land in the name of my daughter . . . But I being given this trust, executed it with care . . . I sold the land, and kept back none of the price of the land but gave all the money to the poor.
>
> (*Papyrus Berolinensis* 8502)

Similarly, the Chryse episode (where Peter accepts a contribution from a notorious woman) establishes that money may be accepted from any benefactor if it is used for the community's good.

But the reader also learns a number of seemingly gratuitous financial details; that, for example, the converted ship captain had to stay and sell his cargo before following Peter to Rome (53.11–12), that people were charged a fee to see the contest between Peter and Simon (70.28), that the widows received a gold piece for gathering at Marcellus' house (66.15). The value of Eubula's stolen property is precisely described (63.18–20). We are told of Nero's anger at Marcellus for planning to use his money to help Christians, and Marcellus is himself depicted as angry that he wasted his money on Christians after his conversion by Simon, and so on throughout the narrative (55.5–18). The *Acts* is thick with references to money. Like the references to the emperor and patronage, this emphasis on money is also part of the social web of meaning in the narrative. There are no more powerful signifiers for social networks than sexuality and property. With respect to the former, Peter Brown has demonstrated the strong social significance of the Church's call for continence in the early empire. By ending sexual congress, Christians displayed their hopes for ending the contemporary society (Brown 1988: 64). The emphasis on continence is not so pervasive in the *Acts of Peter* as it is in many of the other *Apocryphal Acts*, but it was the effect of Peter's preaching on continence – "many other women besides fell in love with the doctrine of purity and separated from their husbands, and men too ceased to sleep with their wives" (86.8–11) – that resulted in his martyrdom.

Sharing with other Christian groups the goal of ending contemporary society, the community of the *Acts of Peter*, through its repeated emphasis on money and property, also envisions the construction of an alternate society in its place. Property as a social or literary signifier acts to represent an extension of the social body; by its nature property allows the body to be extended into social space through accumulation and exchange and through the social and economic interaction involved in such accumulation and exchange (Chidester 1988: 97). By suffusing the text with financial references, the *Acts* insists on this Christian community's substance, on its determination to have material existence. When he triumphs over Simon, raising the dead and healing the sick, Peter exhibits Christ's and the community's power; when he transfers control over and the honor due the donation of money from the wealthy to Christ (the control being under the direction of Christian leaders), he exhibits a changed social reality to control this power. For centuries the wealthy had manifested their substance and power through patronage. The *Acts* projects a community that, by its possession of money and dispensing of it, similarly displays its substantive nature and framework for power (Stoops 1982: 317).

It is difficult to define the actual composition of the community to whom the *Acts* was directed. If one subtracts the senators as unlikely converts, the text mentions the kinds of people other sources have led us to expect – wealthy women, a prison official and his wife, a shipper, an innkeeper, a goldsmith (Meeks 1983: 51–73). There is one anomalous social indicator in the text; it contains what Dimitris Kyrtatas has called "the strongest statement in favor of manumission in Christian literature" (Kyrtatas 1987: 66). Before he will resurrect the young senator, Peter persuades the young man's mother to allow the slaves she manumitted upon his death to remain free. She agrees and even guarantees to continue to supply their support (77.13–15). Peter explains his request: "For I know that some will feel injured on seeing your son restored to life, because these men will become his slaves once again" (77.8–10). "Some" (*quorundam*) were freedmen, perhaps, who would be able to identify with the blow of being freed and then having freedom snatched back. The detailed description of the revenge that Marcellus' slaves worked on Simon likewise shows a certain sympathy for the sensibilities of slaves. The sympathy for the underclasses seems fitting in a text that affirms its belief in a "carpenter and son of a carpenter" (71.24–25); as Peter insists, "none of you should expect another (saviour) than him who was despised and mocked by the Jews . . ." (54.28–29).

The *Acts of Peter* appears to reflect a group that would have little difficulty feeling allegiance with a craftsman, a carpenter. By its rejection of the emperor, his cult, and the natural leadership of the upper classes, and through its revised notion of patronage, the *Acts* reflects an estrangement from the surrounding political and social culture that devalued classes other than the wealthy and the wellborn. The *Acts* seems written for a community that connected religion with a social and political agenda. In the *Acts of Peter*, we overhear a group that proves the validity of the anachronistic warning Dio Cassius puts into the mouth of Maecenas: "Do not, therefore, permit anyone to be an atheist or a sorcerer . . . For such men, by speaking the truth sometimes, but greatly falsehood, often encourage a great many to attempt revolutions" (52.36).[14] If not revolution, at least change. The *Acts* displays an ease with the notion of forms broken, being reformed, and existing anew – a statue shattered and refashioned; a dried fish, revivified, swimming again; and three dead men resurrected. Such repeated images not only represent, but make conceivable, the possibility for radical change, embodying a promise of reformation and restructuring after what appeared to be destruction. The social and political implications are plain.

There is evidence for an audience ready for such a message in Asia Minor, the most likely location for the *Acts'* genesis.[15] The *Orations* of Dio of Prusa, for example, testify to social and political unrest and factionalism throughout the region, unrest precisely among those groups receiving attention in the *Acts of Peter* – artisans and tradespeople (34.16ff., 19ff.). Rioting as a form of collective action manifests strains in a society and a challenge to existing social and political systems (Smelser 1962). Thus the rioting, to which contemporary sources testify, corroborates the existence of the social strains we have seen articulated in the *Acts*, and these pressures perhaps explain the challenge to the contemporary operating systems of power that are implicit in the *Acts*.

The *Acts* is very much a radical document. It works to construct a new site of power in the culture – the Christian community – whose superior healing powers manifest its strength. The *Acts* then displays a Christian community intent to separate out and constitute new categories of people for social attention: the poor, the sick, the suffering. These new categories call forth new social structures to contain and deliver Christian power. (These are the categories around which Christianity's later social and political power would grow.) Such a message plainly contests the prevailing systems of power.

It is not a particularly unusual occurrence in the context of the early empire for the *Acts of Peter* to be both a religious tract and a social and political text. Political subversion rather routinely operated under the guise of pagan religiosity in the provinces, as G. W. Bowersock has shown (Bowersock 1987), and Simon Price (1984) has established the close connection between the exercise of political power and the operation of the imperial cult. Fictive prose narratives may have been particularly amenable to combining within themselves such various levels of signification. For Reinhold Merkelbach (1962) has suggested that many of the ancient romances, apparently entertaining secular texts, may, in fact, embody the ritual concerns of contemporary mystery religions.[16] My reading of the *Acts of Peter* would seem to lend support to Merkelbach's supposition, demon-strating that related prose narratives likewise join the religious and the secular. As Merkelbach reads the ancient romances as religious narratives, so I have contended that the *Acts of Peter*, a religious text, should be read as projecting a social and political agenda. It is part of the rhetoric of Christianity to separate the religious and the political, but, in the early Roman empire, this rhetoric had not yet prevailed, and its assumptions should not be allowed to constrict our readings of the prose narratives of the period.

6

THE SICK SELF

The *Acts of the Martyrs* and the *Acts of Peter* offered their readers and listeners a self-understanding of themselves as sufferers, empowered by the experience of suffering. These Christian narratives show that Christians did not reject the body; rather they had invested it with new significance. The body's pains were profitable as, Peter had claimed, was the paralysis of his daughter. Perpetua's suffering allowed her to overcome both the devil and her gender, and Peter's upside-down crucifixion joined him with Christ's effort to set the world aright again. Epictetus had rejected the body's claims and had instructed his students to master and ignore them. Bodily suffering instead provided Christians with their community identity. Christian narrative assumed an audience that could embrace a message for sufferers as "for them." As, over a hundred years ago, Harnack perceived an innate principle of early Christianity: "it was and it remained a religion for the sick . . . it assumed that no one, or at least hardly anyone was in normal health, but that men were always in a state of disability" (Harnack 1904–1905: 109).

It is my contention that Christianity found a subject for itself already being prepared in the Greco-Roman world of the early empire. This was a period of intense interest in medicine and prestige for doctors. Medical discourse was popular and two examples – Galen's autobiographical *On Prognosis* and a section of an epistolary novella describing a purported meeting between Hippocrates and Democritus – will provide evidence that medical narratives were offering inhabitants of the early empire a self-understanding similar to that in Christian texts. These medical narratives scripted a subject that was essentially a sick body located in a flawed world. This representation and the ideological tendencies it embodied helped in

142

the creation of a subject that would be present for the call of Christianity – in its beginnings, as we have shown, a radical social institution focused on, and articulated through, the suffering body.

Modern scholarship has identified the early empire as a critical period in the development of the concept of the human "person" or "self," that would eventually evolve toward the notion of the individual important to modern ideology – "an independent, autonomous, and thus essentially non-social moral being" (Dumont 1985: 94). In his monumental *History of Autobiography in Antiquity*, Georg Misch determined that Augustine was the first individual with sufficient "inner life" to write a true autobiography (Misch 1951: 1.17). Misch associated Augustine's new-found capacity with the rise of Christianity. Michel Foucault more recently has shown this turn toward the person to be part of a wider cultural movement that predated Christianity. Foucault observed that this concern for the individual "self" began with a pronounced and intense attention on the human body, a turn toward the body in the period of the late Republic and early empire (Foucault 1988: 43). Foucault's observations are persuasive: Epictetus, as well as the Christian narratives, gives evidence of this attention on the body. It needs to be recognized, however, that a simple "turn toward the body" would not necessarily have led to a self-reflexive, inner-directed subject. A particular conception of the body was needed to enable this type of subject. The trajectory toward the individual "self" might well have gone differently, for in this period the body itself was a matter of debate. It was significant for the development of the "individual" that Galen, whose influence on medical thinking was to have a profound impact for centuries, chose to champion a particular kind of body, namely a body that could indicate its inner workings. Galen's *Prognosis* is a document in a cultural debate. It is Galen's narrative performance of one particular way of conceiving the body and it was the sort of "body" that Galen represented that fostered a conception of an inner directed "self" and helped to prepare a subject present for Christianity's call.

In the *Prognosis*, written around A.D. 164/165, Galen described his rise to fame and prestige in the competitive climate of Roman medicine. Although he was to become the pre-eminent authority in medicine for fourteen centuries, Galen's early career was typical of that of many other upper-class inhabitants of the Roman empire. He was born in Pergamum around A.D. 129, and his father, an architect, provided him with a superior general education. He studied with representatives of all the major philosophical schools, Platonists, Peripatetics, Stoics, and Epicureans (*De Affectum Dignotione*; V.41K).[1] After being instructed by a dream, his father directed him at sixteen to the study of medicine (*De Ordine Librorum Propriorum*; SM II.88). Galen not only studied with the best doctors in Pergamum, but spent five years in Alexandria, the center for contemporary medical studies. Returning to Pergamum, he was appointed the doctor to a gladiatorial school. Around A.D. 162, Galen left Pergamum for Rome and recorded in his *Prognosis* (*De Praecognitione*)[2] how he achieved medical success in the city – how he became an imperial physician.

According to Vivian Nutton, its editor, the *Prognosis* is one of Galen's most polished works, one that he obviously intended for a wide circulation. But it is also according to Nutton, a rather odd text yoking together diverse genres; it was part autobiography, part social diatribe, part medical text (Nutton 1972: 55). Its form – fusing narratives of the self, the larger society and the body – showed the *Prognosis'* concern with the complex of related topics that was experiencing transformation during the early empire. Cultures traditionally have used the physical body to represent and figure the social body, and the fusion of these two concepts, physical body and social body, has significant influence for a cultural definition of the "self" (Stallybrass and White 1986: 192). That Galen explicitly treated all these topics in the same discourse suggested that his narrative had a stake in the cultural debate over these terms and may throw some light on the particulars of the debate.

One can read the *Prognosis* as Galen's record of his successful performance of his epistemology that the body signified, that its surface revealed inner meanings that were able to be read and interpreted. The narrative's implicit tone of contest, as it describes Galen's victories over his rivals, signaled its performative nature. In the *Prognosis*, medical practice was presented as a competition. Just as it was explicitly described in the *Methodo Medendi* (MM), where Galen used the metaphor of public performance and contest when he derided Thessalus, the founder of a rival school of medicine. He taunted Thessalus, for example: "What kind of theater is it in which you are victorious over Hippocrates?" (MM 10.13K), or, in another place: "Who will judge the winner? Who will pack the theater for him? Who will announce the victor? Who will crown him?" (MM 10.18K).[3] Galen conceived of his medical practice not simply as an occupation, or a humanitarian project, but as a contest being played out before an audience in which his rivals were displaced and vanquished. His *Prognosis* had a role in a contest to establish his method of medicine and his notion of a particular kind of body – one that could indicate its inner functioning. It was the kind of body, as represented by Galen and other doctors of his persuasion, that helped to constitute a subject for Christianity. Galen's body, when known inside and out, was discovered to be essentially at risk; it was always verging toward dysfunction, needing careful, constant monitoring and outside control. It was a body that mattered, that signified and was significant, very unlike the body offered in Epictetus' narratives that was to be bracketed off from the "real" self.

In Galen's period, the possibility of knowing the body was only one among a number of areas of contested knowledge. Philosophers and doctors disagreed whether, in fact, any valid knowledge was possible. To place the *Prognosis* in its context, some background for this disagreement must be provided, although any brief summary of the complex topic of the differences among medical sects tends to oversimplify it. Galen's writings will be used for the particulars of the debate among doctors, even though his descriptions of medical history likely reflect his own biases. Galen's perspective at least shows how one influencial doctor interpreted medical theory and its history and framed the debate around it in the late second century. Galen described three main medical sects in his day: the rationalists or dogmatists, the empiricists, and the methodists. Doctors in these schools, or sects, were divided by competing notions of what could be known about the inner workings of the body and how much knowledge was necessary to treat the body (Frede 1981).[4] Galen's descriptions of the "primary sects" focused on such differences of epistemology:

> Those who rely on experience alone are accordingly called empiricists. Similarly, those who rely on reason are called rationalists . . . The one proceeds by means of experience to the discovery of medicines, the other by means of indication [*endeixis*].
>
> (*De Sectis ad Ingredientis* 1; SM III.1/2)

A fundamental question separating the medical sects was their attitude toward medical theory. In early Greece, philosophic and medical theorizing had arisen in close conjunction. They were components of the same enterprise – to understand the nature and function of the natural world. Early medical theorists had tended to relate their medical investigations to some larger system of natural philosophy. But, by the third century B.C., a number of competing theories explaining medical phenomenon had arisen, and it was perhaps in reaction to such competing claims that the so-called empiricists began to deny the need for any theoretical grounding for medicine (Frede 1986: 224). The empiricists claimed that a doctor's experience, augmented with the record of the experience of other doctors, could provide all the necessary medical knowledge with no need for extended theoretical explanations. These "empiricists" began to label other doctors as "rationalists," whatever their individual differences, who held that medical theory had to explain the inner workings of the body or the hidden causes of disease or any other phenomena that had to be disclosed through reason rather than observation (*De Sectis ad Ingredientis* 1; SM III.1; Frede 1982: 2). Empiricists denied the necessity of knowing anything that was not manifest and open to observation; the extensiveness of their denial of the non-manifest can be seen in Galen's description:

> The empiricists, on the other hand, do not grant that anatomy makes any discoveries or that it would be necessary for the art, even if it did. Furthermore, they do not grant that there is such a thing as indication [*endeixis*] or that one thing can be known on the basis of another thing, for one has to know all things on the basis of themselves. Nor do they grant that there is such a thing as a sign of something which is not manifest. Furthermore they argue that no art has any need for logic . . . claiming there is no such thing as proof anyway.
>
> (*De Sectis ad Ingredientis* 5; SM III.10–11)

Galen's description suggested that when empiricists turned toward the body, they stopped at its surface. Nevertheless, according to Galen, although they differed so radically on the grounds for their medical practice, the empiricists and dogmatists often arrived at the same medical treatment. Using different methods they reached the same results (Frede 1982: 2, citing *De Sectis ad Ingredientis* 1.12, 7.16, 12.12). Indeed Galen commented that the two sects might abandon their long arguments if they would only allow that both their methods of discovery had validity (*De Sectis ad Ingredientis* 4; SM III.9).

Galen claimed that he belonged to no sect, but that he borrowed the best from each (*De Libris Propriis* 1; SM II.95). Apparently, his insistence that all knowledge gained through the rational method stand the test of experience had separated him from an orthodox rationalist position. He shared many of the beliefs associated with the rationalists (Frede 1981: 78). Clearly, Galen held that medicine was founded on rational principles; indication was the basis of his method of medicine (Kudlien and Durling 1991; Frede 1982: 4–8).

> Everything that is distinct from experience is called indication. Thus anyone who wishes to constitute the therapeutic method in the appropriate way must necessarily begin from the first indications, and proceed from those to the subsequent things, and then to the things that depend upon them, and do this without letting up until he arrives at the goal itself.
>
> (MM 10.127K)

The "goal itself" for Galen was full comprehension and understanding of a disease and its causes, authenticated through the very rigor of the rational method by which these were discovered (De Lacy 1987: 298).

The particular deficiency that Galen found in empiricism was its retreat from any search for complete understanding. Michael Frede has summarized the limitations of this method: "Though technical, it [empirical knowledge] is not scientific because it does not provide us with any understanding of why the things we know from experience are the way they are; experience can just give us facts, but not their explanation" (Frede 1981: 81). The facts, without an understanding of causes and natural systems, were not sufficient for Galen, and, therefore, empiricism by itself was not sufficient. But Galen did acknowledge the worth of at least getting the facts straight, as he proved by his suggestion that an empiricist doctor might be less dangerous to a patient's well-being than an insufficiently trained rationalist doctor; that is, a doctor so unfamiliar with logic as to be unable to discriminate between sound and unsound arguments (MM 10.37K). Galen always recognized that his method of medicine premised on a thorough knowledge of logic, physics, and physiology was arduous and demanded a high level of intellectual ability and lengthy training, and he never denied that experience could produce an adequate practical medicine (MM 10.122K; Frede 1981: 77).

Galen acknowledged no value, however, in the third medical sect – methodism. This sect, like empiricism, had been influenced by scepticism, and rejected any concern for discovering hidden causes: not because these hidden causes were unknowable as the empiricists held, but because it was unnecessary to know them (*De Sectis ad Ingredientis* 6; SM III.14).[5] For the methodists, all necessary medical knowledge was manifest. As they put it, "a knowledge of manifest communities" (*De Sectis ad Ingredientis* 6; SM III.14; Frede 1982: 3). According to Galen, the methodists refused to consider any evidence other than the disease itself:

> claiming that the indication as to what is beneficial, derived from just the affections themselves, is enough for them, and not even from these taken as specific particulars, but assuming them to be common and universal. And hence they also call these affections which pervade all particulars "communities."
> (*De Sectis ad Ingredientis* 6; SM III.12)

The methodists held that there were only three communities of diseases; constriction, dilation, or a combination of these (see Frede 1982: 15 for the influence of Asclepiades on methodism). By the "disease indicating the treatment," the methodists meant that all a doctor had to do was recognize the community that a disease belonged to; for example, recognize that something was constricted and remedy that condition – in this case, loosen it. Disease indicated treatment in a direct way; the analogy of people suffering from thirst was used. To remedy someone's thirst, drink was given (Sextus Empiricus *Outline of Pyrrhonism* 1.238). Nothing more subtle was necessary; no inquiry, for example, of what prompted the thirst. Only the condition of thirst mattered or was relevant for its remedy.

By limiting the number of diseases and relying on the principle that diseases themselves indicate their treatment and thus there is no need to delve into hidden causes or to consider the individual circumstances of each patient, the methodists made the art of medicine a relatively simple matter. Galen said, in fact, that they explicitly inverted the Hippocratic aphorism that "the art [of medicine] is long and life, short," claiming "that life is long and the art short" (*De Sectis ad Ingredientis* 6; SM III.14–15).

Galen vehemently rejected the methodists' teachings, in part for opening medicine to the undereducated and the socially inferior, but also for having reduced so drastically the art of medicine and what he considered was traditional to it (Frede 1985: xxxi).[6] The methodists, according to Galen, were uninterested in causes, in patients, and lumped diseases into a few large categories. In his estimation, they neglected almost everything necessary for correct diagnoses; he listed some of their most egregious omissions:

> They claim that neither the part affected has anything useful to offer toward an indication as to the appropriate treatment, nor the cause, nor the age, nor the season, nor the place, nor the consideration of the strength of the patient, nor his nature, nor his disposition. They also put aside habits ...
>
> (*De Sectis ad Ingredientis* 6; SM III.10)

Galen claimed that the methodists considered only the manifest and general and rejected all that was specific and individual.

Even this brief summary of the disagreements separating the medical sects has shown that the nature of their debate was essentially epistemological. The sects' differences centered on what could be known about the body and its inner workings. Galen believed that, with rigorous, long-term study, nearly every aspect of the body was open to discovery and comprehensible. He based his method of medicine on his belief that all aspects of the body revealed themselves by specific indications to the properly trained doctor (that is, one trained in logic with a sufficient knowledge of the body's inner physiology, and the physical principles underlying this physiology). He believed that the body indicated its nature and doctors could use such indications to understand the body and its inner nature:

> And what we have just established in the case of disease goes equally well, in my view, for symptoms and affections, health and wholeness, strength and powers and everything else whose names and conceptions are predicated of something that underlies them. All of these are found in bodies, some as dispositions, some as activities, some as affections. Some of them are natural, others unnatural; and all of them have their specific indications, although the majority of doctors have failed to discern them.
>
> (MM 10.156K)

The empiricists and methodists, in contrast, renounced all knowledge of the inner recesses of the body or the hidden causes of its functioning as either unknowable or useless.

The premises and points of debate between the medical sects, at least as Galen offered them, have obvious relevance for the development of the "self" as an inner-directed person with an interior life, albeit physical, capable of being examined, understood, and deciphered. In the empiricist or methodist model, the turn toward the body would have stopped at the surface; any examination of the "bodily self" would have been, in the most literal sense, superficial. In Galen's model, founded as he said on Hippocratic practice, the body indicated its inner nature, signified its individual interior and the specific particularities that resulted from its unique circumstances. It was methodism's refusal to entertain individual elements that particularly provoked Galen. He ridiculed their practice:

> The fluid affection never needs laxatives but always constictives, in winter, in spring, in summer, in fall and whether the patient be a child, in the prime of life, or old, and whether he happens to be in Thracia, in Scythia, or in Ionia. Hence they say, none of these factors is of any use, but all are a matter of idle concern. And what about the parts of the body? Are not these, too, useless for an indication of the treatment?
> (*De Sectis ad Ingredientis* 7; SM III.17)

This debate between the sects, on the possibility or necessity of knowing the body, indicates that the trajectory toward the modern "self" did not proceed without contest. Galen's influence and his premise that the interior of the body could be known, and known only as the body of a specific individual in a specific context, helped set the course for an inner-directed, reflexive "self." For Galen, the body did indicate its interior, and it is this knowable body, this signifying body, that he represented and re-represented in the narrative of the successful prognoses that comprised the plot of his *Prognosis*. This work described Galen's rise to prominence as the direct result of his demonstrated knowledge of the interior workings of the body. Galen offered the case that initiated his ascendancy in great detail. This was his successful prognosis of the condition of his countryman, the Aristotelian philosopher, Eudemus. The depiction of this case and Eudemus' concentrated, protracted attention to his body vividly illustrates the turn toward the body discussed by Foucault. Galen described Eudemus slowly recognizing the onset of his disease:

> One day he began to feel a little indisposed after his bath, and at the eighth hour he had a shivering fit which prevented him from taking food. Although he passed the next day

without incident, he thought it best to let the eighth hour go by. When nothing unpleasant occurred then, although he fasted until the ninth hour, and there was no apparent change, he took a bath and a light meal. On the third day he came to visit me, as was his custom, but for safety's sake he thought it best on that day also to let the suspected hours go by. He waited until after the ninth hour to take his bath, had a comfortable meal and was then convinced that nothing untoward would happen to him.

$$(2.2–3; 14.606K)^7$$

Eudemus kept up the close scrutiny of his body. On the fourth day he consulted his friends whether he should bathe or not. All agreed that he should, except Galen who suspected quartan fever. And indeed, on the fourth evening, Eudemus "felt a hot sensation throughout his body, which he ascribed to the drink he had taken – for he had drunk some old wine" (2.10; 608K). Eudemus discussed this symptom with his doctors, but they also dismissed it. Nevertheless, as his fever continued to develop, he began to give credence to Galen's prognosis. He called together all the best doctors in the city to discuss treatment. All agreed that he should be treated with theriac. Galen, however, counseled against using the drug at this stage, saying that it would only increase the effect of the fever.

The unanimity of the other doctors' recommendation overwhelmed Eudemus and he did take the drug, but to no effect. The doctors then recommended a second dose; this immediately caused the fever to strike again, earlier than expected and more vehemently. At this point, his doctors gave up on Eudemus; only Galen still predicted a recovery. The narrative gave a distasteful view of the other doctors praying for the failure of Galen's prognosis, and with it, Eudemus's demise (3.9; 616K).

Galen is, however, vindicated. Soon Eudemus sent for him, "wanting me to pass judgement on the feeling of well-being which he had (3.10; 617K). When Galen arrived, Eudemus immediately instructed him to take his pulse to see if he was really well. Assured that he was indeed on the way to recovery, Eudemus asked Galen to explain how he had been able to make such a confident prognosis about the course of his disease. Galen's explanation embodied his epistemological assumptions about the knowable body. He explained to Eudemus that the proper prognosis was "revealed to me through his pulse beats by the nature which governed his body, which was then aroused and active in expelling from the body all that was noxious in the bodily humours" (3.13; 617K). Galen peered inside Eudemus' body, into the hidden interior, through his proper interpretation of external signs. At this point, Eudemus explicitly questioned Galen on how the body could be said to signify: "What do you mean 'this has been shown by nature?' – for surely it did not tell you so by speaking" (3.13; 617K). Galen explained this was "Because it has caused an upward movement of the arteries even more than a lateral expansion . . . which it always does when it is trying to discharge an irritant from the body" (3.14; 617–618K). Galen traced his ability to read Eudemus' body, to interpret its hidden interior to his understanding of the nature of the body and his ability logically to infer the body's interior functioning from external signs. His prognosis proceeded first from his knowledge of physics: his explanation assumed that all physical entities were the products of four elements (fire, earth, water, air) and the four Hippocratic qualities (hot, cold, moist, dry) associated with these elements. These qualities, in turn, generated in human bodies four fluid humours: yellow bile, blood, phlegm, and black bile. His explanation also revealed his physiology, for it assumed that good health resulted from the proper blend of these humours in the body, and dysfunction, as in Eudemus' case, involved some bad mixture. Galen demonstrated the logical foundation of his prognosis as he explained why Eudemus could anticipate a particular conclusion for his disease.

> "Well now," I said, "this group of indications [*semeia*] precede an impending hemorrhage, just as these portend sweats." I then added to my argument also those that precede an attack of vomiting. "We have no particular special sign for a wholesale critical evacuation through the lower belly: but since none of the other particular indications is present, it remains to hope that will happen to you."
>
> (3.16; 618K)

Eudemus, himself a philosopher, recognized and explicitly praised Galen's rational method: "You have made a truly logical exposition of how you reached this prognosis" (3.16; 618K). Galen's explication exemplified how far removed his medicine was from a mere recognition of the manifest and a reliance on experience. Galen's method assumed a body that was a subject to be understood, a text to be read.

Eudemus was clearly delighted with Galen's method of medicine and his cure: "he abandoned his habitual moderation and shouted to all of us his friends . . . that Pythian Apollo deigned to prophesy to the sick through the mouth of Galen, and then to treat them and cure them completely on the day predicted" (3.17; 618–619K). Eudemus' excitement here is curious; what precisely was it that excited him so much? That the obvious cause, his cure, may be only part of the reason is suggested by a later episode in the *Prognosis* when the emperor Marcus Aurelius showed a similar extravagant enthusiasm.

Marcus Aurelius exhibited the same close scrutiny of his body as had Eudemus. Galen described how Marcus Aurelius and his doctors believed that the emperor was about to fall ill with a fever.

> On the previous day he had taken a draught of bitter aloes at the first hour and then some theriac at about the sixth, as was his daily custom. He had a bath at sunset and a light meal. All night long there followed colicky pains and evacuations through the lower belly, which made him feverish, and when his court doctors saw him in the morning, they advised him to rest and fed him some thick gruel at the ninth hour . . . they agreed that this was apparently the opening of an attack of an illness.
>
> (11.2–3; 658K)

Galen, on the basis of his reading of the emperor's pulse, gave a different diagnosis: "I said that there was no attack of fever, but his stomach was overloaded with the food he had taken, which had turned to phlegm before excretion, and that this was now quite clear" (11.5; 659K).

At this, Marcus Aurelius complimented Galen three times, saying: "That's it, what you have said is just it . . ." (11.5; 659K). Later, the emperor magnified his compliment with the remark: "We have one doctor and he is *eleutheron*." And Galen explained: "As you well know, he was continually speaking of me as the first among physicians and unique among philosophers" (11.8; 660K). The term Marcus uses of Galen, *eleutheron*, is, as Vivian Nutton has pointed out, highly complimentary; it reflected "a philosophical ideal only rarely attained, the wisdom of the sage that brings spiritual and moral liberty" (in Galen 1979: 219). Why would Galen's diagnosis of what was essentially an upset stomach have elicited such enthusiasm and magnanimous compliments from the emperor? The emperor's description of Galen as a philosopher would have had particular meaning for Galen who himself entitled a treatise "The Best Physician is Also a Philosopher" (1.53–63K). Galen always maintained that the true physician possessed all the parts of philosophy – "the logical, the scientific and the ethical" (SM II.7) and that denying the title of philosopher to a doctor was mere quibbling:

> Should you, then, still quarrel about names and dispute over trifles, maintaining that one ought to describe the doctor as firm, temperate, incorruptible, and just, but not as a philosopher? and admitting that he knows the nature of bodies, and the action of organs, the uses of parts and the classification of diseases, and the indication of drugs, but not that he engages in logical contemplation?
>
> (SM II.7)[8]

Why, however, did Marcus Aurelius praise Galen so highly in this particular situation? I suggest that the excited reactions of both Marcus Aurelius and Eudemus to Galen's prognoses resulted from their realization and acceptance that he did in fact "know the nature of their bodies"; that he had proved he was indeed able to discern what was going on inside them. The thrice repeated cry of Marcus Aurelius, "that's it, what you have said is just it" (11.5; 659K) emphasized that his appreciation resulted from his recognition that Galen had properly understood his internal condition. And this compliment comes from the man who now is perhaps best known for the record of his own efforts to understand himself in his *Meditations*. Marcus was so excited because Galen had shown his valid understanding of the emperor's inner functioning. The debate between the medical sects has relevance here. Living in a world of MRIs and cat-scans, it takes effort to conceive of a mental geography where the interior of the body was primarily hypothetical, debatable, largely unknown, indeed, for many, unknowable terrain. But these episodes of the *Prognosis* allow us to enter this thought-world. Marcus Aurelius' excitement was caused by his recognition that he had been an object of valid knowledge to Galen. Galen's practice of his medical method was making visible the interior of the individual, opening space for an inner life – one that was not mental, but physical. Galen's method, based on indication, unlike that proposed by the empiricists or the methodists, allowed the body to be a signifier of internal depths. The reactions of Marcus Aurelius and Eudemus to his ability to decipher their bodies indicated the importance this knowledge had for them; it cautions us not to disregard its importance because of our very different mentality.

The entire structure of the *Prognosis*, as well as its title, functioned to offer the body as an object of knowledge. The narrative presented each patient as a subject to be understood by the doctor. The various cases seem chosen specifically to present various manifestations of the doctor's knowledge. Near the center of the text, for example, Galen narrated three related cases. He admitted that his diagnoses in these did not demonstrate a particularly sophisticated grasp of medicine. He included them rather as examples of a particular kind of knowledge – the doctor's ability to recognize mental aberrations from bodily indications, specifically from the action of the pulse. As demonstration, Galen first presented the case of a woman "who was said to lie awake at night, constantly tossing and turning" (6.2; 631K). Galen examined the woman and found her to be without fever and unresponsive to him and so he surmised that she suffered either "from a depression caused by black bile or from some worry she was unwilling to confess" (6.4; 631K). When he introduced this case, Galen noted its similarity to a famous case, Erasistratus' diagnosis of the passion of Antiochus for a concubine. In fact, Antiochus had been in love with his stepmother, and Galen's slip here showed he was conflating this case with a similar one where Hippocrates discerned the love of Perdiccas for his father's concubine. By calling up these examples Galen included his case in the context of earlier famous doctors' cases (Galen 1979: 194). He introduced the case of this woman, he said, to dispute the contention of "sophistic doctors" that these earlier doctors had detected the lover's arteries pulsing with love. Galen argued that the pulse could only indicate that a patient was psychologically troubled, not the specific nature of the troubled condition. Galen admitted that he had discovered only by chance the exact cause for his woman patient's illness – that she was in love with a dancer, Pylades. Someone had happened to mention the dancer's name and Galen saw that the woman's color changed, and, taking her pulse, found it to be irregular. On this basis, he deduced she was in love with Pylades (6.7–10; 632–633K).

Galen took a certain risk when he introduced this case. By this point, diagnoses of lovesickness were so conventional that Galen's contemporary, Apuleius, could mock them in his *Metamorphoses*:

Alas, the ignorance of doctors' minds! They cannot interpret this throbbing of the veins, unsteadiness of the complexion, labored breathing and frequent tossing back and forth from side to side. Good gods, how easy it is for any educated man – even if not a medical specialist – to recognize sexual desire . . .

(10.2)[9]

Galen, while agreeing that such diagnoses did not depend on much medical learning, nevertheless introduced this case to remind his readers that doctors had the ability to read even mental conditions on the basis of physical signs. He emphasized this ability by introducing two more similar cases (the steward who feared a review of his accounts and Boethus' son who remained sick because he had eaten hidden food). He explained what the other doctors had overlooked in their examination of the lovesick woman and the fearful steward: "They have no clear conception of how the body tends to be affected by mental conditions" (6.15; 634K). Galen introduced these cases as testament that mental conditions also could be indicated by bodily signs.

After his son's cure, Boethus marveled that other doctors shared neither Galen's knowledge nor his logical abilities in these areas:

"they seem," he said, "not only to be ignorant of the particular pulse beat of men under stress but also, if one of them happens to know your conclusions, they cannot reason them out for themselves because they are not naturally intelligent and have not trained their logical faculty by learning."

(7.18; 641–642K)

These three cases allowed Galen to display that his knowledge based on logical principles had opened his patients' inner lives to him. The *Prognosis* demonstrated that patients' mental selves, as well as their physical ones, became subject to the well-trained doctor's knowledge.

Galen introduced another case to demonstrate how useless it was for patients to try to evade the doctor's knowledge. At the request of Peitholaus, the emperor's chamberlain, Galen had been called in to treat a young man, Sextus.[10] He gave a prognosis, that a crisis in his fever would occur either on the sixth or seventh day. If it occurred on the sixth day, Galen predicted that the fever would then reoccur (10.1–3; 652K). Sextus did fall ill on the sixth day, and the narrative described how he sought to evade Galen's foreknowledge.

When a crisis came in this way on the sixth day, Sextus, who was extremely stubborn, in order to prove me wrong by not having a relapse, took a daily bath and abstained from wine and food except for barley gruel, either on its own or with small pieces of bread. Often bread dipped in water would be enough for him. When he had kept this up until the twelfth day, he boasted that he had thus defeated my prediction.

(10.4–5; 652–653K)

But Sextus did not escape Galen's knowledge; knowledge that Galen insisted throughout his narration of this episode was available to every well-trained doctor. On the fourteenth day, Sextus finally succumbed to the fever Galen had predicted. This case served to illustrate that the doctor's knowledge of the interior processes, of the nature of the body, could not be evaded by the object of his knowing. The subject was subjected to the functioning of his or her body and, thereby, subject to the doctor's knowledge. Sextus read the doctor's knowledge as control and, in a certain sense, the turn toward the body can be associated with a turn away from the ideal of self-control, of self-mastery that served as one of the "few genuine commonplaces in Greek moral thought" (Edelstein 1967: 206).

In this respect, the *Prognosis* had a double representational project. It presented its subjects as objects of knowledge; specifically, they were objectified as bodies, often sick bodies. At the same time the narrative repeatedly presented subjects discovering for themselves their own subjectivity – that of a body in need of inter-pretation and care. The narrative provided numerous examples of subjects carefully scrutinizing their bodies. When they were not examining their own bodies, they were portrayed as seeking to understand the inner body through description or dissection. The intense collective interest in medicine displayed in the *Prognosis* speaks to an extensive cultural attention on the body in the society. Medicine is the primary cultural institution for locating attention on the bodily. Thus, the concentrated general interest in medicine indicates a cultural focus on the body in the Greco-Roman thought-world. Romans had a long tradition of medical self-sufficiency and knowledge, and comments such as Plutarch's, that every individual should know his own pulses, reflected this tradition of general awareness and concern for the functioning of one's own body (*De Tuenda Sanitate* 136). But Galen's narrative provided evidence of

157

a much more extensive and sophisticated attention to the body. Eudemus and Marcus Aurelius scrutinized their bodies for any sign of illness; they had multiple medical consultations with multiple doctors. The general nature of this interest in medicine was also indicated in Galen's discussion of his public medical demonstrations of anatomy. Such public demonstrations appeared to have been a regular feature of the period; Galen gave them frequently in his early days in Rome (*De Libris Propriis* 1; SM II.96). Dio Chrysostom described the effects on a general audience of the less reputable medical lecturers:

> the so-called physicians who seat themselves conspiciously before us and give a detailed account of the union of joints, the combination and juxtaposition of bones, and other topics of that sort . . . And the crowd is all agape with admiration, and more enchanted than a swarm of children.
>
> (*Discourses* 33.6)

The *Prognosis* describes an interest in Galen's anatomical demonstrations as a topic of conversation at Eudemus' bedside. An illustrious group had gathered there composed, as Galen said, "of almost all the social and intellectual leaders of Rome" (2.24; 612K). The public importance of the guests is noted: "Sergius Paulus, who was made prefect of the city not long after, and Flavius Boethus, who was also himself an ex-consul then and a student of Aristotelian philosophy, like Paulus also" (2.24; 612K). These men were portrayed as discussing Galen whom Boethus announced he had already invited to give a demonstration on "how speech and breath are produced and by what organs." All those present expressed their eagerness to attend such a demonstration:

> for Paulus agreed that he certainly lacked the opportunity of observing phenomena revealed by dissections. Similarly, Barbarus also, the uncle of the emperor Lucius, who was then ruling the area called Mesopotamia, requested instruction, like Paulus, and later also Severus, a consul and enthusiast for Aristotelian philosophy.
>
> (2.26–7; 612–613K)

That these very active, public men (Boethus would become governor of Syria Palaestrina and Severus was a son-in-law of Marcus Aurelius) were ready to be instructed in anatomy denotes the serious level of interest in medicine in Rome among non-doctors (Galen

1979: 164). Boethus' request that Galen allow shorthand writers to transcribe the demonstration suggests the existence of an even more extended audience (5.20; 630K).[11]

The occasion of Galen's first anatomical demonstration provides a vivid glimpse into the ongoing cultural debate about the possibility of knowing the body during the period. Galen described how he was about to begin his demonstration and had just announced that he would show how cutting the nerves of the larynx rendered an animal voiceless, when Alexander of Damascus (perhaps to be associated with the Aristotelian philosopher, Alexander of Aphrodisias) interrupted him to dispute his first point: "Should we agree with you on your primary point, that we should all believe in the evidence of the senses" (5.14–15; 628K). At this, Galen stormed out, calling his audience "boorish pyrrhonists" (sceptics).[12] This scene explicitly dramatizes Galen's attitude toward those who questioned the reliability of the bodily senses. For Galen, medicine depended on at least some trust in clear sense perception (De Lacy 1987: 306).

The *Prognosis* gives evidence for a general interest in medicine in Rome that appears unusual. Even discounting that the narrative reflects a doctor's perspective, the general zeal for medical information seems extraordinary. The *Prognosis* testifies to a general avidity for medical knowledge; people encountered in the street wished to accompany Boethus to the bedside of his son to see Galen's examination (7.3; 636K). Severus stationed a man outside a patient's house to conduct Galen to him immediatedly after he had examined the patient to report on the progress of the case (10.10; 654K). Such prevalent public and private discourse on the body testifies to a general cultural focus on the topic.

This focus on the body effected a redirection of the society's traditional concerns about the individual's relation to her or his "self." The emphasis in traditional Hellenistic thinking on self-mastery, on understanding and controlling oneself through rational analysis, was, to a certain extent, abrogated before the medicalized "self" as represented by Galen. Epictetus had idealized the mind/soul's mastery of its bodily nature. In the *Prognosis*, Sextus construed Galen's knowledge of his body as control, and, if it was not that, it at least exhibited Sextus' own lack of control over his body's functioning. The body that Galen represented had a complex bodily inner life in need of external interpretation. Galen consistently reminded his readers that his knowledge of the body was not magical and was available to anyone as intelligent and as well-trained as he was, but his narrative conveyed how complicated a business the proper interpretation of the body was. The structure of the *Prognosis* itself showed the necessity for external guidance in the management of the body. Everyone it depicted needed a guide for understanding his or her body, free and slave, men and women, philosophers, even an emperor: all are shown to need such guidance. In the *Prognosis*, all the usual barriers that separated the social orders fell away, subsumed in the universal category of body. In a hierarchical society such as the Roman state, the ruler's body was the cynosure of all eyes, the special focus of attention. But in this narrative, the emperor's body was represented as no more privileged than any other. All bodies are equal in their dysfunction and their need for the expert's help. In fact, the emperor was represented specifically as one misled concerning his body. At one point, the text referred to him simply as "the emperor [*autokratora*] who believed he suffered the onset of a feverish paroxysm" (14.11; 673K). He was defined by his mistaken prognosis; in this, at least, he was neither as absolute, nor self-ruled as his title implied.

In Galen's narrative, not only was every body in need of external guidance, but nearly every body was in need of treatment. This was a corollary of Galen's theoretical understanding of the body. He subscribed to the traditional notion as he testified: "It has been adequately demonstrated by them of old time, the most distinguished both of philosophers and of physicians, that the bodies of animals are mixtures of hot, cold, dry, and moist" (*De Temperamentis* 1.1; Helmreich II.72). For Galen, health resulted from a proper balance of the humours formed from these elements in the body. Maintaining the body in good balance was difficult. Galen enumerated nine possible kinds of mixtures for humours; only one of these was completely well-balanced (*De Temperamentis* 1.8; Helmreich II.29–32). Edelstein described the effect of this kind of medical paradigm:

> In ancient medicine, wherever human health is understood as a balance of certain elements, or where certain elements are thought to course, constantly changing, through the body, there is neither in theory nor in practice a healthy man. For health has no being but is a continuous becoming.
>
> (Edelstein 1967: 84)

In the *De Temperamentis*, Galen described the balance of the interior body as affected by multiple variants such as foods, climates, and heredities. The difficulty in managing these different mixtures clearly presumed both a body verging continually toward disequilibrium and the need for expert advice. Different foods affected the mixtures of the body differently and even the foods themselves might be of one mixture before they were eaten and another mixture after. Different parts of the body had various mixtures at one and the same time, and Galen warned that it was not possible to infer from one part of the body the mixture of the whole. Galen's definitions of disease and health in themselves reflected the inherent difficulty of keeping the body in equilibrium: "disease is that departing most from the well-tempered, but health is that departing least" (*De Temperamentis* 2.4; Helmreich II.63). The standard appeared to be seldom maintained.

In the *Thrasybulus*, a treatise where Galen argued that health belonged to the province of doctors rather than trainers, he included a vivid image for the difficulty he saw in maintaining the equilibrium of the human body.[13] Galen used a metaphor to support his case that the body needed the continual supervision of a doctor to maintain good health. He compared the body to a wine jar:

> just as if you imagine two wine jars, both bored through with holes in many places, both at first full and both emptying equally through the holes and this with somebody always taking care of one and constantly replacing as much as flowed away, but no one should pay attention to the other until it was completely empty.
>
> (20; SM III.57)[14]

The image chosen for the body – a leaky vessel, its contents ever flowing away – was a graphic representation of the body, always deteriorating, ceaselessly verging toward dysfunction. This vessel was so constructed that it needed a manager always attending to it. This image of the wine jars, in fact, picked up language Galen had used of the body in the paragraph before – equally leaky and equally in need of an overseer:

> For the person skilled in health needs to be such a person. Perceiving and remedying every small damage and injury. But if the body remained wholly uninjured and the same as the creator left it, it would not need any repairer at all. But now, since it does dissolve and deteriorate, it needs some competent supervisor, who will both recognize what is lacking, what it

is and how great, and will remedy it immediately by replacing
the same and as much.

(19; SM III.57)

In the *Prognosis*, Eudemus had listed some of the body's normal
routes of leaking away: "vomiting, gastric evacuations, urinations,
sweats, hemorrhage and normal bleeding piles" (3.15; 618K). Galen's
image of the body implied both a continual disintegration and a
need for constant external management. This representation in the
medical discourse, so popular in Roman society, can be assumed to
have had an impact on the culture's "self"-representation. Self-
mastery must be given over, at least where it pertained to the body.
Galen suggested that the body needed constant oversight and an
expert monitor to keep watch over it.[15] The "turn toward the body,"
it seems, correlated to a certain extent with a turn away from
self-mastery, away from the ideal that one's own rationality was
in total control. Ancient philosophic thought had a tradition of
exempting bodily functions from the control of the self (Plato
Timaeus 86ff.), but as the body began to hold a more important
position in the activities of self-regard, the domain for an individual's control of the self can be seen to recede.

In his later life, Galen moved the body even more centrally into
territory traditionally occupied by "other" than the body whether
this was called "soul" or "mind." In his treatise, "That the
Capacities of the Soul Follow the Mixtures of the Body" (*Quod
Animi Mores Corporis Temperamenta Sequuntur* [QAM]), Galen
came very close to defining the soul as the mixtures of the body.[16]
In his early works, Galen had held that a good doctor was a philosopher; in this later work, he went further, showing that the complete
philosopher must be a doctor. Galen opened the QAM with a
statement that made it immediately apparent that this work was
appropriating the traditional subject matter of philosophy for medicine (Ballester 1988: 133). Galen proclaimed that he had not only
found the proposition true that the capacities of the soul followed
the mixtures of the body, but also that it was useful for those
wishing to govern their minds (1; SM II.32). He implied that
those who wished to regulate their minds/souls must turn their
attention to their bodily mixtures (*crases*). In fact, Galen explicitly
stated that it was through a good mixture that the mind could be
influenced to virtue (*arete* 1; SM II.32.11). Galen turned away here
from the traditional schema of pursuing virtue through rational

162

self-mastery toward a pursuit of virtue through attention to the body (and the expert guide that this would assume). Galen recognized that his thesis in QAM would move medicine into the domain of philosophy. He did not wish to destroy the benefits of philosophy. He maintained, rather, he wished to explain and teach philosophers certain things that they had ignored; for example, that humans become friends or enemies of justice through the mixtures of their bodies (11; SM II.73). If philosophers had come to this recognition, it would have displaced one of their major concerns into the medical field. Rather than pursuing virtue through the rational control of desires and passions, its pursuit would be linked with the careful control of the body's balance.

Galen made every effort in the QAM to support his thesis that the capacities of the soul followed the mixtures of the body by invoking the authority of the ancient philosophers and doctors. Geoffrey Lloyd, in an illuminating analysis, has shown how Galen manipulated these sources to the point of serious distortion to make them appear as though they had supported his point of view (Lloyd 1988). Galen chose his texts selectively, for example, to prove that Aristotle had held that soul was the mixture of the four qualities of heat, cold, wetness, and dryness. In what Lloyd defined as a "convoluted argument" (24), Galen first established that Aristotle had held that the soul was the form (*eidos*) of the body. And since the body was a construct of both its material and form, and the material of bodies was supplied by the four qualities, the mixture of these four qualities must be their form.[17] If all these premises were granted, then the mixture of the four qualities was the soul (3; SM II.37). Galen offered this argument in hypothetical terms, but nevertheless, according to Lloyd, extrapolated more than Aristotle's words could warrant to support his case.

Again, by choosing selectively from Plato's work, Galen also used him to support his thesis that the faculties of the soul followed the mixtures of the body (Lloyd 1988: 18–23). Galen maintained that the two parts of the soul Plato held to be mortal, the spirited and the desiderative which were situated, respectively, in the heart and the liver, were clearly the bodily mixture itself (SM II.44). He claimed, for example, that "the mixture of the heart is the spirited form of the soul" (SM II.44). Galen approached his discussion of the third part, the rational part of the soul, more cautiously. He recalled that Plato had held that the rational soul was immortal and said that he did not want to argue this point with Plato (3.773K; SM II.36). But if Galen did not actually argue, he did indirectly question Plato's conception. He mused, for example, that he was not sure what the substance of the soul could be, if it belonged to the class of incorporeals. "For in bodies I see numerous mixtures all distinct from each other . . . but of incorporeal substance which . . . is neither a quality or a form of a body I cannot conceive of any differentia" (3.776K; SM II.38).

Galen further insisted that if the rational soul was not corporeal, it was, nonetheless, susceptible to bodily influences. Galen substantiated this point with repeated examples. He wondered for instance, why physical events caused the soul to depart the body in death: "Why does the soul emigrate when the brain is too cold, or too hot or very moist? Why does the loss of a great deal of blood also make it leave; or taking hemlock; or a burning fever?" (3.775K; SM II.38; Ballester 1988: 132). He also pondered why the humours had such an effect on mental states: "I do not know why delirium is produced by an excess of yellow bile in the brain or melancholia is the result of black bile . . ." (3.777K; SM II.39). Galen also noted the effects of wine on the rational soul – "it relieves all pain and trouble," or again, "It likewise makes our souls at once milder or bolder-acting, of course, through the mixtures of the body which are produced by means of the humours" (3.779K; SM II.41). Galen showed his uneasiness with the notion of an incorporeal soul so obviously affected by physical causes: "For how could it be driven by association with the body into a nature opposite its own, if it were neither a quality of the body, nor a form, an affection, or a faculty?" (5.778K; SM II.48).

In any event, Galen insisted that whatever its substance, it was clear that the soul was subservient to the body:

> Hence those who assert that there is a distinct substance for the soul must recognize that it is subservient [*douleuein*] to the mixture of the body since the mixture can separate it from the body, carry it to delirium, deprive it of memory, make it sad, timid and depressed.
>
> (3. 779K; SM II.41; Ballester 1988: 133)

Galen recognized that his physiology has consequences for moral philosophy. He imagined someone questioning him "how can humans be blamed or praised for their actions, if the soul is subservient to the body?" If they are good or evil "not through themselves but because of their mixture" (11.814–815K, SM II.73). His answer – that there is in all of us a capacity to love the good and hate the bad without considering whether it originated in the body or not – was a harsh one (as his example made clear). He pointed out that humans destroyed scorpions, venomous spiders, and adders, although they are bad by nature. Galen suggested that humans are able to judge and punish behavior whether or not it is innate. Just as they killed scorpions because they sting and did not pardon them because it was in scorpion nature to sting, so they can condemn persons who are bad "without considering whether it originated in the body or not" (Pigeaud 1989: 66). Even if bad actions were a result of bad mixtures, individuals were not guiltless, for Galen further believed that people must be held accountable for achieving the best balance possible for their bodies (Siegel 1973: 215).

Quite plainly in the QAM, Galen was relocating elements into medicine that in the Hellenistic philosophical tradition had been the concern of moral philosophy. Within this context, the turn toward the body acquired a moral dimension. According to Galen, the complex physical interior life of the body influenced many elements that had been thought to be under the control of the rational faculty. Galen suggested that the rational faculty was, rather, influenced by the body. And in this scheme, it was the doctor and not the philosopher who offered advice and remedies in areas previously outside his domain. Galen's argument in the QAM removed from the control of the self much that traditional Greek thought had located there (Walzer 1962).

Galen had made clear in his *De Temperamentis* how complicated the business of balancing the mixtures was. An overseer was necessary to explain people's bodies to them and help them keep them in balance, just as the overseer in the *Thrasybulus* had tended the perforated wine jar, and just as Galen explained Marcus Aurelius's body's functioning to him. Galen's work suggested that at the same time as inhabitants of the early Roman empire turned toward their bodies and discovered a complex individual interior that could be read and interpreted, they also became aware of its fragile stability that needed external supervision and control to help set it right. The "turn toward the body" initiated a retreat from the ideal of self-mastery and tokened a change in cultural subject, a redirection from a subject as a controlling rational mind or soul to a subject as body, a dissolving body tending toward disequilibrium, that needed interpretation, attention, and external control. For those with access to doctors, the necessity for expert attention may have posed no problem; what, however, about all the others without such access? What of people like those in the crowd described by Dio Chrysostom, attending the medical demonstrations and affected by representations of the body, which may, like Galen's, have offered that it was disintegrating and needed attention? Plato had supplied one answer centuries earlier in his attack on those "turned toward the body" during his period. In the *Republic*, he castigated Herodicus for "lingering out his death ... living in perpetual observance of his malady" and compared him with a carpenter who had no leisure to be sick, who, faced with long treatment, preferred to die and be freed from his troubles (III.14; 406B).[18] The fact that so many inhabitants of the early empire turned to healing religions such as Christianity and Asclepius worship suggests that an answer like Plato's did not satisfy them.

Galen depicted a human body at risk and verging toward disequilibrium, and he matched this with an image of the contemporary social body seriously out of balance.[19] He opened the *Prognosis* with a highly rhetorical invective against contemporary doctors:

> For since those who are eager for the semblance of ability rather than the reality have come to predominate in medicine as well as in the other arts, the finest aspects of these arts are now neglected and attention is lavished upon what may bring them a high reputation with the general public – a gratifying word or act, a bit of flattery, a toadying salutation each day of the rich and powerful men in the cities, accompanying them when they go out, staying at their side ...
>
> (1.1; 599K)

Galen painted a graphic picture of these doctors with their "expensive clothes and rings, their abundant retinue and their flashy silver equipment" duping the credulous, impressed by such appearances (1.2; 600K). These doctors were only one symptom of the general decline of the whole society. Galen emphasized the prevailing "injustice" of what he referred to as "life now" (1.11; 603K). He, like other members of the Second Sophistic, saw little good in the contemporary period: "the causes of all this in the world lie in the materialism of the rich and powerful in the cities, who honoring pleasure above virtue, consider of no account those who possess some finer knowledge and can impart it to others" (1.13; 604K). Things were in such a bad way that most doctors, according to Galen, were so ignorant of what had been discovered by their "predecessors and especially by Hippocrates, our guide to all that is good" (1.9; 602K) that they greeted the prognoses of a properly trained doctor with charges of sorcery (1.8; 602K). Galen himself was labeled a sorcerer by his rivals. After his correct diagnosis of Eudemus, for example, he reported that the renowned doctor Martianus:

> slanderously maintained that my forecasts derived not from medicine but from divination. When some people asked what sort of divination he meant, he sometimes said that it came from observing the flight of birds, sometimes from sacrifices, sometimes from chance happenings or from consulting horoscopes.
>
> (3.7; 615K)

Galen's comments on his rivals were also hostile. He described his medical opponents as not simply misguided and ignorant practitioners, but as, actually, evil. He called their actions a "life of crime." In the *Prognosis*, Galen implied that his talents had actually put his very life at risk. Early in the text Eudemus warned Galen about the doctors in Rome who, he said, had only come to the city to practice their villainy in anonymity (4.10; 622K). Eudemus likened these doctors to brigands: "Robbers in our own country band together to harm others and spare themselves: similarly those here combine against us, the only difference from bandits being these men operate in the city, not in the mountains" (4.11; 622K).

Eudemus described these doctors as belonging to the lower, uneducated classes in their own cities, and warned Galen to fear even poisoning from them. The philosopher concluded his warning with an admonitory example:

> He told me in his discourse of a young man who had arrived in the city some ten years earlier and who had been poisoned, together with the two servants who accompanied him, because, like me, he had given a practical demonstration of his proficiency in medicine.
>
> (4.16; 623–624K)

Eudemus described a society so flawed that the most talented were at risk of actual harm.

In his *Prognosis'* introduction, Galen similarly stressed the danger and jeopardy for the doctor dedicated to his art. He offered the hypothetical case of a well-trained doctor unable to explain his medical knowledge to other doctors because of their ignorance. This doctor eventually incited such envy that the other doctors "conspire against him, first by plotting poisoning, secondly by the trap in which they caught Quintus, the best physician of his generation, who was expelled from Rome on a charge of murdering his patients" (1.9; 602K). In the *Prognosis*, Galen portrayed a world, a society where the very lives of "whoever wants to pursue the art of medicine in a philosophic manner worthy of the sons of Asclepius" (1.25; 602K), were in danger. Galen's narrative described the rivalry between doctors as more than a matter of professional differences, but literally a matter of life and death.

Vivian Nutton noted the conventional aspects of this opening of the *Prognosis*, as well as its similarity to the very similar abuse (that Nutton calls the "rhetoric of hate") leveled at the methodists and one of their founders, Thessalus, in the opening of Galen's *De Methodo Medendi* (Nutton 1991: 15). There Galen also described contemporary doctors as ignorant flatterers of the rich and lower class (10.5K). He described them as originally being practitioners of menial trades "cobblers, carpenters, dyers" (10.5K). He particularly castigated Thessalus for his menial origins, depicting him as the son of a wool-worker: "it would have been impossible for you to form a judgement . . . raised as you were in the women's quarters by a father who carded wool in a shameful manner" (10K). Nutton doubted the validity of this description of Thessalus' origins, suggesting that he more likely "came from the higher stratum of society, the owners of the land over which the sheep grazed" (Nutton 1991: 19).

Nutton also noted the similarities between Galen's list of the occupations of the incompetent doctors and his contemporary, Celsus', denigration of Christians, as illiterate wool-workers, cobblers, and dyers (Origen *Contra Celsum* 3.4). The similarity helps to explain the implicit atmosphere of violence and threat created in the introductions of both the *Prognosis* and the *De Methodo Medendi*. The conventional nature of these insults showed that the doctors of the period were involved in an inherently cultural debate – one that extended beyond a simple matter of disagreements between professional rivals. The level of insults and the implied threat of danger both signal that the differences over how the body was to be perceived touched a sensitive cultural nerve. Neither side of the debate could conceive of how someone holding the opposite view could function in the culture as they understood it to be. When a Galen, or a Celsus, or a Eudemus located a person among the lower classes, for example, he was consigning them to cultural otherness – "that which can not be and still be part of the culture" (Armstrong and Tennenhouse 1989: 4). In this period only the upper classes had a cultural existence; that is to say, no one other than the educated wealthier classes had a place in the ideological conceptual world of the culture makers – the wealthy and the educated. When one of the upper classes labeled others as belonging to groups outside this world, it suggested that those so labeled had breached some ideological barrier, had placed themselves outside the bounds of what was held acceptable in the particular thought-world.

Cultures have only a limited number of places to assign to those who do not belong. In the ancient world, as we have seen, one such place was among the low-born, the poor, and unimportant; another was among the criminal – bandits and murderers. Yet another was among those with more than human powers: sorcerers and wonder-workers. That in these arguments between medical practitioners all these categories come into play discloses the ideological nature of the struggle in their disputes. These patterns of insult alert us to the fact that, in their discourse about how the body was to be understood, the doctors had entered sensitive cultural terrain. They were involved, in fact, in helping to bring about a change of cultural subject. All the discursive attention occurring in Rome on medicine and topics associated with bodies that is evidenced by the *Prognosis* points to a shift in the cultural attention toward the body. Galen's narratives in particular worked to create a cultural "self" as body – a body able to signify its inner life, but difficult to keep in order and needing outside supervision; in many instances, a sick body, needing a doctor. The cultural shift toward the body also worked to downplay differences of class and gender. As Galen's narrative has shown, the body was one aspect of human being where all shared equally the need for external help – whether slave or emperor, man or woman.

Galen concluded the QAM with an argument that he hoped would clinch his thesis that, in Geoffrey Lloyd's words, "the krasis you are born with (as also the krasis of the country in which you are born) makes an appreciable difference to your character ..." (Lloyd 1988: 37). Galen reminded his readers how geography affected rationality: "In fact, in Scythia there has been only one philosopher, but in Athens many; in Abdera there are many stupid people, but in Athens few" (11.822K; SM II.79). This proverbial stupidity of the people of Abdera was the genesis of another example of popular medical writing from the Hippocratic pseudepigrapha, which shows that an understanding of the self as a sick body in a flawed world was not limited to Galen. Among the pseudepigrapha are a group of letters describing a meeting between Hippocrates and Democritus. Of particular interest is *Letter Seventeen*, called by Wesley Smith, a recent editor of the pseudepigraphic writings, "the climax and intellectual center" of the group (Smith 1990: 21). Smith suggested, on the ground of its anatomical interests, that this letter was a late addition to the collection, after Herophilus' anatomy had become well-known, perhaps even after Marinus revived interest in anatomy in the first/second century A.D. (Smith 1990: 26).[20]

In these letters the people of Abdera, known for their stupidity, have summoned Hippocrates to treat Democritus, their famous citizen, whom they believe has gone mad because of his continuous laughter. *Letter Seventeen* described Hippocrates' arrival in Abdera, his meeting with Democritus, and his conversion to the philosopher's world-view. By the end of this letter, Hippocrates would declare that Democritus was not only sane but "has tracked down and understood the truth of human nature" (17.10).

Hippocrates' description of his first sight of Democritus is significant:

> And Democritus himself was sitting under a low plane tree, in a coarse shirt, alone . . . , on a stone seat, pale and emaciated, with untrimmed beard. Next to him on the right a small stream bubbled down the hill's slope softly. There was a sanctuary on top of the hill, which I conjectured was dedicated to the nymphs, roofed over with wild grapes. He had a papyrus roll on his knees in a very neat manner, and some book-rolls were laid out on both sides. And stacked around were a large number of animals, generally cut up. He sometimes bent and applied himself intensely to writing, sometimes he sat quietly attentive, pondering within himself. Then after a short time of this activity he stood up and walked around and examined the entrails of the animals, set them down and went back and sat down.
>
> (17.2)

Commentators have pointed out the conventional nature of parts of this depiction. Democritus' garb, physique, beard, intense study, and reflection identified him as a philosopher. The secluded grove, near a temple to the nymphs, evoked the traditional setting for philosophical dialogue (Smith 1990: 21, citing Plato *Phaedrus* 230B). But there was one anomalous element in this scene – the stacked up, dissected animals. The letter added an experimental, physical component to the traditional picture of the philosopher. After observing Democritus, Hippocrates approached and tested his rationality. He asked him what he was writing. Democritus explained that it was "a treatise on madness . . . what it is, how it comes on men, and how to relieve it" (17.3). He dissected the animals to discover the nature and location of the bile, for, as he said, "its overabundance generally causes dementia" (17.3).

The initial picture depicted the philosopher turning to the physical body for an understanding of human behavior. The narrative explicitly offered the body as a text to be consulted in comprehending the human subject. Hippocrates pressed Democritus to explain his continual and seemingly inappropriate laughter, and Democritus answered with a rather conventional, cynic-flavored indictment of humanity (Stuart 1958): "you think that there are two causes for my laughter, good things and bad. But, I laugh at one thing, humanity, brimming with ignorance, void of right action, childish in all aspirations . . ." (17.5). For Democritus, everything associated with the human condition was laughable.

Just as the *Prognosis* had, *Letter Seventeen* held greed as a primary cause of human problems: "Of all this, greed is the cause" (17.8), and similarly depicted competent medical practice as an occasion for jealousy. Democritus, as Galen did, described the prevailing envy at acquired skill:

> Really, I expect that your medical science is not even pleasing to them. They are disaffected from everything by their wantonness and they consider wisdom madness. Yes, I suspect that they have slandered most of your learning through jealousy or ingratitude . . . And the majority, void of knowledge or training themselves, in their ignorance destroy what is superior, for the votes belong to the imperceptive. Even those who have experience of it do not want to associate with it, nor fellow practitioners to bear witness to it, for they are full of jealousy.
>
> (17.9.90)[21]

Because of his anatomical efforts, Democritus included himself in his general denunciation of humanity: "Do you not see that I, too, am a portion of the evil? In looking for a cause of madness I stretch animals out and cut them up, but I should be seeking the cause from humankind" (17.9). Democritus held out little hope for humanity. He used medical terminology to convey the human situation: "Don't you see that even the cosmos is full of misanthropy? It has collected an infinity of affections [*pathea*] for men. Man as a whole is an illness [*nousos*] from birth" (17.9). In the context of this letter, beginning with the portrayal of dissections, and Democritus' search for the physical causes of human behavior, this diction retained some of its medical force. At first, Hippocrates rejected this dark picture of the human condition. Early in the letter he had ironically challenged Democritus: "Speak by the gods! Maybe, without it being apparent, the whole world is sick and has no place to send an embassy for therapy. For what could there be outside itself?" (17.4).[22] Building on the beliefs of the historical Democritus, the fictive Democritus answered, chiding Hippocrates: "There are many infinities of worlds, Hippocrates, and never, my friend, belittle the riches of nature" (17.4).

In the cultural world brought into being by narratives such as the *Prognosis* and *Letter Seventeen*, that offered an image of contemporary society as deeply flawed and out of equilibrium, matched with a conception of the self as a physical body similarly tending to disequilibrium and sickness, inhabitants did, indeed, begin to look to other "worlds" for therapy. The initial image in *Letter Seventeen*, of Democritus reading the physical body as one among a number of other texts, is suggestive. Christians, as the *Acts of the Martyrs* have shown, offered their bodies as texts for their neighbors to read as proof for the reality of another world.

7

IDEOLOGY, NOT
PATHOLOGY

It has been my contention in this study that the early Roman empire saw the construction of a new cultural subject. Narratives issuing from different cultural points – medicine, Christian martyr literature – brought into cultural consciousness a representation of the human self as a body in pain, a suffering body. At the same time, others, like those of Epictetus and the Greek romances, confirmed a more traditional Hellenic subject – a mind/soul controlling and directing a body whose pain and suffering mattered little to the self's real essence. A debate was taking place over key terms concerned with human being in the world, and its site was the human body. The recognition of this discursive struggle will help to explicate emphases in second-century texts that have often puzzled – even, at times, offended – modern sensibilities. Commentators have described Aelius Aristides' *Sacred Tales*, the letters of Ignatius of Antioch, and the *Meditations* of Marcus Aurelius as neurotic or pathological. In a recent book, for example, R. B. Rutherford introduced a discussion of Aristides with the deprecatory comment: "peculiar and unpleasant though his personality may seem to us today" (Rutherford 1989: 199). The same offense, moreover, is ascribed to all three men, namely, an inordinate fixation on bodily pain and suffering. Interpreting these authors' textual emphasis on pain as merely a reflection of the pathology of aberrant individuals of the early empire is an unfair simplification of the texts. Such a reading prevents the recognition that their emphasis on pain and suffering reflects a widespread cultural concern, which during the period was using representations of bodily pain and suffering to construct a new subjectivity of the human person.

Chapter 6 examined the role of medical discourse in this construction. Medicine is one of the most important institutional

173

elaborations of the body in any society, but in the early empire the cult of Asclepius offered a parallel social institutionalization of the body. This cult, as the general interest in medicine, also had wide and increased popularity during the early empire. Both Edelstein and Ruttimann note expanded building at all cult centers, and the inscriptional evidence supports the cult's prominence (Edelstein and Edelstein 1945: 2.109, 255; Ruttimann 1986: 8, 17, 21, 33, 85).

The texts of Ignatius and Aristides in particular need to be considered within this general framework of an increased attention to the body. These texts provide evidence for an important moment in the representation and regulation of the self. This moment was pivotal in the transformation from the civic person of ancient society (who located authority externally, in various social institutions), into the person of late antiquity who searched within for other-worldly authority. In one of his most suggestive statements, Foucault located the body as the "site of all control" (quoted in Turner 1984: 250). The focus on the body in Ignatius and Aristides should not be interpreted as aberrant, but as part of a far-reaching cultural discourse that constructed new locations for social control and power.

Charles Behr has established the basic outline of Aristides' life. Born in A.D. 117 in upper Mysia of wealthy parents, Aristides received the best education available. He had just embarked on what was already a successful oratorical career when he fell ill in A.D. 143. Unable to regain his health, Aristides eventually retired to the temple of Asclepius in Pergamum in A.D. 145. It was customary for Asclepius worshipers (called incubants) to sleep in the temple to await dream visitations and cures from the god. For two years, Aristides remained in the temple receiving divine advice and prescriptions, part of a group of incubants. In A.D. 147, he recovered sufficiently to leave the temple and resume his career, but he maintained his close relationship with Asclepius for the rest of his life, especially after he again fell sick with smallpox in A.D. 165. Aristides died in A.D. 171.

In *The Sacred Tales*, six orations composed at the end of his life, Aristides recounts his long interaction with the god and its effects. *The Sacred Tales* are not unparalleled in content, although they may be unusual in their length. Numerous inscriptions testify that worshipers of Asclepius were expected to record the god's interventions; there is also contemporary papyrological evidence that a book-length account of the god's help was not exceptional. It is necessary to emphasize this fact because modern commentators often interpret Aristides' account of his bodily symptoms and the god's concern as manifestations of an egotistical self-regard rather than as an accepted aspect of cult practice. Aristides himself testified: "Straight from the beginning the god ordered me to write down my dreams. And this was the first of his commands" (ST 48.2).[1]

The god's orders resulted, according to Aristides, in a record that was 300,000 lines long. But *The Sacred Tales* are not this record; rather, as Aristides explained, it is a narrative, ordered in a dream vision, summarizing his long relation with Asclepius. By contrasting this work with the lost dream diary, Aristides underlined his perception that his text is a shaped discourse, not simply a record, but a representation. It was his attempt to allow others to share with him his experience of the god's beneficence.

Aristides' detailed narrative of his illnesses, dreams, and physical treatments have won him few admirers. Misch, although admitting "here again we seem close to an appearance of the record of the inner life," denies the *Tales* the status of true autobiography. He finds missing Aristides' "ability to conceive his visions psychologically" (Misch 1951: 2.508). Even worse is Aristides' persistent focus on the physical, the bodily; Misch asks rhetorically how Aristides could publish "such stuff" (Misch 1951: 2.506).[2] Peter Brown also appeared disappointed with Aristides' constant, mundane physical focus: "we obscurely resent the fact that a degree of intimacy with the divine which would make a saint or a martyr of any of us should merely serve to produce a hypochondriacal gentleman of indomitable will" (Brown 1978: 41). In my view, Misch and Brown expected something from the text that the text itself did not intend (as Brown, in fact, said). In his text, Aristides described a relationship with the divine that is neither psychologically nor spiritually based, but physically based. Aristides' text is about the body, and in his representation, divine power is focused and inscribed on the body in palpably material terms.

Modern problems with Aristides' narrative originate from commentators' unwillingness to entertain the stated terms of the discourse and the representation of the discursive subject it offers. *The Sacred Tales* is a narrative concentrating on the body. Moderns find this focus difficult to maintain, but contemporaries seemingly did not. Rather, this focus is another reflection of the cultural turn toward the body noted by Brown and Foucault. The *Tales* constructed a subjectivity around what is essentially a body, and in particular a suffering body. In the role of the patient, the attention of the divine is caught and held. Aristides was explicit about his relationship with the divine – it shares the modality of patient and doctor: "I decided to submit to the god, truly as to a doctor, and to do in silence whatever he wishes" (ST 47.4). *The Sacred Tales* provides another discursive example of the period's particular and intense attention to the body.

Aristides' paradigm of the doctor/god, patient/devotee informed and explained the nature of his narrative. The represented subject of the narrative was essentially a body presented for observation and treatment. Aristides clearly stated his focus. Early in the first *Tale*, for example, he began a major section, "But now I wish to indicate to you the condition of my abdomen. I shall reckon each matter day by day" (ST 47.4). And so he does for the fifty-seven chapters that follow until he concludes "so much for my abdomen" (ST 47.61). This close scrutiny and record of the body, as well as Aristides' testimony of the god's interest in such minutiae, are what moderns find offputting. In *On Prognosis*, however, Galen showed that Aristides' contemporaries were not similarly unsettled. Galen's sketches of wellborn gentlemen monitoring and discussing their pulses, their diets, their medical regimes, offer testimony for the general interest in the care of the body.

It is necessary to understand Aristides' narrative in this context; it is an example of a text emanating from fixed attention on the body. The *Tales* maintains a focus that is unwaveringly physical: "I bathed at evening and at dawn I had pains in my abdomen, and the pain spread over the right side and down to the groin" (ST 47.8). Passage after passage details symptomatology. Other passages record the therapies, most of them physical, ordered by the god as interpreted by Aristides. "Vomiting was also ordered through many tokens, and this was the fifth day in a row without bathing" (ST 47.15). "On the twenty-third, vomiting in the evening, and this according to a dream" (ST 47.21). "The following of not bathing; the day after that of not bathing and vomiting" (ST 47.40). This representation of the subject's interaction with the divine in terms of symptoms and prescriptions from the contemporary medical panoply – vomiting, blood-letting, bathing and not bathing – may offend modern sensibilities. It seems, however, a necessary product of the relationship between the subject and the divine constructed in the narrative – a relation between a self understood as a body, specifically a patient's body, and a god who treats this body.

Aristides did not depict the "journey of the soul" Misch (1951) sought because his discourse focused instead on the body. And his "this-worldly" focus was a necessary result of an attention fixed so on the operations of the body. Rather than making such observations, judgements, however, it is more productive to recognize how the focus on the body affected the construction of the relation between divine and human in the text. Aristides constructed a relationship that had as its premise a material body needing constant divine inspection and treatment. A summary reflects the extent and duration of the god's attention:

> I have not bathed for five consecutive years and some months besides, unless, of course, in winter time, he ordered me to use the sea or rivers or wells. The purgation of my upper intestinal tract has taken place in the same way for nearly two years and two months in succession, together with enemas and phlebotomies, as many as no one has ever counted, and at that with little nourishment and that forced.
>
> (ST 47.59)

Aristides represented his "self" as a body undergoing treatment. His relation with the divine was completely derived from this doctor/patient paradigm. The god's vision and methods may have surpassed mortal doctors, but this sphere of operation was the same – the physical body. Aristides has a personal relation with his god, that was primarily directed toward his material body.

At this point my stress on the physicality of the self-representation in the *Tales* might be questioned because so much of the narrative describes Aristides' dream life. In fact, much of the critical discussion of the *Tales* has centered on these dreams but has removed them from their context. The dreams in the text are linked to a physical effect in almost all cases. Aristides introduces dreams only to show how he physically implemented them. Modern scholars interested in the workings of the mind may search the dreams for psychological evidence, but Aristides, as a worshiper of Asclepius, searched them for instructions concerning his body.

Many of the dreams refer quite literally to the body, depicting foods or episodes of bathing, but some seem to reflect Aristides' concern over his interrupted career, his anxieties, his need for reassurance, his aspirations (Stephens 1982: chapter 6; Michenaud and Dierkens 1972). Nevertheless, even for these, Aristides supplies a physical interpretation. Aristides' hermeneutic reveals more of his thought than his dreams can. Recollections of dreams are notoriously dependent on the dreamers' cultural and experiential networks. Interpreters separated from these networks by nearly 2,000 years are not well-situated as psychoanalysts. Aristides' repeated physical interpretations of his dreams, however, quite patently manifest both his project and how dreams function in *The Sacred Tales*. For Aristides, dreams were basically staging areas for physical treatments, and for this reason they are included in the narrative.

The tenacious reductionism of some of his readings of dreams only underscores this point. Near death with smallpox, he dreams of Athena:

> Then not much later, Athena appeared with her aegis and beauty and magnitude and the whole form of the Athena of Phidias in Athens. There was also a scent from the aegis as sweet as could be . . . She reminded me of the *Odyssey* . . . I myself was indeed both Odysseus and Telemachus and she must help me.
>
> (ST 48.41–42)

To modern commentators, Athena's appearance in this dream demonstrates megalomania (Dodds 1965: 41). Aristides gives the dream a physical interpretation: "And it immediately occurred to me to have an enema of Attic honey, and there was a purge of my bile" (ST 48.43). Having understood that the juxtaposition of Athens and a sweet aroma indicated a prescription, Aristides displayed his basic, physical reading of his dream no matter how distracting or uplifting its content might be.

He performed a similar interpretation of another dream that featured the emperors Marcus Aurelius and Lucius Verus:

> I dreamed that I was staying in the Palace and that the care and honor, which the emperors showed to me in all their activities, was marvelous and unsurpassable. . . . Later they took me along on a tour. They went off to inspect some drainage ditch . . . I also saw the excavation of this ditch taking place. They behaved marvelously to me during the trip. For many times I was between the two of them . . .
>
> (ST 46–47)

The dream continues to detail the emperors' kindnesses, but again the focus of Aristides' interpretation is noteworthy: "So I bathed and vomited at evening, for I took note of the excavation" (ST 47.50). From his dream of intimate interaction with the emperors, Aristides considered important the point that enabled a physical reading – the excavation, which he translated into vomiting. The unswerving focus of the *Tales*, even in the dreaming, is the same focus as that imputed to the divine – namely, the body. Aristides did not psychologize his visions, as Misch desired him to; rather, he somatized them.

In the *Tales*, Asclepius's attention was explicitly represented as enacted on Aristides' body. Devotees experienced the god's regard in their treatments. Asclepius often demanded treatments, it seems, that exceeded in rigor even those of the contemporary medical practice. Aristides interpreted his god as ordering difficult physical challenges for him. Even in his weakened physical condition, Aristides was commanded to undertake barefoot runs in the coldest weather, to smear his body with cold mud, to take icy plunges in rough waters (ST 47.59, 65, 74; 48.18, 50, 51; 51.49).[3] Such demands cannot be dismissed simply as indicators of Aristides' masochistic yearnings (Dodds 1965: 42). A comment of Marcus Aurelius allows them to be recognized as common Asclepeian practice. In an analogy that would make sense only if he were describing a commonplace and understood the treatments to be rigorous, Marcus Aurelius wrote: "we have all heard 'Asclepius has prescribed for so and so riding, or cold baths, or walking barefoot'" (*Med.* 5.8). It appears that it was normal practice for devotees to manifest their obedience through their endurance and bodily submission to painful commands. Worshipers performed their devotion with bodies that accepted pain.

Aristides described an episode that shows how, within the divine relationship, pain can be transmuted. In Smyrna, Aristides had an apparition of Asclepius which he interpreted as ordering him to bathe in a river:

It was the middle of winter and the north wind was stormy and it was icy cold, and the pebbles were fixed to one another by the frost, so that they seemed like a continuous sheet of ice, and the water was such as is likely in such weather. When the divine manifestation was announced, friends escorted us and various doctors, some of them acquaintances, and others

179

who came either out of concern or even for the purposes of investigation. There was also another great crowd, for some distribution happened to be taking place. . . . But being still full of warmth from the vision of the god, I cast off my clothes, and not wanting a message, flung myself where the water was deepest. Then as in a pool of very gentle and tempered water, I passed my time swimming all about and splashing myself all over. When I came out, all my skin had a rosy hue and there was a lightness throughout my body. There was also much shouting from those present and those coming up, shouting that celebrated phrase, "Great is Asclepius". . . . My mental state was also nearly the same. For there was neither, as it were, conspicuous pleasure, nor would you say it was like human joy. But there was a certain inexplicable contentment which regarded everything as less than the present moment, so that when I saw other things, I seemed not to see them. Thus I was wholly with the god.

(ST 48.19–23)

This scene is instructive for understanding the relationship that is central to *The Sacred Tales*. Aristides submitted himself to what he understood to be the god's orders to endure a painful experience and the result, contrary to what the natural circumstances warrant, was not pain, but well-being and union with the divine. Onlookers explicitly interpreted Aristides' ability to endure the freezing swim as a manifestation of the god's power. The crowd greeted his emergence from the river with shouts honoring Asclepius. Aristides, who regularly represented himself as in almost constant pain, found bodily ease and divine union as a result of his obedience. This entire episode represents how the experience of suffering changes when it is undertaken at divine behest. Interpretation affects experience.

Aristides' experience of refreshment and union with the divine through the physical endurance of the body appears similar to the experience described of Christian martyrs in the same period. In Lyons, for example, also during the reign of Marcus Aurelius, Blandina, a martyr undergoing torture, received "renewed strength with her confession of faith: her admission, 'I am a Christian; we do nothing to be ashamed of', brought her refreshment, rest, and insensibility to her present pain." Later she is described as insensible to pain because of her "communion" with Christ (ACM 1.19, 56).

For both Aristides and Blandina, the god's epiphany was evidenced by altered human somatic perceptions. Others also recognized the god in such episodes. The crowd shouted "Great is Asclepius"; how else could Aristides' chronically infirm body have endured the icy plunge except supported by some external power? Aristides' representational project displays the power of the divine in the negated weakness of the body.

Like *The Sacred Tales*, the medical discourse also represented the human body as constantly at risk, needing careful monitoring to remain in balance – baths to add moisture, blood-letting and vomiting to produce dryness. The *Tales*, which shared with the medical texts the subject of a body that is constantly susceptible to risk and that requires supervision and regulation, solved the problem of management. The narrative constructed a subject that was open to the penetrating surveillance and regulation of the divine, a subject that had turned over mastery of the "self" to the divine. Asclepius displayed his control by demanding difficult physical trials of his worshiper; the ability of the devotee to carry out these challenges was taken as evidence of the god's presence. Proof that Aristides had turned over control of his body was precisely the body's ability to endure what it could not have endured without the support of the god. The god's regulation was so complete that, as the episode of the wintery plunge made clear, it altered the experiences of the senses. Aristides' account shows how vividly the god's real and manifest presence is felt in such altered somatic testimonies. Aristides constructed a subjectivity that understood itself as completely surveyed, regulated, and informed by the divine.

Aristides represented himself as so completely under the god's control that he willingly risked even death. At one point, for example, Aristides interpreted a dream as prescribing enemas, but he was so weak he had difficulty procuring treatment: "the doctor did not have the courage to apply them, when he saw the thinness and weakness of my body. But he believed that he would, as it were, kill me" (ST 47.73). Aristides, nevertheless, insisted on the therapy. By giving himself up to divine regulation, Aristides had abdicated all authority: "for I said it was impossible for me to do anything, either important or trifling, without the god" (ST 50.102). Aristides was completely submissive to divine commands:

> As regards my blood, I said I did not have the authority to
> do one thing or the other, but that while the god commanded

the letting of my blood, I would obey, whether willing or
not, or rather never unwillingly.

(ST 49.9)

The god's regulation extended even to levels of such basic physical
details as bloodletting, purging, vomiting.

The Sacred Tales constructed a subjectivity that was under divine
surveillance and control even in its innermost workings. This
subjectivity was not regulated by an impersonal control, such as
Fate or Providence, but by control as intimate as the body itself.
It is this intimacy which is so arresting. As inhabitants of the early
empire moved further away from a civic conception of themselves
and looked for new paradigms of regulation, Aristides' text suggests
one of their first stops was a very private place; namely, the body
and its regulation. The cult of Asclepius offered one institutional
answer for the regulation of the body: turning it over to the divine
regulation of the god, Asclepius.

In this context, healing itself becomes less important, since
suffering can be validated as the basis for the divine relationship
(Festugière 1954: 86). Aristides explained how he had come to
understand his illnesses and treatments themselves as sources of
honor:

If someone should take these things into account and consider
with how many and what sort of sufferings and with what
necessary result for these he bore me to the sea and rivers
and wells, and commanded me to contend with the winter,
he will say that all is truly beyond miracles, and he will see
more clearly the power and providence of the god, and will
rejoice with me for the honor which I had, and would not
be more grieved because of my sickness.

(ST 48.59)

In fact, Aristides began to value his relationship with the god more
than any human happiness: "And who on this account regard their
disease as profitable, and who in addition have won approval, in
place of which I would not choose all the so-called felicity of
mankind" (23.16).

Handing the regulation of the body over to divine inspection and
control altered the significance of some basic experiences. Pain and
suffering were easily endured by means of divine approval that came
to matter so much to Aristides. His comment following a dream in

which he pictured himself shouting to the God, "The One," only to be answered, "it is you" (ST 50.50), shows how the relation with the divine had altered even his attitude toward his sickness: "For me this remark, Lord Asclepius, was greater than life itself, and every disease was less than this, every grace was less than this. This made me able and willing to live" (50.51). When Asclepius did not cure Aristides, Asclepius gave him something to do with his pain and allowed him to understand pain as profitable and as the basis for his relation with the god. Pain is always easier to bear if a nomic structure can be provided for it. The cult of Asclepius provided such a structure, and, in this period that was focused on the body, particularly the body at risk, the cult enjoyed marked growth. Aristides' text suggests that part of his adherence to the cult was the construction of a subjectivity that was understood as a body turned over to the constant surveillance and regulation of the divine. Within the epistemology of the Asclepius cult, the body was no longer a place for civic or personal self-mastery or regulation. Aristides quite explicitly represented the body, the site of all control, as under divine, not human, regulation. He expressed a subjectivity that valued itself and won the approval of the divine through suffering. This subjectivity placed greater value on transcendent approval than on worldly achievement. Self-erasure in the face of the divine was part of Aristides' sense of his own worth. Being eclipsed by the power of the god was a sign of the honor given him. Aristides' conception of the "self" centered on the physical, but it entailed a transfer of the regulation of the physical self from the human to the divine sphere. It used suffering to supply not only the need for the divine control, but also the validation of this control.

Aristides has been called a hypochondriac on the evidence that he survived so long despite all the symptoms he enumerated.[4] I argue, rather, that the physical emphasis of the text reflects not hypochondria, but the kind of close scrutiny of the body prevalent in the period and the Asclepius cult's response to this cultural preoccupation. There is ample evidence that Aristides was often ill, especially after contracting smallpox (Festugière 1969: 138). It is significant, however, that even during his earlier illnesses, his doctors did not seem to dismiss Aristides' sickness; they were simply unable to cure him (ST 48.5, 69). Moreover, it is important that Galen, a contemporary, far from citing him as a malingerer, vouched for Aristides' heroic endurance despite his infirmity. In a text preserved in Arabic, he wrote:

As to them whose souls are naturally strong and whose bodies are weak. I have only seen a few of them. One of them was Aristides, one of the inhabitants of Mysia. And this man belonged to the most prominent rank of orators. Thus it happened to him since he was active in teaching and speaking throughout his life, that his whole body wasted away.

(*Commentary on Plato's Timaeus*, quoted by Behr 1968: 162)

Charles Behr rejected Galen's testimony on the grounds that his diagnosis (chronic consumption) was incorrect. Behr believed Galen never actually saw Aristides, but only heard about him from his teacher and Aristides' doctor, Satyrus (Behr 1968: 162–163). Even if Galen's comment was based on hearsay, however, the testimony of a notable doctor of the period and one who had contacts with Pergamum, where Aristides spent so much time, deserves some consideration. Galen obviously believed that Aristides suffered from a chronic illness, but nevertheless stayed active and achieved prominence because of his unusual fortitude. Galen's picture also coincides closely with Aristides' self-representation.

The *Tales* is, to a certain extent, Aristides' description of the process by which Asclepius empowered him to continue his oratory despite his physical weakness. When the god first ordered him to continue his work, his command seemed absurd to Aristides: "for the prescription was like an order to fly, the practice of oratory, for one who could not breathe" (ST 50.17). Nevertheless, Asclepius ordered Aristides, while he was still an incubant in the temple, to keep on with his work composing speeches and reading them to the other incubants (ST 50.14). Thus, empowered by the god, as he believed, Aristides pursued his oratorical work while enduring his harsh regime:

But despite all the fastings, . . . we spent the whole period, nearly to the winter paradoxically, in writing and speaking and correcting that which had been written. And mostly we worked on until at least midnight. Next on each following day, having performed our usual routine, we took some little food. And when fasting followed upon vomiting, this work and study was my consolation.

(ST 47.60)

Aristides recognized that the god was the source of his rhetorical ability as much as of his physical feats. He gave the god, for example, equal credit for an icy bath and the address following it: "The spectators wondered no less at the bath than at my words. But the god was the cause of both" (ST 48.82). In Aristides' estimation, it was Asclepius who had enabled him to overcome his physical liabilities and continue with his oratory, making his success possible. Aristides' presentation of himself matches Galen's description closely. Galen's comment shows he also knew both Aristides' achievement and his physical weakness. What Galen calls "strength of soul," Aristides calls "Asclepius." Both men agree, however, that Aristides' physical infirmities were such that only some extraordinary factor, by whatever name, could have explained his accomplishments. Regardless of his diagnosis, it is clear that Galen had information about Aristides that supported the orator's description of himself, and his comment testifies that he had never sensed from the doctors in Pergamum that Aristides was a hypochondriac. Galen bears witness, moreover, that Aristides was not considered aberrant by at least one eminent contemporary. It is important to recognize this, for it is necessary to posit that Aristides' discursive emphasis was appropriate and that Aristides himself was not obviously abnormal if we are to use his work as a entrance into the cultural preoccupations and compensatory maneuvers of his time. Galen testified to Aristides' reputation as an eminent orator who overcame physical impediments to achieve success.

Aristides was successful as a prolific and respected orator in a time when the highest social value inhered in oratorical achievement. This point must be emphasized, for some commentators have explained Aristides' supposed hypochondria psychologically as his excuse for the failure of his oratorical aspirations. Such interpretations would be more convincing if "the crippling regime" (Brown 1978: 43) of the invalid had in fact ruined Aristides' career, but it did not. Aristides was among the most admired orators of his day. Philostratus, who was nearly a contemporary of Aristides, includes him in his *Lives of the Sophists* (*Vitae Sophistarum*) and reflected only positive estimations of him. Philostratus knew *The Sacred Tales* and appeared to have found nothing pathological in them. He simply commented on the usefulness of such "diaries" for teaching the art of speaking well. Philostratus called Aristides "gifted," and referred to his "erudition" and "force and power of characterization" (*Vitae Sophistarum* 2.9.589). Philostratus also included Marcus Aurelius' estimation of Aristides: "The Emperor was greatly pleased with the man's personality, so unaffected was it and so devoted to study . . ." (2.9.589).

For contemporaries, Aristides' personality does not seem to have been the problem that it has been for moderns. Certainly, it did not affect his reputation or success. As a result of his illnesses, Aristides may have been less traveled than his contemporaries, but he achieved the highest prominence, nevertheless. In sum, Aristides was admired in his society.

The testimony of Philostratus and Galen help us to formulate an alternate interpretation of Aristides' narrative self-representation. No longer the record of a "deeply neurotic, deeply superstitious, vainglorious man," or of a "hypochondriacal gentleman of indomitable will," it becomes the representation of a man suffering from chronically poor health, who, by turning to the Asclepius cult, encountered a paradigm that allowed him to use his suffering body for empowerment and to see his pain as in some sense beneficial. Aristides' relationship with Asclepius provided him with a nomic structure for understanding his infirmities and living with them. Aristides comes to see himself as under the god's control and empowered by such control he achieved more success than his weakened body would otherwise have allowed him. Within such a restatement of this sort, which conforms to his own statements and those of his contemporaries, Aristides no longer appears abnormal. Rather, he provides invaluable evidence for understanding the relation created between devotee and god in a cult that was very popular in the early empire.

Aristides' representation of an embracing divine control can help explain what commentators have characterized as his most egregious example of egotism – his reaction to the death of two of the children of his "foster" sister (i.e., grandchildren of the servant whom Aristides considered his second father). Aristides held a deep conviction that he lived only because of Asclepius' special care for him:

> Some say that they have been resurrected when they were dead, and their stories are accepted, of course, and it is an old practice of the god. We have received this benefit not only once, but it is not even easy to say how often. To some he has given added years of life from his predictions. We belong to this group. For this is the least offensive way to express it.
>
> (*Oration* 42.6)

The more offensive way to say it is that Asclepius added years to Aristides' life by deducting them from the lives of others. Aristides explained the procedure:

> The fever, however, did not completely leave me until the most valued of my foster children died. He died, as I later learned, on the same day as my disease ended. Thus I had my life up to this time as a bounty from the gods, and after this, I was given a new life through the gods, and as it were, this kind of exchange occurred.

(ST 48.44)

Aristides has been chided for his lack of sympathy here. But the words "most valued" testifies to his regret and sense of loss. His remark and his method of supporting it can better be understood as another example of Aristides' use of his relation with Asclepius to explain one of life's tragedies. This is no Alcestis situation. Aristides did not pray that someone might die so that he could live. Rather, when he learned of the child's death, he attempted to make sense of it and saw in what would otherwise be a pure tragedy the god's salvific purpose, which extended his own life. There is certainly egocentrism here, but there is also an effort to find a religious explanation for tragic events.[5] Later, the dead boy's sister, Philumene, also fell sick. Aristides sent a doctor, but it was in vain, since this child also died. Aristides' explanation of how he came to understand this death through a dream has struck many readers as utterly macabre. He dreamed that he saw the child's body: "All of Philumene's trouble had been inscribed on her body and on her insides, as it were on the entrails of sacrificial animals" (ST 51.23). Aristides was able to read his own name on her intestines, as well as other signs that "heralded safety and declared that Philumene had given a soul for a soul and a body for a body, hers for mine" (ST 51.24).

Aristides again made sense of a child's premature death by seeing it as extending his own life. In his retelling of his dream experience, he portrayed Asclepius as inscribing his intent on the body of the child herself (Pearcy 1988). In Aristides' representation, bodies become texts on which the god's purposes and intentions are written. Within such a context the fact that the child died and Aristides lived must mean something. That Aristides took it to mean that his own life was extended because of the child's death permitted him to transform the death from a senseless tragedy into another occasion for renewed gratitude to the god. His attitude shows not only his egocentrism (and few upper-class men would not have thought their lives worth more than that of a retainer's child), but also how completely he understood that the god was managing his life.

Aristides was vain, ambitious, egotistical (no more so than Galen, however) but his personality did not fall so far outside the parameters of what was normal for the period that it should cause us to dismiss his testimony. *The Sacred Tales* provides an indispensable narrative representation, revealing how an upper-class inhabitant of the early empire positioned himself as a worshiper of Asclepius. This narrative also shows what assumptions about himself and his body lay behind Aristides' actions.

In the first instance, Aristides constructed his "self" as a body. This self-representation appears to have been part of a wider cultural performance that was taking the body as an important locus for observation. In particular, Aristides depicted himself as a suffering body, and, in fact, suffering constituted the medium of encounter between the "self" and the divine. In the representation of the *Tales*, Aristides experienced his god in his ability to withstand his suffering and therefore came to redefine pain as more beneficial to him than its absence might have been. The subjectivity constructed in the *Tales* – that of suffering body – is matched, moreover, by a divine subject attending to this body, treating, regulating, fixing it. In Aristides' text, the place for self-regulation has shifted, it seems, from the traditional Hellenic model of self-mastery, of an administration of the body for the society (Foucault 1988: 57). Instead, self-mastery is relinquished; the "self" is displayed recumbent, exposed inside and out to the survey and management of the divine. The "self" is incapable of even life itself; for Aristides the "self" is no longer controlled by either self or society, but directly by the god. Aristides attributed all his actions and achievements to Asclepius. In this text, the "self" is erased within the power of the divine. Paradoxically, this representation reflects the ideological trajectory toward the autonomous, individual "self," for as Aristides posited a divine control he slipped the bonds of any earthly mastery – witness his repeated rejection of medical advice, his adamant refusal of public office, his failure to greet the emperor, as Philostratus relates, on the ground that he was "contemplating" (*Vitae Sophistarum* 2.9.582).

If, as Foucault has suggested, the body is the site of all control, *The Sacred Tales* relocates control, not to the self, or the contemporary society, or the political structures, but to the realm of the transcendent. Part of the discursive project of the *Tales* is a radical relocation of power from the earthly to the divine. My reading of the text has shown that, in certain parts of the early empire, probably as part of the cultural turn toward the body, pain and suffering began to take new significations. Aristides validated pain as beneficial, and as a channel for encountering the divine. He constructed a subject who relinquished control of his body to a deity, and who, moreover, recognized the presence of the divine in his own self-erasure. In sum, Aristides provided evidence that, in addition to Christian martyrs and ascetics, other inhabitants of the early empire were identifying the body as the place of encounter between human and divine. His work shows that Christians were not the only ones involved in a representational project in which power over the self was relocated from this world to another.

This recognition of the representational project of the *Tales* provides a context for reading the *Letters of Ignatius of Antioch*, which embody a context more similar to Aristides' than differences of class and devotion might suggest.

Ignatius of Antioch died a martyr close to the time Aristides was born; he wrote seven letters as he traveled from Antioch to Rome for martyrdom.[6] Ignatius was as devoted to his god as Aristides was to his (both assumed new names to reflect the new identities provided by their gods, Theophorus for Ignatius, Theodorus for Aristides). Suffering and self-erasure were privileged operators in Ignatius' conception of the relation between human and divine, as they were for Aristides. Indeed, Ignatius' narrative expresses an enthusiasm for his anticipated suffering which has proved as problematic for moderns as did Aristides' zealous recitation of his pains and treatments. Ignatius insisted that the mark of Christians was their willingness to die ("through whom [Jesus Christ] unless we freely choose to die unto his suffering, his life is not in us" (*Ad Magnesios* 5.2).[7] Ignatius was the first writer to use the word *pathos* (suffering) to describe Christ's death, and its choice underlines his focus. Christ's suffering was his essential message, and Christians' acceptance of suffering was the sign of their commitment to his message.

Ignatius, like Aristides, projected the suffering body as the meeting place of human and divine. He wrote to the Christians in Smyrna (the city where Aristides took his icy plunge into the river and was rewarded with divine union): "near the sword, near

God; with the beasts, with God; only in the name of Jesus Christ to suffer with him; I endure all things since he, the perfect human being, empowers me" (*Ad Smyrnaeos* 4.2). Like Asclepius, Jesus, whom Ignatius called "the one physician" (*Ad Ephesios* 7.2), empowered sufferers and enabled them to endure. Ignatius understood pain not as something to be avoided, but as providing a benefit – union with the divine – just as Aristides did. This attitude explains his urgent pleas to the Church in Rome not to help him and thus thwart the martyrdom for which he longed:

> May I benefit from the wild beasts prepared for me, and I pray that they will be found prompt with me, whom I shall even entice to devour me promptly ... Indulge me; I know what is to my advantage; now I begin to be a disciple.
>
> (*Ad Romanos* 5.2–3)

Ignatius portrayed his suffering body as explicitly as Aristides did and likewise saw it as a route to divine attention: "the wrenching of bones, the mangling of limbs, the grinding of my whole body, evil punishments of the devil – let these come upon me, only that I attain Jesus Christ" (*Ad Romanos* 5.3).

Attaining Christ quite explicitly entailed suffering and martyrdom for Ignatius. His attitude exceeded that of Aristides, who was willing to risk death in carrying out the god's commands, but for whom death would have meant the end of his relation with the divine. Aristides transferred control of his body to the divine, but it was a temporal control. Ignatius not only transferred control of the body from this earth to the transcendent, but he also constructed a subjectivity that relocated along with this control. In Ignatius, the "self" did not really come into being until it suffered; suffering was not simply something that happened to a person. Rather, it was the means of achieving real selfhood. Ignatius told his readers that he was not yet "someone" and would not be until he was perfected in Jesus Christ, that is, martyred (*Ad Ephesios* 3.1). For Ignatius, discipleship entailed death: "I write to you (fully) alive, longing to die" (*Ad Romanos* 7.2). Ignatius completely rejected this world and its power: "of no profit to me will be the ends of the world and the kingdom of this age: it is 'better for me to die' to Jesus Christ than to rule the ends of the earth" (*Ad Romanos* 6.1). Ignatius understood his real existence as beginning with his suffering and martyrdom; "if I suffer, I shall become a freedman of Jesus Christ, and I shall arise free in him"

(*Ad Romanos* 4.3). He renounced his life in this world: "I no longer want to live in human fashion" (*Ad Romanos* 8.1). Although Ignatius shared certain themes of Aristides (bodily suffering, transfer of mastery of the self to the divine), his letters project a more radical representation than does Aristides' narrative. Aristides' subject is erased within divine empowerment, but this erasure does not entail bodily destruction as it does in Ignatius. Aristides' narrative displays a shift and relocation of power out of this world into another, but it does not suggest an absolute end of all contemporary modes of power. The bodily destruction on which Ignatius' letters insist acts as a powerful and stark signifier of the end of all contemporary social and political authority and control. Ignatius' letters insisted on the necessity for the dissolution of the body, the site of all control. There could be no more radical signifier for a complete rejection of this world's systems of power and control than his fervent desire for martyrdom.

Ignatius' letters were able to demand such a complete rejection because, at the same time as they represented a denial of all earthly control, they also constructed a human institution to embody the divine control that bodily destruction substantiates. Aristides, although he lived in a sanctuary of Asclepius as part of a group and consulted the temple priests, represented himself interacting with his god as essentially an individual. Ignatius, on the contrary, portrayed himself as a member of a community that was united around their suffering bodies. He exhorted the Smyrnaeans, for example: "Labor together with one another, contend together, run together, suffer together. Rise together as God's servants, assistants and servants" (*Ad Polycarpum* 6.1).[8] Ignatius linked the ideas of suffering and community, for he placed as strong a discursive emphasis on the community validated by suffering as on the suffering itself. A main focus of Ignatius' *Letters* was to urge the obedience of each Christian community to the church structure, established in a hierarchy of bishop, presbyters, and deacons. Ignatius testified that he had the authority to speak about such obedience because he was on the way to perfection through death (*Ad Trallianos* 5.1–2). His *Letters* project his death, in fact, as the emblem of his commitment to the structural integrity of the community. In Ignatius' text, as William R. Schoedel has pointed out, there is very nearly a correlation between submission to suffering and submission to the bishop (Schoedel 1985: 111). This correlation makes better sense when it is recognized that martyrdom works to signify the end of contemporary power systems, which the bishop also replaces as he marks the place of the divine: "One must regard the bishop as the Lord himself" (*Ad Ephesios* 6.1). Ignatius explicitly linked conformity with the Christian community to Christ's passion: "If anyone talks in an alien purpose that person does not conform to the passion" (*Ad Philadelphios* 3.3).

Just as the suffering validated the community, the community on earth had sufferers as its focus. Ignatius reflected that the mark of false teachers was that "for love they have no concern, none for the widow, none for the orphan, none for the distressed, none for the imprisoned, . . . for the hungry and thirsty" (*Ad Smyrnaeos* 6. 2). Not only false teachers but, in fact, most other contemporary social institutions likewise shared such a lack of concern. Ignatius named precisely those categories exempted from the prevailing social power relations. By putting suffering at its center and signifying sufferers as its focus, Ignatius' discourse represented a radical reordering and reversal of contemporary social systems. That reordering is predicated by the text's construction of a subject that achieves true worth by suffering and dying. The letters offer the very form of subjecthood around which the Christian community as an institution will form – the suffering, the sick, the poor, and the afflicted.

In summary, both Ignatius' letters and Aristides' *Sacred Tales* proceed out of a concern with the suffering body. Both texts display a subject relinquishing his body to divine surveillance and control, even to the point of submission unto death. Both subjects came to embrace their suffering as the basis of their relationship with the divine; both came to understand their pain as profitable. Aristides' relationship with Asclepius, however, lasted only as long as his illness did. For Ignatius, death did not end transcendent control; he looked forward to a continuing existence with the divine and an enduring earthly community built around sufferers.

It is of particular interest that both these two discourses, despite the many differences between their authors' social positions, construct a body facing pain as a subject. This similarity shows that in the discourse of the second century a new conception of human subjecthood was gaining ground – the subject as sufferer. The emphasis on pain in Ignatius and Aristides ought not to be dismissed as evidence of individual pathology, but recognized as an indication of this discursive project; namely, the construction of a subject centered on pain and suffering.

The emperor, Marcus Aurelius, Aristides' contemporary, left a text that represents a similar subject. The presence of this work strengthens the hypothesis that observes a discursive shift. In his *Meditations*, Marcus, a follower of Epictetus, attended to the same topics as Aristides and Ignatius – suffering and death.[9] Like them, this discursive focus has also earned him the label "pathological" (Misch 1951: 2.487). Since this epithet has now been heard so often, one may suspect that if there is pathology, it belongs to the culture rather than to the psychology of any individual.

Robert Newman has explained the popularity of the genre of *meditatio* in late antiquity: "when personal instead of civic virtue became the chief aim of Stoic philosophy, the *meditatio* became the chief ethical tool" (Newman 1989). The *meditatio* form allowed Stoics to prepare themselves for the proper assessment of life's vicissitudes by reflecting on them beforehand. An assessment of external events as well as their own emotions, attachments, and desires was central to the Stoics' system, as Epictetus' instructions demonstrated. Stoicism was premised on a belief that a natural order, a *logos*, permeates the universe and *is* the universe. And the Stoic ideal was to live in conformity with this order, "with Nature," as it was ofen put. Stoic morality was, in essence, a "morality of consent" (Festugière 1954: 107). The Stoic *sapiens* was one who recognized the natural order, identified with it, and approved it. Such recognition was possible because of the human intellect (recognized variously by Marcus Aurelius as the *nous*, a piece of the divine, a daemon (Rist 1982: 32)). This intellect allowed Stoics to objectify and distance from themselves all human and earthly distractions and focus on the beauty of the divine world order, on Nature, and to recognize that only virtue, that is, identification with this order, actually matters.

Marcus Aurelius wrote the *Meditations* as part of his effort to examine his life and see things as they really were, as Epictetus had counseled Stoics to do (*Discourses* 1.1.25). This text was written during what must have been a difficult period, the last years of Marcus' life when he was involved in almost continual military campaigns to beat back incursions into Roman territories. During this period, nevertheless, he took the time to write these philosophic exhortations to himself, to rouse his intellect to do its work of seeing things plainly. Note his repeated instruction to himself – "always remember" (Brunt 1974: 3). The *Meditations* show Marcus Aurelius' attempt to put Stoic teachings, such as those of Epictetus, into practice.

The *Meditations* seem to have provided Marcus Aurelius with an aid for approaching the Stoic goal Apollonius had taught him: "to look to nothing else even for a moment save Reason alone; and to remain ever the same, in the throes of pain, on the loss of a child, during a lingering illness" (1.8). Marcus Aurelius' list of troubles parallels those besetting Aristides, but Marcus Aurelius turned to philosophy, rather than the transcendent, to master them. The *Meditations* emphasized the areas particularly threatening Marcus Aurelius' Stoic equanimity; the text returned repeatedly to anger, the ephemerality of fame, and especially death. The text frequently recalled Marcus to the proper attitude towards death: "Despise not death, but welcome it, for Nature wills it like all else." For dissolution is but one of the processes of Nature (9.3). Marcus quoted Epictetus with approval:

> A man while fondly kissing his child, says Epictetus, should whisper in his heart: 'Tomorrow peradventure thou wilt die.' Ill-omened words these! Nay, said he, nothing is ill-omened that signifies a natural process. Or is it ill-omened also to talk of ears of corn being reaped.
>
> (11.34)

Marcus insisted that death is a good; death "is a release from impressions of sense, and from impulses that make us their puppets" (6.28).

The frequent repetition of this lesson, however, betrayed Marcus Aurelius' difficulty in learning it.[10] He dwelt, for example, on the irony that physicians, astrologers, philosophers, all of whom dealt professionally with the avoidance of death's pangs, died despite their professional interest (4.48). He rehearsed in several guises the monotonous catenation of death: "One closed a friend's eyes and was then himself laid out, and the friend who closed his, he too was laid out – and all this in a few short years" (4.48). In another place he recollected that all legendary figures are now alike in death and ended a list of the illustrious dead with the names Augustus, Hadrian, and Antoninus (4.33). R. B. Rutherford has commented, "The next term in the progression is unspoken but obvious" (Rutherford 1989: 163). Marcus Aurelius' own death seems to have been constantly on his mind, and he repeatedly offered himself proof for the naturalness of death:

194

Pass then through this tiny span of time in accordance with
Nature and come to journey's end with good grace just as an
olive falls when it is fully ripe, praising the earth that bore
it and grateful to the tree that gave it growth.

(4.48)

Rutherford noted that "no subject in the *Meditations* is treated
with such fascination, such endless variation" as death (Rutherford
1989: 167).

The effect of this repeated textual attention to death, however,
is not a sense of the author's peaceful acceptance, but rather a
feeling that death held a smothering omnipresence for him. Marcus
Aurelius insisted repeatedly that the knowledge that one conformed
with nature provided an anodyne for the brevity of life; he wrote,
for example, "All that thy seasons bring, O Nature, is fruit for
me" (4.23). His continual return to the topic, however, seems akin
to probing an aching tooth with the tongue to see if it still hurts.
He found that it still did. It was a central tenet of Hellenistic
philosophy that reason could master the pain of life's vicissitudes
and the melancholy of death. But Marcus Aurelius' text suggests
that in the discursive climate of the second century even the reason
of the emperor, supported by every material and social benefit, was
barely adequate to the task.

Marcus' rejection of the body in the *Meditations* only exacerbates
the sense of melancholy pervading his work.[11] His contempt for
the body has often been said to be more Platonic than Stoic (Asmis
1989: 2247). As Epictetus had, Marcus Aurelius pictured the body
as nothing but a corpse (4.41). He counseled himself "as one
already dying disdain the flesh: it is naught but gore and bones
and a network compact of nerves and veins and arteries" (2.2). He
pictured the body after death: "all this just a bagful of stink and
filthy gore" (8.37). His sketch of bathing – usually held as one of
the chief pleasures of ancient life – conveyed the depth of his
disgust: "As the process of bathing appears to you – oil, sweat,
muck, greasy water, all that is disgusting – such is every part of
life and all material things in it" (8.24). Indeed Marcus Aurelius
seemed disgusted by all bodily activities. He asked rhetorically,
"What kind of men they are – eating, sleeping, copulating,
excreting and so on" (10.19). All of life's material treasures when
seen aright were also contemptible in his eyes:

seeds of decay in the underlying material of everything –
water, dust, bones, reek. Again, marble but nodules of earth,

and gold and silver but dross, garments merely hair-turfs, and purple only blood. And so with everything else.

(9. 36)

It is not possible to read much joy in such descriptions. Rather, Marcus Aurelius sketched a life that made departure easy. The implied lesson in many of his vignettes is whether death can be so terrible if such is life:

All that we prize so highly in our lives is empty and rotten and paltry and we but as puppies snapping at each other, as quarrelsome children now laughing and anon in tears. But faith and modesty and justice and truth.

(5. 33)

The abstractions listed in this quotation named the virtues that supposedly make life bearable. Life in the aggregate otherwise had little to recommend it.

An empty pageant, a stage play; flocks of sheep, herds of cattle; a tussle of spearsmen; a bone flung among a pack of curs; a crumb tossed into a pond of fish; ants, laden and laboring; mice, scared and scampering away; little marionettes, dancing and jerking on their strings.

(7.3)[12]

Marcus Aurelius was devoted to his philosophic code; his text leaves no doubt of that. He did believe that "everything that befalls justly befalls" (4.10), but his difficulty in maintaining this code is evident in the repetitions of the text itself. The impression that remains with his reader is the sheer joylessness with which he held the Stoic belief that in the last analysis nothing but reason mattered. The body is an indifferent, and it is of little concern. Pain and death are not unnatural and therefore not evil (6.13). This austere answer must serve, Marcus Aurelius insisted. He did puzzle, however, over what happens after death. The intellect was divine, but this did not necessarily imply immortality. John Rist has pointed out that Marcus Aurelius examined a number of approaches to this topic, considering the possibilities of extinction, or reassimilation into the *logos*, or being scattered into atoms (6.24), but that he tended toward extinction (8.5) with the possibility that the soul might exist for some limited period (4.21).

Although on the surface Marcus Aurelius' text is quite different from those of Aristides and Ignatius, it is very much the same in one sense. All three texts constructed a subject focused on suffering and death. The discursive response to death and pain in the *Meditations* was situated in the mainstream of the Hellenic philosophic tradition; Marcus Aurelius' self-mastery entailed the submission of his desires, fears, and emotions to the domination of his reason. Within this model, an individual's reason scanned the body only to reject the body's fears and desires as either unreal or unimportant. The *Meditations* do not share the resolution offered by the other texts, namely, to turn the body over to the divine. Perhaps it is this difference, the turn away from the body, that contributes to the sense of the impersonal nature of this text, even though it was addressed "To Himself."

Earlier texts from Marcus Aurelius' hand display a quite different self-representation. A number of the emperor's early letters survive from the correspondence of Fronto, an eminent orator and rhetorician as well as Marcus Aurelius' tutor.[13] These letters reveal a young man, serious, devoted to his studies, and openly loving to his teacher and family. They also show that at this point Marcus shared the kind of fixed attention to the body seen in Aristides' work and which he was depicted showing in Galen's *Prognosis*.

This correspondence between Fronto and Marcus Aurelius has been labeled hypochrondriacal, but I would suggest that this mistakes the function of the body in the letters (Bowersock 1969: 72).[14] Discussion of body symptoms comprises the entire text of some of the letters. By discussing their bodies, Marcus Aurelius and Fronto signaled the personal nature of their communication. They communicated their affection by opening their bodies to each other. We again see how the body functioned as a privileged medium for talking about the self. Many of the letters of Marcus Aurelius and Fronto focused quite narrowly on the body in pain. One short letter from Fronto reads in its entirety: "I have been troubled, my Lord, in the night with widespread pains in my shoulder and elbow and knee and ankle. In fact I have not been able to convey this news to you in my own writing" (*Ad Marcum Caesarem* 5.73; Haines 1.187).

One of Marcus Aurelius' letters shared a similar focus. Almost the whole letter is devoted to human pain and risk:

> This is how I have passed the last few days. My sister was seized suddenly with such pain in the privy parts that it was dreadful to see her. Moreover, my mother, in the flurry of

the moment, inadvertently ran her side against the corner of the wall, causing us as well as herself great pain by the accident. For myself, when I went to lie down I came upon a scorpion in my bed; however, I was in time to kill it before lying down upon it. If you are better, that is my consolation. My mother feels easier now, thank the gods.

(*Ad Marcum Caesarem* 5.23; Haines 1.196)

In this correspondence, talking about the personal and talking about the body at risk seem to have become almost conflated.

In another letter, Marcus frightened Fronto, who believed that the symptoms being enumerated belonged to Marcus and was relieved when he learned they were really Marcus Aurelius' daughter's (reflecting an attitude not so unlike Aristides' attitude regarding his retainer's children). Marcus Aurelius' letter began:

Thank the gods we seem to have some hopes of recovery. The diarrhea is stopped, the feverish attacks got rid of; the emaciation is extreme, and there is still some cough. You understand, of course, that I am telling you about our little Faustina.

(*Ad Marcum Caesarem* 4.11; Haines 1.202)

For the young Marcus Aurelius, the body and its workings, even its excretions, caused little if any contempt. What happened to make the author of the *Meditations* disgusted to such an extent at bodily functions? One can only suggest age, experience, and a rigorous turn to philosophy. In another letter, Marcus described his desire to live a life more completely informed by higher principles: "Time and time again does your pupil blush and is angry with himself, for that twenty-five years old as I am, my soul has drunk nothing of nobler doctrines and purer principles" (*Ad Marcum Caesarem* 4.13; Haines 1.217).[15] Marcus went to the traditional philosophical wells to drink his nobler doctrines; through these, he was taught to master his self and his body under the direction of his reason. His *Meditations* shows he had taken his lessons to heart, and portrays his determined retreat from a sense of his "self" as a body experiencing the pain of being. They also show that his turn from the body involved a turn away from the joy he exhibited when Galen successfully read his symptoms in the *Prognosis*.

Marcus Aurelius, buttressed by every material and political advantage, maintained his adherence to traditional modes of self-mastery. The history of the next few centuries, however, suggests that many would abandon the answers that Hellenic philosophy offered or would graft them onto new stocks. My contention is that the kind of subjecthood forged in the narratives I have examined in this chapter would provide the basis for the new political, social, and religious unities that would follow. From many different perspectives the discourse of the early empire had begun to represent the human subject as a body in pain, focused on suffering and death. Despite the various particularities seen in the texts by Aelius Aristides, Ignatius of Antioch, and Marcus Aurelius, each author represented a subject focused on his own suffering body and approaching death. Two of the texts depicted a response to this "self" that involved relinquishing control and regulation to the divine. The *Meditations*, however, represented the more traditional reliance on self-mastery. Although written by an emperor who was in better health than Aelius Aristides, and not under sentence of death as Ignatius of Antioch was, this text is, nevertheless, the least joyful of the three.

8

SAINTS' LIVES
The community of sufferers

Hagiographic narratives, accounts of saints' lives, first began to appear in the middle of the fourth century. They followed the popular *Acts of the Martyrs*, and early Lives focused on the institutions of eremitism and monasticism. Later saints were discovered in varying milieux from the airy isolation of the stylites to the social centrality of wealthy women. The quick translation into Latin versions and wide circulation of the earliest example, the *Life of Antony*, attributed to Athanasius, attest to the genre's immediate popularity – a popularity that continued throughout the Latin middle ages and the Byzantine period.[1] Jean Bolland began the critical study of hagiography in the seventeenth century with the publication of *Acta Sanctorum*, a collection of texts. His followers, the Jesuit Bollandists, as well as many others, have continued this textual work. Attention has also been directed toward assessing the historicity of the saints' Lives and the usefulness of their historical information.[2] My attention on these texts, however, will focus on how they continued the representation of Christianity as a community of sufferers.

Current critical theory has drawn attention to the politics of representation. Representation by its nature is partial and selective and inevitably excludes material which might have been represented or represented differently. A culture's reality, its sense of the way "things really are," is now recognized to be a function of its systems of representation, the processes and particularities used to bring its cultural world to consciousness. What gets represented, how, and by whom are essential questions not just for making sense of literary texts themselves, but for coming to understand the cultures producing such texts and in turn reproduced through them. Humans come to understand themselves, their roles, and

200

their world through the scripts their cultural representations offer them.

The function of narrative in the formation of the self is not a modern notion; the authors of hagiography acknowledged it. The texts of a number of saints' Lives expressed an acute awareness of the close connection between discourse and self-understanding. Quite explicitly, hagiographers wrote to offer their readers models for human action. In this sense all saints' Lives, whether based on historical figures or otherwise, can be considered "fictions," fashioned models for emulation rather than historical portraits. The prologue to the *Life of Antony* (251–356), was clear about the work's purpose:

> Since you have asked me about the career of the blessed Antony, hoping to learn how he began the discipline [*askesis*], who he was before this, and what sort of death he experienced, and if the things said concerning him are true – so that you might lead yourselves in imitation of him . . .
>
> (Athanasius 1980: introduction)

The Lives repeatedly made references to the effect texts have on "real" lives. Both Antony and Simeon the elder (387–459), for example, are depicted as choosing the ascetic life after having heard passages from the Gospels read in church (Athanasius 1980: 2; Lent 1915–1917: 112). Saint Augustine testified that reading the *Life of Antony* led some men to abandon their careers and the world. Female saints had female literary models. The *Life of Olympias* (d. early fifth century) opened by linking Olympias with Thecla the female heroine of the second-century *Acts of Paul and Thecla*: "Thecla, a citizen of heaven, a martyr who conquered in many contests . . . Olympias walked in the footsteps of this saint, Thecla, in every virtue of the divinely inspired way of life" (Clark 1979: 1). Quite clearly the writers of hagiography would have agreed with contemporary literary theorists on the important consequences in actual human lives of narrative representation.

The identification of Christianity's representational strategies offers a key to understanding how Christianity acquired power and influence in the ancient world. A basic premise of this study has been that it is difficult for us as heirs to the representational coup effected by Christianity not to view the texts of the early Christian period with simplifying hindsight, overlooking their radicalism in the light of its centrality in our own tradition. B. P. Reardon's statement in his *The Form of Greek Romance*, that the popularity of hagiography put an end to the writing of Greek romance, is therefore suggestive (Reardon 1991: 167). The eclipse of Greek romance by hagiography obviously belonged to the far-reaching ideological rearrangements that Christianity accomplished in the Greco-Roman world. Reardon's comment suggested an avenue for examining the working-out of this ideological shift in a limited representational space. Comparing the saints' Lives with the romances they replaced allows them to be historicized, set into their historical situation, so that what is distinctive about them can emerge. The representational enterprise of the early Greek saints' Lives was similar with that of the martyr *Acts*, namely, to generate the centrality of a particular kind of human subject – the subject as sufferer, as poor or sick. Saints' Lives continued to produce the model of subjecthood that Christianity needed in order to form as an institution. Christianity formed around this subjectivity of sufferer, not only conceptually, but also actively – collecting funds, acquiring power, administering hospitals and poorhouses to succor various categories of sufferers.

Representation in hagiographic narratives as in the earlier martyr narratives functioned to bring to cultural consciousness a reality different from that previously provided in the prose narratives of the Greco-Roman world and it introduced new types of actors onto the cultural stage. The specific parameters of this difference can emerge through a comparison of the Lives with the Greek romances. That these two prose narrative forms shared similarities of plot and incident has often been noted; trials, travels, adventures, sufferings are features of both. Elizabeth Clark, in her discussion of the *Life of Melania* (385–439), however, defined the salient difference between the two forms. Clark noted the close correspondence between the heroines of romance and the saint. Melania, a beautiful adolescent of high birth, kept from her heart's desires by her kin, traveled throughout the Mediterranean world; she was shipwrecked and beset by pirates (Clark 1984: 155). In spite of these romantic plot elements, Clark maintained that Melania's ascetic lifestyle and the reality of its depiction separated her from the world of romance. As Clark commented: "lice are not the stuff from which romances are made" (Clark 1984: 165). Clark's perception deserves extrapolation, for lice *are* conspicuously the stuff of hagiography. The Lives are filled with the specifics of the more wretched aspects of human existence; lice, worms, pus, and rotting flesh featured significantly in them. If a culture's reality results from the particularities of human existence represented in the cultural media, saints' Lives functioned to construct a reality radically different from that of the narrative representations of the Greek romances.

As was outlined in Chapter 2, the typical romance began when two wellborn and handsome young people fell in love and somehow became estranged. During their separation, they suffered both because of their longing for one another and because of the many misfortunes and dangerous situations they found themselves in or threatened by – shipwrecks, slavery, prison, pirate attacks, disembowelment, crucifixion, torture. But fundamental to the depiction of suffering in the romance was that it was offered as specifically a condition that was to be passed through or avoided in the nick of time. The suffering and trials of romance existed primarily to provide piquancy to delay the happy ending that every reader anticipated would be the conclusion of the romance. The marriage, or reunion providing the finale of each romance, functioned as a celebration of the social collectivity. Each romance ended with an implicit promise that no more suffering would follow and that the hero and heroine returned to or commenced a life characterized by "wealth, marriage and luxury" as a character in Achilles Tatius defined the ideal life (6.13.1; Reardon 1989). The plot of romance, in essence, narrated its heroes' and heroines' escape from a world where poverty, pain, and loneliness could touch them. Romance affirmed that the protagonists' "real" life, their "real" community, excluded exactly such conditions. At times, the narratives emphasized the unreality of their protagonists' suffering by depicting apparent misfortunes as illusory.

Achilles Tatius' heroine, Leucippe, for example, presumably died on three different occasions in the narrative; in one, she appeared to be disemboweled and her entrails roasted and eaten. The narrative description in this scene reflects some of the cultural focus on the body in pain apparent in so many texts from the period, but the real point of the episode was that Leucippe had not, in fact, been harmed. The reader later learns that the whole gruesome spectacle has been staged with the aid of an actors' trunk to fool the robbers holding her (3.15–17).

At another point Clitophon saw Leucippe killed, decapitated, and thrown from a pirate ship (5.7.4–5). The narrative portrayed him sorrowfully gathering up the headless body and burying it. Again the girl's suffering turned out to be an illusion – at least for

Leucippe who later explained that another woman, an unfortunate prostitute, had been substituted and beheaded in her place (8.16.1). In this episode the narrative suggested that the murder was not the tragedy the reader had interpreted it to be because it had happened, not to Leucippe, but to a woman of the lower sort. In the narrative representation of romance the second woman's suffering was invisible. The romance betrayed here its inherent bias against the lower classes, a bias shared by the rest of Greco-Roman culture. In Chapter 2, the prevailing elite bias of the romance perspective was outlined. Achilles Tatius repeatedly represented the lower classes (except for favored slave companions) as "other," savage, dangerous, and deserving little sympathy. Sailors caught in a storm, for example, are shown to have acted like cowards; they seized the lifeboat, abandoned the ship, and fought off the passengers with axes and swords (3.3). After the shipwreck Leucippe and Clitophon are attacked by herdsmen/robbers (*boukoloi*), described in the most negative terms: large, black, with shaven heads, and speaking a foreign language (3.9.2). The narrative nearly identified sailors with pirates. Chaereas, a seaman, was easily able to collect a band of evil-doers to help him abduct Leucippe.

Chariton's romance shared this same perspective. In the scene that depicted the near crucifixion of Chaereas and Polycharmus, the heroes were saved at the last moment, but their fourteen companions, the other workmen (*ergatoi*) died without any authorial comment or sympathy. In the narratives of these romances, only actions that affected the wellborn were expected to elicit readers' sympathy. And for these wellborn characters, pain, poverty, and suffering were only temporary, alien conditions as foreign to the real existence of the protagonists as the exotic lands they often traveled through before their final reunion and return to the authentic human community. The romance narratives functioned as part of a cultural script that represented poverty, pain, and suffering as unauthentic human conditions estranging those experiencing them from legitimate society. Hagiographic discourse offered a radically different script and continued the work of martyr texts by introducing and maintaining different categories of subjects into the cultural consciousness. Two groups of saints' Lives can serve to demonstrate the narrative function of the genre – those depicting Stylite saints and women saints.

The popular and widely distributed *Acts of the Martyrs* presented the message that to be a Christian was to suffer. The earliest saints'

Lives, although focused on the institutions of eremitism and monasticism, continued to depict the physical suffering of the saints and place it in the tradition of the martyrs. Both Pachomius (286–346) and Antony were beaten by the devil, and Pachomius explicitly compared his mortifications to the martyrs' actions. Sick, he considered eating some healthy food, but determined not to, when he remembered: "if the martyrs of Christ, having their limbs cut off and being beheaded or burnt, persevered to death in their faith in God, shall I be a coward in a very minor trouble" (Veilleux 1980: 13). The Lives of the Stylite saints, however, embodied the message that to be a Christian was to suffer much more forcefully than these earlier lives. Stylites were those individuals who chose to take up a position on a pillar (*stylos*) and hold it for years; they remained unprotected from the elements, fasting, praying, experiencing extreme physical hardship and, as a result, achieved immense fame and influence in their time (Delehaye 1923). The earliest Stylites were Syrian, and the rigor of their practice has often been explained by the extremism of the Syrian ascetic tradition. This explanation, however, leaves their popularity still unexplained. Despite their physical and geographical isolation, the Lives attributed to these saints a wide popularity. Simeon the Elder was visited by numerous pilgrims from as far away as Britain; Daniel the Stylite was consulted by emperors and bishops.[3] The Lives themselves were curiously popular, translated into many languages and circulated widely. The depiction of the Stylites centered on the real physicality of their suffering – this was no illusory pain. What strikes a modern reader of these Lives is the brutally graphic delineation of the suffering human body they included. These narratives did not avert their gaze from the noisome reality of actual human suffering. These saints attracted so much attention because, like the martyrs, they enacted for all to see the cultural script that determined that to be a Christian *was* to suffer. The suffering now was located in the afflicted human body of the saint rather than the tortured body of the martyr.

Antony's version of the *Life of Simeon the Elder* contained graphic descriptions of bodily affliction (Harvey 1988: 386–387). Even before Simeon mounted his pillar, the narrative depicted him tightly binding a reed cord around himself under his clothes and wearing it until his body became infected down to the very bones (5). The other monks complained to the archimandrite that Simeon smelled and was full of worms; a description of Simeon's body that is repeated several times in the early chapters. When the archimandrite himself discovered that indeed Simeon was rotting, infested with worms, he tried to have the cord binding him unfastened. Hot water was poured over Simeon's body to separate the cord from his garments and rotting flesh, but finally doctors had to be summoned to cut apart the putrid mass (8). From the beginning of his narrative, Antony emphasized in all its appalling detail the reality of Simeon's physical sufferings. Nor did these sufferings abate when Simeon mounted his pillar; the Syriac text noted, for example, that the ulcers on Simeon's feet (filled with maggots) emitted such a stench that those climbing up to see him were distressed when they had reached only the halfway point up the ladder (Lent 1915–1917: 156). Disciples had to put incense and fragrant ointment on their noses so they could ascend to Simeon.

A later episode in the narrative acted to convey not only the reality of Simeon's suffering but its worth. A Saracen leader arrived under Simeon's pillar just as a worm fell from the saint's leg. The Saracen caught the worm and blessed himself with it. Simeon shouted down for him not to touch it; it was only a stinking worm from stinking flesh (18). The saint's words shock the reader into visualizing the repugnant aspects of the suffering body that the narrative depicted. When the Saracen, however, looked into his hand, he found a pearl, not a worm. In the reversed rhetoric of Christian discourse, suffering in all its horror is transformed into treasure, and sufferers are honored. In the same way, Christian martyrs had insisted that their torture was victory and their death, life. Nevertheless, for Simeon and his body the worms remained worms; the realism of the scene insured that the loathsomeness of the saint's actual physical suffering was explicitly represented. Nor does the narrative displace this suffering onto some "other," as the romance did, but described it as the constitutive action of a major Christian cultural hero. Simeon's condition linked him physically with all those who came to him to be healed. Some commentators have suggested that the rot and worms act as tropes, figuring the saint as already dead to this world (Browning 1981: 126). Perhaps so, but more concretely they graphically convey the similarity between the saint's physical condition and that of all the others depicted in the Lives who suffer from grievous physical ailments.

The *Life of Simeon* influenced the practice and portrayal of later, equally popular, Stylite saints. Daniel the Stylite (409–493), who made himself an imitator of Simeon, was likewise famous and honored for his ascetic exertions. His depiction described him as actually crippled by his life. When he dismounted from his pillar to travel to Constantinople to intercede against the monophysites, the narrative described Daniel descending "with difficulty owing to the pain he suffered in his feet" (Dawes and Baynes 1948: 72). In Constantinople, a woman threw herself at the saint's feet and the reader shared her view: "she saw that on one foot the sole had dropped away from the ankle bone and there was nothing left but the shin bone; she was amazed at the man's endurance" (82). This saint was represented as a sufferer, and the *Life* offered a miracle worker who was as physically maimed as those he healed.

By the sixth century, the Church was a well-established healing institution. Healing was the central focus of the *Life* of Simeon the Younger (521–592). His pillar on the "Wondrous Mountain" attracted a veritable carnival of sufferers. Again, the *Life* illustrated that this stylite prodigy, who had taken up his position on the pillar when he was only seven years old, was himself afflicted and crippled by the life he had chosen. Like Simeon the Elder, Simeon the Younger wound a cord tightly around himself with the same result, namely the offensive odor of rotting flesh (van der Ven 1962: 26). As a further ascetic exercise, Simeon determined to remain in a crouched position for a year. This practice caused the flesh of his thighs and hams to rot, so that it melted together until he was unable to straighten out his legs (van der Ven 1962: 26). His crouching deformed his knees, but these are healed by the Lord. The text portrayed in detail Simeon's gruesome physical suffering and described the numbers of those appealing to him for help; namely, for exorcism, for in most cases the sufferers' afflictions are ascribed to Satan. The *Life of Simeon* records so much terrible suffering that it wearies the modern reader. So many sick – the dropsical, lepers, those with plague, snakebite, hemorrhage – paraded through the text. The reader is taken aback by the unflinching realism in the depiction. In one case described in the narrative, for example, a woman who was unable to expel excrement through her anus but only through her female organ, presented herself. At Simeon's word, the demon who had obstructed her departed and, thereafter, the *Life* noted, she excreted naturally (van der Ven 1962: 114).

One can understand from such descriptions why hagiography has proved itself an important source for medical historians (Magoulias 1964). With the exception of certain specifically medical writings, hagiographic texts focused as did no others on the particulars of human disease and suffering. The representation of the saint's suffering, and that of his clients, functioned to bring into cultural consciousness in realistic particularity specific categories of cultural subjects – the sick and the suffering. Their task of generating and regenerating this subject explains the insistent noisome realism of the texts. The Lives insist on the presence of these subjects excluded from earlier literary narratives and urge their centrality. Romance projected as its goal an ideal human community without suffering. Like the *Acts of the Martyrs*, the Lives constructed a human community focused on suffering and made up of sufferers – their goal an escape from all human community to another place. Human life is defined as a state of suffering in the Lives.

The narrative emphasis in women saints' Lives contributed to this creation of a subjectivity of sufferer. Christians were the first, it seems, to write biographies of women and the choice of subject itself testifies to a new and changed representational world (Meredith 1984: 181). The *Life of Melania* (385–439) offers a developed example of the conventional plot for women saints; namely the story of a rich woman who reconstituted herself as a poor person by disposing of all her wealth. The Gospels may assert that the "poor are always with us," but that was not the situation in the represented world of Greco-Roman culture. The poor existed outside its focus.

The narrative of the *Life of Melania* stressed its heroine's real poverty. It depicted in detail the tremendous exertions it took for this fabulously rich woman to rid herself of her fortune. At times there appeared almost a fixation on money in the text with its strict attention to precise accounting: "They sent money to different regions, through one man 40,000 coins, through another 30,000, by another 20,000, through another 10,000, and the rest they distributed as the Lord helped them to" (Clark 1984: 15). Some instances of Melania's alms-giving strike the contemporary reader as almost humorous. In Egypt, for example, Melania visited the hermit Hephestion; she was moved by the sight of the holy man's poverty – his sole possessions, a mat, a few biscuits, and some salt. The hermit refused her offer of gold, so before she left his cell, she hid some in his salt. When Hephestion discovered her ruse he chased after her and demanded that she take the gold back. He finally had to throw it into the river (38). In Christian representation, no one was depicted willing to accept the wealth of this world. Hagiography, like the *Acts of the Martyrs*, inverted the values of its contemporary society.

Melania's personal sacrifice, however, was not humorous, but very real. When the devil tempted her to recall the beauty of one of her estates, the pain of her renunciation could be overheard in her description:

> We had an extraordinary piece of property, and on it was a bath that surpassed any worldly splendor. On one side of it was the sea, and on the other, a forest with diverse vegetation in which wild boar, deer, gazelles, and other animals used to graze. From the pool, the bathers could see boats sailing on one side and the animals in the wood on the other . . . there were sixty-two households around the bath.
>
> (18)

The devil baited Melania by shifting the discourse from the discipline of poverty to the economics of exchange, enacting a temptation in her own motivation: "What sort of place is this Kingdom of Heaven that it can be bought with so much money?" (17).

Despite temptation, Melania persisted in her ascetic choice and rid herself of all her wealth. The genuineness of her poverty is emphasized by real effects. The Empress Serena called her servants to witness the toll paid by the saint for her poverty:

> Come, see the woman who four years ago we beheld vigorous in all her worldly rank, who has now grown old in heavenly wisdom . . . she has trod underfoot the softness of her upbringing, the massiveness of her wealth, all the delights of the things of this life.
>
> (12)

Melania lived the life of the very poor, eating only on Saturday and Sunday (and then only moldy bread), wearing haircloth, and during Lent sleeping on sackcloth and ashes. In the *Life*, Gerontius quoted her servant: "At the time of Holy Easter, when the blessed woman emerged from the exceedingly narrow cell, we shook the sack that lay under her and enormous lice fell out" (40). Although she still continued to consort with empresses and received imperial favors, her life of poverty was squalid and real. Upon her arrival in Jerusalem, for example, Melania testified that she had so successfully divested herself of her wealth that her condition met the criteria for being registered upon the poor: "we thought of inscribing ourselves on the church's register and of being fed with the poor from alms" (35).

The *Life* of Melania displayed its heroine as belonging to the category of the poor. Nor did the narrative offer this as a category of the "other," or a temporary detour from valid social life, but rather as a subject position anyone could and everyone should occupy.[4] Melania is shown to recognize that her renunciation only equated her with the many others who suffered from deprivations:

> And again, when I see the Evil One [the devil] suggesting a vainglorious thought to me (for example, that far from linen and numerous dresses of silk, I now wear haircloth), I think myself as very lowly. I bear in mind that there are those who lie in the marketplace naked, or only on mats, freezing in the cold.
>
> (62)

Melania's narrative allowed the reader to see and identify with those left usually outside the traditional focus of Greco-Roman representation. Hagiographic narratives often provided such glimpses and opportunities for identification – Palladius' *Lausiac History* (419–420), for example, depicted a cripple without hands or feet lying in the marketplace (Meyer 1965: 21.3) and a poor woman giving birth all alone among the poor sleeping on the Church porch in Alexandria (Meyer 1965: 68.3). Just as the Stylite saints' Lives showed their heroes as afflicted, women saints are depicted as poor. Greek hagiography in the Stylites' afflictions and the poverty of saintly women provided new roles for cultural heroes.

In a similar fashion, Gregory of Nyssa's depiction of his sister Macrina (*d.* 379) strove to express the reality of her poverty. During her last illness, Gregory found his sister lying on a board, on the ground. After she died, he searched for garments appropriate to lay her out in and asked her companion if there wasn't something suitable in the storage closets. She answered: "What closets? You have everything she possessed in your hands. Look at her dress, the covering of her head, her worn sandal. This is her wealth; this her property. There is nothing beyond what you see . . ." (Gregory of Nyssa 1967: 189). Just as the lice did in Melania's *Life*, the worn sandal served to convey the actuality of Macrina's poverty. Neither are the stuff of romance, but they are precisely the material of the new cultural representation replacing it.

The highly romanticized story of the Antiochene actress, Saint Pelagia, only emphasizes this change of cultural focus. The narrative presented Pelagia in terms reminiscent of the traditional romantic heroine, as the very epitome of worldly desire and wealth. At the beginning of the narrative, Pelagia was described walking through Antioch in a cloud of perfume, naked except for the jewels covering her down to her very toes, accompanied by slaves dressed and collared in gold (Petitmengin 1981: 4–5). Her appearance so shocked a group of bishops that they averted their eyes, all except for bishop Nonnus. He gave her instead the long and steady gaze that so often ended in love in the romances (Pavlovskis 1976). In this case its eventual result was Pelagia's conversion. Once she converted, Pelagia acted quickly. She immediately called for an accounting of her riches so that she might turn them over to the Church and, as she said, rid herself of the means by which the devil had ensnared her (36–37). Then she disappeared from Antioch.

Years later, Nonnus asked James the Deacon, who was on his way to Jerusalem, to carry greetings to a certain Pelagius. James visited this monk and talked to him through a small window in his cell. He did not recognize the once beautiful Pelagia; as he said later, how could he have? – Her eyes were so sunken and her body so wasted by her violent discipline (45). James returned for a second visit to find that the monk had just died. He watched the wasted body of the saint carried out of the cell treated by the monks carrying it as if it were more precious than gold and precious stones (49). As the monks prepared the corpse for burial, they discovered that it was the body of a woman, and James recognized that the pitiful corpse was that of Pelagia once called by all Antioch "Margarita" (Pearl), on account of her many jewels (30).

In the representational calculus of hagiography, suffering was the new riches. The body wasted by suffering had become more desirable than one covered in jewels. We may recall the worm dropping from Simeon's leg that was transposed into a pearl. This is a root metaphor in Christian representation, stressing the worth of suffering and poverty. In Christian narrative the female heroine was not a Leucippe, who escaped from human suffering and returned to a human community characterized by marriage, wealth, and comfort, but a Pelagia who left her wealth and beauty for poverty and pain and whose story concluded with her escape from the human community altogether. This plot with its ending rejected the traditional social networks celebrated in the romances and concentrated on a new focus for social unity. By making its protagonists afflicted and poor, hagiography served to introduce and maintain new roles in cultural consciousness. Not to be represented is culturally not to exist. [Before Christianity as an institution could grow, it had to create the subject of its concern. The telling of the lives of saints, their pain, their terrible ailments, their poverty, constructed this subject as a focus of cultural attention.]

Not only what gets represented but who gets to represent is also an important factor in a culture's representational system. It is difficult to generalize about the authors of Greek romance, but the authors of the saints' Lives were all clerics or monks. Their own interests were patently linked to the construction of the suffering subject in the saints' Lives, especially in the depiction of their poverty. The narratives made clear that it was not enough for individuals simply to divest themselves of their goods and embrace personal poverty; their money must also be directed toward those in need and the institutions caring for them, and away from its traditional recipients – family and state. The *Life of Melania* made this point emphatically. Both Melania's father and her husband's relatives were censured for trying to retain a share in the couple's property. The devil was shown to be the source of such misguided thinking:

> For the devil had led her father to such an extent (as we said before) that he, a man of great virtue, had committed a great sin under the pretext of good. It was suspected that he wanted to take their possessions and give them to the other children because he was eager to hinder them from their heavenly project . . .

(Clark 1984: 12)

The text also credited divine providence for having saved the couple's wealth from the public treasury after the prefect of the city had made an attempt to confiscate it:

> by divine providence, it happened that the people rebelled against him [the prefect] because of a bread shortage. Consequently he was dragged off and killed in the middle of the city. All the others were afraid and held their peace.

(19)

Neither the state nor the family were to acquire Christians' wealth.

Palladius, in the *Lausiac History*, offered a sketch that epitomized the case against leaving riches to kin. He told the story of a rich virgin in Alexandria who, the narrative laments, never gave a cent to "stranger, virgin, church, or poor man." Instead the woman adopted a niece, and "night and day without any longing for heaven she kept promising her all her wealth" (Meyer 1965: 6.1). Palladius also denounced such misguided thinking as the devil's work: "For this is one way the devil deceives us . . . in the guise of loving one's relatives" (6.2). Saint Macarius saved this rich virgin by a trick; he offered to obtain for her emeralds and hyacinths at a bargain price if she would give him 500 coins. He took her money and used it for his hospital. When she inquired about her gems, Macarius led her to the hospital and asked:

> what do you want to see first, the hyacinths or the emeralds? . . . He took her to the upper floor, and pointed out the crippled and inflamed women, and said "Look, here are your hyacinths!" and he led her back down again and showed her the men: "Behold your emeralds! If they do not please you, take your money back."
>
> (6.8–9)

Once again in the root metaphor of the saints' Lives, the poor and sick become treasure, an object of cultural desire. Wealth was no longer for the family or the state but was to be given for sufferers, for those poor and sick introduced into cultural consciousness through the narration of the saints' Lives: donated wealth that could be overseen by clerics and monks.

Christian narratives, *Martyr Acts*, *Apocryphal Acts*, *Lives of the Saints*, introduced new categories of subjects – the poor, the sick, the suffering – and functioned to reform the cultural notion of the human community. A vignette from a miracle collection serves to demonstrate and metaphorically encapsulate these reforms. A crowd slept in the Church of Saints Kosmas and Damian; they awaited cures (Deubner 1907: 162–164; Magoulias 1964: 150). The saints appeared in a dream to one of the crowd, a paralyzed man, and instructed him to lie with a mute woman. He demurred, but the saints insisted. At his touch, the woman screamed and the frightened man jumped up and ran away; the result, as the narrative proclaimed, was that of the paralytic who taught the mute woman to speak clearly and the speechless woman who taught the man to run married. Marriage is the traditional social happy ending, and

213

in narratives, functions as an affirmation of the social community. Through the work of Christian narrative and its construction of the notion of the "self" as sufferer, the social community of late antiquity had come to include, conceptually, the mute and the paralytic.

The production of this subjectivity, the recognition and acceptance of a self-definition of sufferer, was essential for the growth of Christianity as an institution. Christianity offered itself as a community of sufferers and could not have developed had it lacked subjects present to respond to its call. In this study, I have tried to show that Christianity did not produce its suffering subject alone, but that this subjectivity was under construction and emanated from a number of different locations in the Greco-Roman cultural world.

NOTES

INTRODUCTION

1 For a general introduction to cultural history or cultural studies, see the introduction in Hunt (1989) or Johnson (1986–1987).

2 See, for example, the essays in Hunt (1989), Veeser (1994), or Greenblatt (1988).

3 An excellent example of this is Nancy Armstrong's *Desire and Domestic Fiction: A Political History of the Novel* (1987). She examines the role of domestic fiction in producing a form of consciousness "so important to the stability of capitalist society . . . writing that constituted the self as such was a primary agent to history" (191). See also the introduction to Hunt (1989).

4 Cohan and Shires (1988) quote Belsey's (1980) definition of ideology: "the sum of the ways in which people live and represent to themselves their relationship to the conditions of their existence" (133).

5 See Peter Brown (1979: 20), "we are only beginning to appreciate the extent to which a relationship with the poor, as such, existed only on the margins of ancient man's view of his society"; and Veyne (1990) sees the concept of the poor as deriving from Judaism and Christianity (30–31). For the topic, see Hands (1968), and contra, Bolkestein (1939) and Constantelos (1991).

6 Consider the attitude toward Philoctetes' malady and suffering inscribed in Sophocles' play and its assumption that sickness and suffering separate a person from the human community as an example of classical Greek thinking about sufferers. See Brown (1988).

7 This text also locates this episode in a context of power, for the pretend monks, although poor, are by that fact powerful and able to exorcise the (pretend) demons troubling the other girls.

8 John Bender, in his *Imagining the Penitentiary*, has clarified my thinking on the relation between writing and the formation of institutions. He cautions that the relation must be viewed as one of enablement rather than cause and effect.

> Belief in causes may well be no more than a conventional acceptance of argumentative categories that are embedded in narrative forms of inquiry. With regard to history, then, I may

suffering and the reward it offered should be viewed as an occasion of joy. See Chapter 4 for a more extended discussion of the *Passion of Perpetua*.

14 This passage concludes "and much less would he be apt to denounce himself when the penalty was death," suggesting that the martyrs Justin observed may have been of the "voluntary" type.

2 MARRIAGES AS HAPPY ENDINGS

1 I am acutely aware that any answers for such large questions will obviously be partial and influenced by their own "from" and "for." I say this to emphasize that my reading of the social implications of the romances is not necessarily intended to supplant other readings, but to augment them in the context of this study's particular interests. The romances, for example, are pervaded with religiosity as was the society that produced them. In my attention to a social reading, I have not focused on the religious structures of the novel that I believe would in fact support my reading. See Merkelbach (1962) and Edwards (1987).

2 Bender (1987) quotes Geertz (1973: 451). Bender in his analysis of the "role of novelistic representation in institutional formation" has provided a valuable discussion of how constructs enable cultural change (1–40).

3 Egger (1990), discusses scholarly "reception" of works with romantic plots. Also see Hagg (1983: 81–108), Pervo (1987), and Bowie (1994). "Juvenile," and "frivolous minded people" were suggested by Perry (1967: 2, 98); "women" were suggested in numerous sources likely stemming from Rohde's (1914) seminal discussion of the genre.

4 Gareth Schmeling (1974) has retreated from his suggestion for a middle-class readership. For the non-existence of a "middle class" in the modern sense, see Ramsay MacMullen (1974: 88–94). By upper class and elite in this study, I intend to refer to those with sufficient means to acquire the major benefits of their society, one example of which would be education. Paul Petit (1957: Appendix 2) in his analysis of the background of the students of Libanius in the fourth century (105 students) indicated that 36 percent were from the imperial aristocracy, 47 percent from the curiales and from fathers in the professions.

5 I have generally used the term romance to refer to the narratives under examination. It would be better if English had a term, as the romance languages do, that did not force a distinction between the romance and the "novel." I usually employ the term "romance," but that does not mean that I am implying a generic difference between the ancient "romance" and the "novel."

6 Longus' romance is not included because it essentially lacks the themes of separation, travel and tribulation that are my focus. Heliodorus' romance, like the three romances treated in this chapter would support my reading of the romance as idealizations of Hellenic society; it was left out only because its explicit incorporation of the themes of lost

218

and regained self and national identity seemed to require a more extensive commentary in a critical reading of its own.

7 That the text was an epitome has been suggested on the basis that the
Suda refers to a ten-book romance of Xenophon, but the extant text
has only five books. Tomas Hagg (1966) has disputed this in his article,
"Die Ephesiaka des Xenophon Ephesios, Original oder Epitome?"

8 See Perry (1967: 7–9) and Reardon (1969, 1971) for the Hellenistic
sense of isolation and search for identity as germane to the novel form.

9 The first initial of the romance author's name will be used before the
citations when confusion might be possible – X for Xenophon; C for
Chariton, and AT for Achilles Tatius.

10 Anderson (1982: 16) thinks the role of the assembly is meant to be
humorous. I suggest the collectivity's concern underlines the civic
importance of marriage. MacMullen (1988: 65–66) comments on
collective civic shouting in the second and third centuries as a manifestation of elite power.

11 See the discussion of Clitophon's "treatment" of Melite later in this
chapter that cures her love sickness. In this case, the text makes an
effort to show that the illicit sex act that cures did not harm
Clitophon's socially sanctioned relationship with Leucippe.

12 Muchow (1988: 100 n. 10) gives a list of places where Callirhoe is
mistaken for Aphrodite: 1.1.2, 2.2.6, 2.3.6, 2.3.9, 3.2.17, 4.7.5, 5.9.1,
8.6.11. Also cf. Edwards (1987: 29–47). He calls Callirhoe "the
human counterpart of Aphrodite" (29).

13 Shaw (1984) cites epigraphical evidence testifying to a family killed
by bandits *causa ornamentorum* (on account of their finery). Hopwood
comments:

> The city elites distanced themselves considerably from the local
> peasantry in their language and social habits like bathing and
> attendance at the gymnasium, many of which activities were
> only open to the elite. . . . It can hardly be a matter of surprise
> that cities were a major target of the "bandits."
> (Hopwood 1989: 174)

14 There is suggestion in the romance that exceptionally high birth offsets
"foreignness." The Great King testifies to his own self-control (C 6.3.8).

15 Konstan (1994: 45–56) points to fidelity as the center of the Greek
novel and the continuation and transformation of passion into
commitment as the basis of the plot. My point is to emphasize that
this commitment is to a socially constructed unity.

16 Merkelbach (1962: 81) saw in this pattern a demonstration of the
connection of the romance to the mystery cults with their patterns
of death, transition, and rebirth.

17 Konstan suggests that chastity is not a "major issue" in the novels,
that "the body is not the primary site on which the problem of love
and fidelity is transacted" (1994: 48). The latter statement is certainly
true, but I would suggest that chastity plays a significant role in these
three romances on the symbolic level; it is used to indicate the
submission of the individual to the social.

22 Konstan (1994: 20) goes on to contrast Polycharmus' behavior with Chaereas' – hiding from his parents and then turning up on the boat. Konstan is using this episode to demonstrate quite correctly, I think, that the "role of rescuing hero is not the primary narrative expression of romance in this genre."

23 That our roles are part of our living according to nature seems implicit in *Discourse* 1.6.12–22. See Long and Sedley (1987: 401). Nor should Chaereas' perceived transgression be considered too minor to warrant voluntary death; the Stoics held that all sins are equal (see Rist 1969 for a discussion).

24 Reardon (1982) lists the frequent displays of ignoble behavior in the romance and notes that its morality hardly reaches heroic standards (23). His description of this romantic world as "civilized and social" (24) is apt in catching an essential difference between the romantic and the heroic/tragic world.

4 SUFFERING AND POWER

1 All references to the martyr *Acts* are from Herbert Musurillo (1972). The translations are his (with some slight changes) unless otherwise noted. For dating of the *Acts*, see T. D. Barnes (1968b, 1978).

2 LaCapra and Kaplan offer a definition of ideology:

> a process in which different kinds of meaning are produced and reproduced by the establishment of a mental set toward the world in which certain sign systems are privileged as necessary, even natural ways of recognizing a meaning in things and others are suppressed, ignored or hidden in the process of representing a world to consciousness.
>
> (LaCapra and Kaplan 1988: 284)

3 Shaw (1993) provides an excellent analysis of how this woman's voice was framed by later Christians to contain its challenge.

4 Mertens (1986) notes that Perpetua's dreams always follow a family scene. My discussion of Perpetua's dreams is indebted to the work of Amat (1985) and Mertens. In comparison with Greek romances, it is noteworthy that no husband for Perpetua is mentioned in the text.

5 Stallybrass (1989: 46) provides a helpful morphology of the carnivalesque including the subordination of the head to the lower body stratum. This is based on Bakhtin (1968). See Babcock (1978). The image of stepping on the devil's head is traditional (*Genesis* 3.15) with Dölger (1932).

6 This is Peter Brown's translation of the passage; from *The Body and Society* (1988: 75).

7 For specialized studies of various aspects of this persecution, see M. LeGlay (1978).

8 Bowersock (1985: 662) suggests caution in using Aristides' oration on Rome as historical evidence: "Aristides is not a representative of any segment of opinion . . . He is a performer."

9 I accept the reading "aethism" over "Asia" here.
10 These charges are mentioned most often in Christian sources. Ste. Croix (1963: 36 n. 109) provides a list of citations.
11 Dewart (1986: 84) discusses the difficulty of comprehending Tatian's notions of the precise nature of the resurrected body.

5 HEALING AND POWER
The *Acts of Peter*

1 Hennecke and Schneemelcher (1991) also has a discussion of dating and location of composition and see Davies (1980: 3–10).
2 See Jones (1993).
3 References are to the page and line numbers in Lipsius and Bonnet (1891–1898 rpt 1959); English translations are from Hennecke and Schneemelcher (1991).
4 Miracles are called "manifestation of Christ's grace" in eight places and "a manifestation of Christ" once. See Stoops (1982: 250 n. 39).
5 For an edition of this text, see Brashler and Parrott (1979).
6 For the emphasis on multiple forgiveness, see 47.20–23, 54.5–6, 58.6–8. There has been debate about whether the first three chapters of the Vercelli manuscript and chapter 41 were part of the original Greek text or a later interpolation. See Poupon (1988) and Vouaux (1922: 28). I am not convinced by the arguments for rejecting these chapters.
7 See Garnsey (1970: 104, 136, 138, 139) for degradation of corporal punishment.
8 For urination, see Price (1984: 195) citing *Historia Augusta, Caracalla* 5.7; for Dio, see Pliny, *Epistulae* 10.81 and C. P. Jones (1978: 114). Celsus accuses Christians of destroying statues of divinities to show their powerlessness (Origen *Contra Celsum* 8.38).
9 Stoops's (1982, 1992) discussion of Marcellus is comprehensive and informative. I have only one addition. Stoops faults Marcellus' supposed belief that he can buy salvation through money. I do not find this disapproved of in the text. Rather, the text seems to share Clement of Alexandria's suggestion that dispensing money is a good way of finding divine favour: "O excellent tradings! O divine merchandise. One purchases immortality for money, and by giving perishing things of the world, receives in exchange for these an eternal mansion" (*Quis dives salvetur* 32).
10 Vouaux (1922: 461 n.3) believes this scene primarily reflects the text's distaste for the corporeal.
11 Galen's pay, see *On Prognosis*, ed. Vivian Nutton (1979: 180). The sums of money expressed, however, seem to be more likely round numbers to convey a general sense of large amounts of money, as is often the case in Latin novels. Cf. Duncan-Jones (1974: 238–259).
12 Cartlidge (1986: 63) calls attention to the "sense of inclusiveness in the polymorphic Christology of the APt."

13 For widespread contempt for the lowly, see MacMullen (1974). Cf. Celsus' attitude in Origen *Contra Celsum* 3.52–55. Dio Chrysostom's comment in *Orationes* 7.115. and 65.7 (Dio Chrysostom 1939) reflect this contempt.

14 Arnaldo Momigliano (1986: 285–297). For the relevance of this speech to Dio's time, see Fergus Millar (1964: 104).

15 See Magie (1950: 2.600, 635) and Dickey (1928: 402–415). For the idea that Christians could be seen as belonging to such alienated groups see Origen's (1953) *Contra Celsum* 1.1.

16 See Merkelbach (1962). Merkelbach's views have been much contested, but the place of religion in the ancient novel is clearly an important one.

6 THE SICK SELF

1 The texts of Galen generally are referred to either from C. G. Kühn (1821–1833) or J. Marquardt *et al.* (1884–1893). The full title and abbreviation are given at the first occurrence; after that, only the abbreviation. The references to Kühn are volume number, followed by page number and a K. The references to Marquardt use SM and page number. The other texts used will be noted upon occurrence. Hankinson (1991) provided in his Appendix 2 a helpful guide to the editions and abbreviations of Galen's works.

2 V. Nutton's edition (1979) is used. References are to chapter numbers and Kühn pages in volume 14.

3 Hankinson's translation (1991) is used in the references to the first two books of *De Methodo Medendi*.

4 My discussion of the medical sects is dependent on the works of Michael Frede (1981, 1982). His translation of the *De Sectis ad Ingredientis* is cited (Frede 1985).

5 See Burnyeat (1980). Scepticism in a certain sense seems to involve a rejection of the body. Burnyeat points out that Pyrrho was said to have regretted the difficulty of divesting one's self entirely of one's humanity (1980: 53). Galen says he was tempted by scepticism, but rejected both Pyrrhonism and Academic scepticism (*De Libris Propriis*) 11; SM II.116).

6 From Galen's description, it would be difficult to believe that a doctor as competent as Soranus belonged to this school.

7 Vivian Nutton's (1979) text, translation, and excellent commentary are used throughout. The Kühn volume number, 14, is omitted in my citations to the text. Chapter numbers and Kühn page numbers are provided.

8 Peter Brain's translation in "Galen on the Ideal of the Physician" (Brain 1977: 936–938).

9 J. Arthur Hanson's translation in *Apuleius' Metamorphoses* (1989).

10 Nutton identified this man as Sextus Quintilius Condianus, son of Sextus Quintilius Maximus, consul in A.D. 151, and himself consul in 180 (Galen 1979: 212–214).

11 Galen's description of people so eager to buy his books that they purchase forgeries also indicates the existence of an avid audience for medical texts (*De Libris Propriis*; SM II.91).

12 See De Lacy (1987) for discussion of Galen and scepticism.

13 Englert (1929) discusses the nature of his argument between doctors and gymnasts.

14 Robert Montraville Green's translation of *Thrasybulus* is cited (Green 1953).

15 In his *Diagnosis and Treatment of the Passions of the Soul* (5.1–57K), Galen suggested that people, especially the young, appoint an overseer for themselves to point out their faults to them.

16 As Oswei Temkin warned in his *Galenism* (1973), Galen's works are filled with statements that "are hard to reconcile even when they do not contradict each other" (6). This seems especially true in his various statements on the soul. Ballester (1988) insists that Galen is not a radical materialist (119) and Lloyd (1988) says Galen leaves vague and open the nature of the soul and the relation between the soul and the body. Pigeaud (1989: 53–67) offers a valuable discussion of this relationship.

17 For a discussion of Aristotle's conception of the soul, see the articles by Frede (1992) and Cohen (1992).

18 Frede (1986: 231) suggests that Herodicus also saw his dietetics as a way to lead the good life: why else would Plato have criticized him so much. They were rivals in the arts of life.

19 See Bowersock (1969) for the attitudes of the Greek Sophists of the period.

20 Smith (1990: 26) is careful to point out that *Letter Seventeen* is not written necessarily in the wake of Marinus and cannot be precisely dated. Late dating would benefit my argument, and the depiction of Democritus practicing anatomy in a popular piece of literature seems to correspond well to the general interest in medicine in the early empire that we have seen reflected in the *Prognosis*. Smith does say that Democritus's effort to investigate madness by locating and examining its seat is "too sophisticated for the period that provides the dramatic date of the letter, and probably before the first century B.C."

21 For a discussion of the historical Democritus' moral theory, see Kahn (1985).

22 Galen had named the number of worlds as one of the areas he believed were undecidable. For an interesting study of Galen's religious beliefs, especially his relationship to Asclepius, see Kudlien (1981: 117–129).

7   IDEOLOGY, NOT PATHOLOGY

1 Edelstein and Edelstein (1945: 2.179–281) for inscriptional evidence; for book-length testimony (2.331; *Oxyrhynchus Papyri* 11.1381), dated to the second century A.D. Behr's (Aristides 1981–1986) translation is used and the Greek text is Dindorf (1829 rpt 1964). ST is used as an abbreviation for *Sacred Tales*.

2 Misch (1951: 2.506) is referring to the names written on Philumene's intestines.
3 Festugière (1954: 91–92) recounts similar prescriptions given to other ancients by Asclepius.
4 Behr (1968: 162); Dodds (1965: 41); Bowersock (1969: 60).
5 Aristides employed the same method to account for Zosius', his retainer's, death. Zosius died because he disobeyed Asclepius' commands (ST 47.76–77).
6 William R. Schoedel (1985: 3–7) discusses the recensions of the letters. Schoedel's translation is used here. See also Bower (1974); Swatley (1973); Stoops (1987); Jay (1981). Robert Joly (1979) holds the middle recension to be a forgery dated to A.D. 150–170, and, although I am not ready to abandon the earlier date, Joly's dating would seem to locate Ignatius toward the end of the century closer to Aristides and Marcus. The three do appear to share a similar thought-world.
7 Jonathan Bayes (1989: 27–31) argues that Ignatius holds not only that the human Christ suffers but also Christ the God. On the use of *pathos*, see Schoedel (1985). Pathos can also refer to physical illness.
8 Schoedel thinks the reference here is to busy servants and does not hold that *sumpaschein* refers to suffering for Christ. But since the verb always continues to refer to the suffering of Christ in the text (Schoedel 1985: 275 n. 6), I suggest that it retains this sense in this passage.
9 Translations from C. R. Haines (Aurelius 1924) unless otherwise noted. See also A. R. Birley (1987); P. A. Brunt (1974); J. M. Rist (1982); R. B. Rutherford (1989) and J. E. G. Whitehorne (1977).
10 Brunt (1974: 19–20, Appendix 2) lists citations for the theme of death. Rutherford (1989: 244) in his helpful study examines several related themes; he notes that Brunt's list indicates that sixty-two – one out of every eight – chapters of the *Meditations* are concerned with death.
11 For the melancholy of the *Meditations* see Birley (1987: 222). Brunt (1990: 219), in a review of Rutherford's book, rejects the general pessimism of the *Meditations*; he suggests instead that Marcus Aurelius' sense of his own imperfections was the cause of the gloom. Brunt describes the *Meditations* as the "only document to tell us what it was like to be a man struggling to live by Stoic principles." This is precisely my point; namely, the new difficulty of living out these precepts.
12 This translation is Rutherford's (1989).
13 The text of the correspondence between Fronto and Marcus Aurelius is found in Marcus Cornelius Fronto (1954). The translation is based on Fronto (1919–1920). For the dating of the letters, see Champlin (1980: Appendix A). See also Stowers (1986).
14 Whitehorne (1977) argues that the letters reflect Fronto's hypochondria rather than that of Marcus Aurelius and gives a list of Fronto's complaints, (415, nn. 13–16). According to Whitehorne, fifty-five of Fronto's letters refer to illness; thirty percent of all his letters refer to

his own illnesses, while eight percent refer to the illnesses of others. Marcus Aurelius has fifty-four letters that mention illness; of these, twenty-seven reply to Fronto's recitation of his illness. Twenty percent of the references are to Marcus Aurelius' own health.

15 Champlin (1974) argues that this letter refers to jurisprudence not philosophy, but Birley (1987: 226) points out, however, that the letter must suggest some "inner crisis" and dissatisfaction with himself, as well as a need for higher things. This letter is dated to A.D. 146.

8   SAINTS' LIVES
The community of sufferers

1 T. Barnes (1986) discusses the authorship of the *Life of Antony*; Barnes disputes that Athanasius is the author.

2 S. Wilson (1983) offers an extensive annotated survey of bibliography on many aspects of the saints' Lives. The works of P. Brown (1971, 1978, 1981, 1983), and E. Patlagean (1976, 1983), as well as a number of the essays in Hackel's (1981) collection, consider the social aspects of the writings of saints' Lives.

3 For texts of the lives of the Stylites, see Lietzmann (1908: Delehaye 1923; van der Ven 1962). For translations, see Dawes and Baynes (1948) for Daniel the Stylite; Lent (1915–1917) for a translation of the Syriac life of Simeon the Elder and Doran (1992); R. M. Price (1985) for Theodoret of Cyrrhus' version of Simeon's life in Chapter 26 of the *Historia Religiosa*. For an excellent guide to the texts and translation of individual saints' lives, see Nesbitt (1969).

4 E. Patlagean's (1983) suggestion that the poor are treated as the "other" in saints' Lives has not persuaded me.

BIBLIOGRAPHY

Amat, J. (1985). *Songes et visions: L'au delà dans la littérature latine tardive.* Paris, Etudes augustiniennes.

Anderson, G. (1982). *Eros Sophistes.* Chico, CA., Scholars Press.

Anderson, G. (1984). *Ancient Fiction: The Novel in the Greco-Roman World.* London, Croom Helm.

Anderson, G. (1993). *The Second Sophistic: A Cultural Phenomenon in the Roman Empire.* London, Routledge.

André, J.-M. (1987). "Les écoles philosophiques aux deux premiers siècles de l'Empire." *Aufstieg und Niederlang der Römischen Welt* II.36.1: 5–77.

Apuleius (1924). *Apulée: Apologie, Florides* ed. P. Vallette. Paris, Les Belles Lettres.

Apuleius (1989). *Metamorphoses* ed. J. A. Hanson. 2 vols. Loeb Classical Library, Cambridge, Harvard University Press.

Aristides, A. (1829 rpt 1964). *Aristides* ed. G. Dindorf. Hildescheim, George Olms.

Aristides, A. (1898). *Aelii Aristides Smyrnaei Quae Supersunt Omnia* ed. B. Keil. Berlin, Weidmann.

Aristides, A. (1976). *P. Aelii Aristidis Opera Quae Extant Omnia* ed. C. A. Behr. Leiden, Brill.

Aristides, A. (1981–1986). *P. Aelius Aristides: The Complete Works* trans. C. A. Behr. Leiden, Brill.

Armstrong, N. (1987). *Desire and Domestic Fiction: A Political History of the Novel.* New York, Oxford University Press.

Armstrong, N. (1992). "Imperialistic Nostalgia and 'Wuthering Heights.'" *Emily Brontë: "Wuthering Heights"* ed. L. Peterson. Boston, Bedford Books. 428–449.

Armstrong, N. and L. Tennenhouse, eds (1989). *The Violence of Representation.* London, Routledge.

Asmis, E. (1989). "The Stoicism of Marcus Aurelius." *Aufstieg und Niedergang der Römischen Welt* II.36.3: 2228–2252.

Athanasius (1980). *The Life of Antony and the Letter to Marcellus* trans. R. Gregg. New York, Paulist Press.

Athenaeus (1927). *Deipnosophists* trans. C. B. Gulick. Loeb Classical Library, New York, G. P. Putnam's Sons.

Athenagoras (1972). *Legatio et De Resurrectione* ed. W. R. Schoedel. Oxford, Clarendon Press.

Aurelius, M. (1924). *The Communings with Himself of Marcus Aurelius Antoninus, Emperor of Rome, Together with Speeches and Sayings* trans. C. R. Haines. Loeb Classical Library, New York, G. P. Putnam's Sons.

Babcock, B., ed. (1978). *The Reversible World*. Ithaca, Cornell University Press.

Bagnani, G. (1955). "Peregrinus Proteus and the Christians." *Historia* 4: 107–112.

Bakhtin, M. (1968). *Rabelais and His World* trans. Helene Iswolsky. Cambridge, Harvard University Press.

Bakhtin, M. (1981). *The Dialogic Imagination*. Austin, University of Texas Press.

Ballester, L. G. (1988). "Soul and Body, Disease of the Soul and Disease of the Body in Galen's Medical Thought." *Le Opere Psicologiche di Galeno* ed. P. Manuli and M. Vegetti. Napoli, Bibliopolis. 117–151.

Barnes, J. (1991). "Galen on Logic and Therapy." *Galen's Method of Healing* ed. F. Kudlien. Leiden, Brill. 50–102.

Barnes, J., *et al.*, eds (1982). *Science and Speculation*. Cambridge, Cambridge University Press.

Barnes, T. D. (1968a). "Legislation against the Christians." *Journal of Roman Studies* 58: 32–50.

Barnes, T. D. (1968b). "Pre-Decian Acta Martyrum." *Journal of Theological Studies* 19: 509–531.

Barnes, T. D. (1971). *Tertullian*. Oxford, Oxford University Press.

Barnes, T. D. (1978). "Eusebius and the Date of the Martyrdom." *Les Martyrs de Lyon* (177) ed. M. LeGlay. Paris, Centre national de la recherche scientifique. 137–143.

Barnes, T. D. (1986). "Angel of Light or Mystic Initiate." *Journal of Theological Studies* 37: 353–367.

Barnes, T. D. (1993). *Athanasius and Constantine*. Cambridge, Harvard University Press.

Barton, C. (1993). *The Sorrows of the Ancient Romans*. Princeton, Princeton University Press.

Barton, C. (1994). "Savage Miracles: The Redemption of Lost Honor in Roman Society and the Sacrament of the Gladiator and the Martyr." *Representations* 45: 41–71.

Bartsch, S. (1989). *Decoding the Ancient Novel: The Reader and the Role of Description in Heliodorus and Achilles Tatius*. Princeton, Princeton University Press.

Bayes, J. (1989). "Divine 'ἀπάθεια in Ignatius of Antioch." *Studia Patristica* 21: 27–31.

Beek, C. J. M. J. van (1936). *Passio Sanctarum Perpetuae et Felicitatis*. Nijmegen, Dekker and Van de Vegt.

Behr, C. A. (1968). *Aelius Aristides and the Sacred Tales*. Amsterdam, Hakkert.

Belsey, C. (1980). *Critical Practice*. London, Methuen.

229

Bender, J. (1987). *Imagining the Penitentiary: Fiction and Architecture of Mind In Eighteenth Century England.* Chicago, University of Chicago Press.

Berger, J. (1972). *Ways of Seeing.* New York, Penguin.

Bernard, L. W. (1976). "Athenagoras: *De Resurrectione.*" *Studia Theologica* 30: 1–42.

Betz, H. D. (1958). "Lukian von Samosata und das Christentum." *Novum Testamentum* 3: 226–237.

Birley, A. R. (1987). *Marcus Aurelius: A Biography.* New Haven, Yale University Press.

Bolkestein, H. (1939). *Wohltätigkeit und Armenpflege im vorchristlichen Altertum.* Utrecht, A. Oosthoek.

Bovon, F. (1988). "The Synoptic Gospels and the Noncanonical Acts of the Apostles." *Harvard Theological Review* 81: 19–36.

Bovon, F. and M. Esbroeck, eds (1981). *Les Actes Apocryphes des Apôtres.* Geneva, Labor et Fides.

Bower, R. A. (1974). "The Meaning of ΕΠΙΤΥΧΑΝΩ in the Epistles of St. Ignatius of Antioch." *Harvard Theological Review* 80: 1–14.

Bowersock, G. W. (1969). *Greek Sophists in the Roman Empire.* Oxford, Clarendon Press.

Bowersock, G. W. (1985). "Aelius Aristides." *Cambridge History of Classical Literature* ed. P. E. Easterling and B. M. W. Knox. Cambridge, Cambridge University Press. 658–663.

Bowersock, G. W. (1987). "The Mechanics of Subversion in the Roman Provinces." *Opposition et resistances a l'empire d'Auguste à Trajan* ed. A. Giovannini. Geneva, Fondation Hardt. 291–317.

Bowersock, G. W. (1994). *Fiction as History.* Berkeley, University of California Press.

Bowie, E. L. (1985). "The Greek Novel." *The Cambridge History of Classical Literature* ed. P. E. Easterling and B. M. W. Knox. Cambridge, Cambridge University Press. 683–699.

Bowie, E. L. (1994). "The Readership of Greek Novels in the Ancient World." *The Search for the Ancient Novel* ed. J. Tatum. Baltimore, Johns Hopkins University Press.

Brain, P. (1977). "Galen on the Ideal of the Physician." *South African Medical Journal* 52: 936–938.

Brashler, J. and D. M. Parrott (1979). "The Act of Peter: BG, 4: 128, 1–141, 7." *Nag Hammadi Codices V, 2–5 and VI with Papyrus Berolinensis 8502, 1 and 4* ed. D. Parrott. Leiden, Brill. 473–493.

Brock, A. J. (1929). *Greek Medicine.* London, Dent.

Brophy, R. and M. Brophy (1985). "Deaths in the Pan-Hellenic Games II: All Combatant Sports." *American Journal of Philology* 106: 171–198.

Brown, P. (1971). "The Rise of the Holy Man in Late Antiquity." *Journal of Roman Studies* 61: 80–101.

Brown, P. (1978). *The Making of Late Antiquity.* Cambridge, Harvard University Press.

Brown, P. (1979). "Response." *The Role of the Christian Bishop in Ancient Society* ed. H. Chadwick. Berkeley, Center for Hermeneutical Studies.

230

Brown, P. (1981). *The Cult of the Saints*. Chicago, University of Chicago Press.

Brown, P. (1983). "The Saint as Exemplar." *Representations* 1: 1–25.

Brown, P. (1988). *The Body and Society*. New York, Columbia University Press.

Brown, P. (1992). *Power and Persuasion in Late Antiquity: Towards a Christian Empire*. Madison, University of Wisconsin Press.

Browning, R. (1981). "The 'Low Level' Saint's Life in the Early Byzantine World." *The Byzantine Saint* ed. S. Hackel. London, Supplement Sorbornost 5. 117–127.

Brunt, P. A. (1974). "Marcus Aurelius in His Meditations." *Journal of Roman Studies* 64: 1–20.

Brunt, P. A. (1977). "From Epictetus to Arrian." *Athenaeum* 50: 19–48.

Brunt, P. A. (1990). "Review of *The Meditations of Marcus Aurelius: A Study*." *Journal of Roman Studies* 80: 218–219.

Burnyeat, M. F. (1980). "Can the Sceptic Live His Scepticism?" *Doubt and Dogmatism: Studies in Hellenistic Epistemology* ed. M. Schofield *et al*. Oxford, Clarendon Press. 20–53.

Burrus, V. (1987). *Chastity as Autonomy: Women in the Apocryphal Acts*. Lewiston, Edwin Mellen Press.

Butler, H. E. (1909). *The Apologia and Florida of Apuleius of Madaura*, Oxford, Clarendon Press.

Cameron, A. (1991). *Christianity and the Rhetoric of Empire*. Berkeley, University of California Press.

Carrithers, M., *et al.*, eds (1985). *The Category of the Person*. Cambridge, Cambridge University Press.

Cartlidge, D. (1986). "Transfigurations of Metamorphosis Traditions in the Acts of John, Thomas and Peter." *Semeia* 38: 53–66.

Champlin, E. (1974). "The Chronology of Fronto." *Journal of Roman Studies* 64: 136–159.

Champlin, E. (1980). *Fronto and Antonine Rome*. Cambridge, Harvard University Press.

Chidester, D. (1988). *Salvation and Suicide*. Bloomington, Indiana University Press.

Cicero, M. T. (1956). *De Officiis* trans. W. Miller. Loeb Classical Library, Cambridge, Harvard University Press.

Clark, E. (1979). *Jerome, Chrysostom, and Friends*. New York, Edwin Mellen Press.

Clark, E. (1984). *The Life of Melania the Younger: Introduction, Translation, and Commentary*. New York, Edwin Mellen Press.

Clarke, G. W. (1974). *The Octavius of Minucius Felix*. Ancient Christian Writers Series, New York, Newman Press.

Clay, D. (1992). "Lucian of Samosata: Four Philosophical Lives (Nigrinus, Demonax, Peregrinus, Alexander Pseudomantis)." *Aufstieg und Niedergang der Römischen Welt* II.36.5: 3406–3450.

Clement of Alexandria (1919). *Works* trans. C. Butterworth. Loeb Classical Library, New York, G. P. Putnam's Sons.

Cohan, S. and L. Shires (1988). *Telling Stories: A Theoretical Analysis of Fiction*. London, Routledge.

231

Cohen, S. M. (1992). "Hylomorphism and Functionalism." *Essays on Aristotle's "De Anima"* ed. M. C. Nussbaum and A. O. Rorty. Oxford, Clarendon Press. 51–73.

Coleman, K. M. (1990). "Fatal Charades: Roman Executions Staged as Mythological Enactments." *Journal of Roman Studies* 80: 44–73.

Constantelos, D. (1991). *Byzantine Philanthropy and Social Welfare*. New Rochelle, Caratzas.

Cyprian. (1964). *Saint Cyprian: Letters* trans. S. R. B. Donna. The Fathers of the Church, Washington, Catholic University of America Press.

Daremberg, C. (1854). *Oeuvres anatomiques, physiologiques et médicales de Galien*. Paris, Baillière.

Davies, J. G. (1972). "Factors Leading to the Emergence of Belief in the Resurrection of the Flesh." *Journal of Theological Studies* 23: 448–455.

Davies, S. L. (1980). *The Revolt of the Widows: Social World of the Apocryphal Acts*. Urbana, Southern Illinois University Press.

Dawes, E. and N. H. Baynes (1948). *Three Byzantine Saints: Contemporary Biographies Translated from the Greek*. Oxford, Basil Blackwell.

De Lacy, P. (1972). "Galen's Platonism." *American Journal of Philology* 93: 27–39.

De Lacy, P. (1977). "The Four Stoic *Persona*." *Illinois Classical Studies* 2: 164–172.

De Lacy, P. (1987). "Galen's Response to Scepticism." *Illinois Classical Studies* 16: 283–306.

De Lacy, P. (1988). "On the Third Part of the Soul." *Le Opere psicologiche di Galeno* ed P. Manuli and M. Vegetti, Napoli, Bibliopolis.

De Ste. Croix, G. E. M. (1954). "Aspects of the 'Great' Persecution." *Harvard Theological Review* 47: 75–113.

De Ste. Croix, G. E. M. (1963). "Why Were the Early Christians Persecuted." *Past and Present* 26: 6–38.

Delehaye, H. (1923). *Les Saints stylites*. Brussels, Subsidia Hagiographia 14.

Den Boeft, J. and J. Bremmer (1982). "Notiunculae Martyrologicae II." *Vigilae Christianae* 36: 383–402.

Deubner, L., ed. (1907). *Kosmas und Damian: Texte und Einleitung*. Leipzig, Teubner.

Dewart, J. E. M. (1986). *Death and Resurrection*. Wilmington, M. Glazier.

Dickey, S. (1928). "Some Economic Conditions of Asia Minor Affecting the Expansion of Christianity." *Studies in Early Christianity* ed. S. J. Case. New York. 393–416.

Dio Chrysostom (Dio of Prusa) (1939). *Dio Chrysostom: Discourses* trans. J. W. Cohoon and H. L. Crosby. Loeb Classical Library, Cambridge, Harvard University Press.

Diogenes Laertius (1925). *Lives of the Eminent Philosophers* trans. R. D. Hicks. Loeb Classical Library, New York, G. P. Putnam's Sons.

Dobbin, R. F. (1989). "The Sense of Self in Epictetus: Prohairesis and Prosōpon." Unpublished dissertation, University of California at Berkeley.

Dodds, E. R. (1965). *Pagan and Christian in an Age of Anxiety*. Cambridge, Cambridge University Press.

Dölger, F. J. (1932). "Der Kampf mit den Ägypter in der Perpetua – Visio, das Martyrium als Kampf mit dem Teufel." *Antike und Christenum* 3: 177–188.

Doran, R., trans. (1992). *The Lives of Simeon Stylites*. Kalamazoo, Cistercian Publications.

Douglas, M. (1970 rpt 1980). *Natural Symbols: Explorations in Cosmology*. New York, Pantheon.

Droge, A. J. and J. D. Tabor (1992). *A Noble Death: Suicide and Martyrdom among the Christians and Jews in Antiquity*. New York, Harper San Francisco.

Dronke, P. (1984). *Women Writers of the Middle Ages*. Cambridge, Cambridge University Press.

DuBois, P. (1991). *Torture and Truth*. London, Routledge.

Dumont, L. (1985). "A Modified View of our Origins: The Christian Beginnings of Modern Individualism." *The Category of the Person* ed. M. Carrithers *et al.* Cambridge, Cambridge University Press. 93–122.

Duncan-Jones, R. (1974). *The Economy of the Roman Empire*. Cambridge, Cambridge University Press.

Durham, D. B. (1938). "Parody in Achilles Tatius." *Classical Philology* 33: 1–19.

Durkheim, E. (1966). *Suicide*. Glencoe, Free Press.

Durling, R. J. (1991). "'Endeixis' as a Scientific Term." *Galen's Method of Healing: Proceedings of the 1982 Galen Symposium* ed. F. Kudlien and R. J. Durling. Leiden, Brill. 112–113.

Eagleton, T. (1990). *The Ideology of the Aesthetic*. Oxford, Basil Blackwell.

Edelstein, E. J. and L. Edelstein (1945). *Asclepius: A Collection and Interpretation of the Testimonies*. Baltimore, Johns Hopkins University Press.

Edelstein, L. (1967). *Ancient Medicine*. Baltimore, Johns Hopkins University Press.

Edwards, D. (1987). "Acts of the Apostles and Chariton's Chaereas and Callirhoe: A Literary and Sociological Study." Unpublished dissertation, Boston University.

Edwards, M. J. (1989). "Satire and Verisimilitude: Christianity in Lucian's *Peregrinus*." *Historia* 38: 89–98.

Egger, B. (1990). "Women in the Greek Novel: Constructing the Feminine." Unpublished dissertation, University of California at Irvine.

Egger, B. (1994). "Women and Marriage in the Greek Novels: The Boundaries of Romance." *In Search of the Ancient Novel* ed. J. Tatum. Baltimore, Johns Hopkins University Press. 260–280.

Elsom, H. E. (1992). "Callirhoe: Displaying the Phallic Woman." *Pornography and Representation in Greece and Rome* ed. A. Richlin. Oxford, Oxford University Press. 212–230.

Englert, L. (1929). *Untersuchungen zu Galens Schrift Thrasybulos*. Studien zur Geschichte der Medizin 18. Leipzig, Barth.

Epictetus (1925). *Epictetus: Works* trans. W. A. Oldfather. Loeb Classical Library, Cambridge, Harvard University Press.

Felix, M. (1931). *Minucius Felix* trans. G. Randall. Loeb Classical Library, New York, G. P. Putnam's Sons.

Festugière, A. J. (1954). *Personal Religion Among the Greeks.* Sather Classical Lectures, Berkeley, University of California Press.

Festugière, A. J. (1969). "Sur les *Discours sacrés* d'Aelius Aristides." *Revue des Etudes Grecques* 82: 117–153.

Foley, H. P. (1982). "Marriage and Sacrifice in Euripides' *Iphigenia in Aulis.*" *Arethusa* 15: 159–180.

Foucault, M. (1965). *Madness and Civilization: A History of Insanity in the Age of Reason* trans. R. Howard. New York, Pantheon.

Foucault, M. (1977). *Discipline and Punish: The Birth of the Prison* trans. A. Sheridan. New York, Pantheon.

Foucault, M. (1980). *The History of Sexuality* trans. R. Hurley. Vol. 1 of *The History of Sexuality.* 3 vols. New York, Vintage Books.

Foucault, M. (1984). "Truth and Power." *The Foucault Reader* ed. P. Rubinow. New York, Pantheon. 51–75.

Foucault, M. (1988). *The Care of the Self: The History of Sexuality.* Vol. 3 of *The History of Sexuality* trans. R. Hurley. 3 vols. New York, Vintage Books.

Francis, J. (1995). *Subversive Virtue: Asceticism and Authority in the Pagan World of the Second Century C.E.* State College, Penn State Press.

Frede, M. (1981). "On Galen's Epistemology." *Galen: Problems and Prospects* ed. V. Nutton. London, Wellcome Institute. 65–86.

Frede, M. (1982). "The Method of the So-Called Methodical School of Medicine." *Science and Speculation* ed. J. Barnes. Cambridge, Cambridge University Press.

Frede, M. (1985). *Galen: Three Treatises on the Nature of Science.* Indianapolis, Hackett.

Frede, M. (1986). "Philosophy and Medicine in Antiquity." *Human Nature and Natural Knowledge* ed. A. Donagan *et al.* Boston, D. Reidel. 211–232.

Frede, M. (1992). "On Aristotle's Conception of the Soul." *Essays on Aristotle's De Anima* ed. M. C. Nussbaum and A. O. Rorty. Oxford, Clarendon Press. 93–107.

Frend, W. H. C. (1965). *Martyrdom and Persecution in the Early Church.* Oxford, Oxford University Press.

Frend, W. H. C. (1978). "Blandina and Perpetua." *Les Martyrs de Lyons (177)* ed. M. LeGlay. Paris, Centre national de la recherche scientifique.

Fronto, M. C. (1919–1920). *The Correspondence of Fronto* trans. C. R. Haines. Loeb Classical Library, New York, G. P. Putnam's Sons.

Fronto, M. C. (1954). *Marcus Cornelius Fronto, Epistulae* ed. M. P. J. van den Hout. Leiden, Brill.

Frye, N. (1957). *Anatomy of Criticism.* Princeton, Princeton University Press.

Frye, N. (1976). *The Secular Scripture: A Study of the Structure of Romance.* Cambridge, Harvard University Press.

Fusillo, M. (1988). "Textual Patterns and Narrative Situations in the Greek Novel." *Gröningen Colloquia* 1: 17–31.

Gager, J. (1982). "Body Symbols and Social Reality." *Religion* 13: 345–363.

Gagier, R. (1990). *Subjectivities.* New York, Oxford University Press.

Galen (1821–1833). *Claudii Galeni Opera Omnia* ed. C. G. Kühn. 22 vols. Leipzig, Cnoblock.

Galen (1884–1893). *Claudii Galeni Pergameni Scripta Minora* ed. J. Marquardt, I. Müller and G. Helmreich. 3 vols. Leipzig, Teubner.

Galen (1905 rpt 1969). *Galenus: De Temperamentis* ed. G. Helmreich. Stuttgart, Teubner.

Galen (1979). *Galen: On Prognosis* ed. and trans. V. Nutton. *Corpus Medicorum Graecorum* 5.8.1. Berlin, Akademie-Verlag.

Galen (1980). *De Placitis Hippocrates et Platonis* ed. and trans. P. De Lacy. *Corpus Medicorum Graecorum* 5.4.1, 5.4.2. Berlin, Akademie-Verlag.

Garnaud, J.-P., ed. (1991). *Achille Tatius: Le roman de Leucippé et Clitophon*. Paris, Les Belles Lettres.

Garnsey, P. (1970). *Social Status and Legal Privilege in the Roman Empire*. Oxford, Oxford University Press.

Garnsey, P. and G. Woolf (1989). "Patronage of the Rural Poor in the Roman World." *Patronage in Ancient Society* ed. A. Wallace-Hadrill. London, Routledge.

Geertz, C. (1972). "Religion as a Cultural System." *Reader in Comparative Religion* ed. W. Lessa and E. Vogt. New York, Harper Row, 3rd ed. 167–178.

Geertz, C. (1973). *The Interpretation of Cultures*. New York, Basic Books.

Geertz, C. (1992). "Local Knowledge and its Limitations: Some Obiter Dicta." *Yale Journal of Criticism* 5: 129–135.

Gellius, A. (1927). *The Attic Nights of Aulus Gellius* trans. J. C. Rolfe. Loeb Classical Library, New York, G. P. Putnam's Sons.

Gennep, A. van (1960). *The Rites of Passage* trans. M. B. Vizedom. Chicago, University of Chicago Press.

Georgemans, H. (1983). "*Oikeiosis* in Arius Didymus." *On Stoic and Peripatetic Ethics* ed. W. Fortenbaugh. New Brunswick, Transaction Books.

Gibbon, E. (1946). *The History of the Decline and Fall of the Roman Empire* ed. J. B. Bury. New York, Heritage Press.

Gordon, R. (1990). "The Roman Empire." *Pagan Priests* ed. M. Beard and J. North. Ithaca, Cornell University Press. 177–255.

Grant, R. M. (1988). *Greek Apologists in the Second Century*. Philadelphia, Westminster.

Green, R. M. (1953). "Galen's De Temperamentis, Thrasybulus." Unpublished typescript, Yale University.

Greenblatt, S. (1980). *Renaissance Self-Fashioning*. Chicago, University of Chicago Press.

Greenblatt, S., ed. (1981). *Allegory and Representation: Selected Papers of the English Institute*. Baltimore, Johns Hopkins University Press.

Greenblatt, S. (1988). *Shakespearean Negotiations: The Circulation of Social Energy in Renaissance England*. Berkeley, University of California Press.

Gregory of Nyssa (1967). *Gregory of Nyssa: Ascetic Works* trans. V. W. Callahan. Fathers of the Church Washington D.C., Catholic University of America Press.

Groce, D., ed. (1962). *Vie de Sainte Mélanie*. Sources chrétiennes 90. Paris, Editions du Cerf.

Hackel, S., ed. (1981). *The Byzantine Saint*. London, Supplement Sorbornost 5.

Hagg, T. (1966). "Die Ephesiaka des Xenophon Ephesios, Original oder Epitome?" *Classica et Mediaevalia* 27: 118–161.

Hagg, T. (1971). *Narrative Technique in Ancient Greek Romances*. Stockholm, Svenska Institutet i Athen.

Hagg, T. (1983). *The Novel In Antiquity*. Berkeley, University of California Press.

Hagg, T. (1987). "*Callirhoe* and *Parthenope:* The Beginnings of the Historical Novel." *Classical Antiquity* 20: 184–204.

Hall, J. (1981). *Lucian's Satire*. New York, Arno.

Hands, A. (1968). *Charities and Social Aid in Greece and Rome*. Ithaca, Cornell University Press.

Hankinson, R. J. (1991). *De Methodo Medendi: Books I and II*. Oxford, Clarendon Press.

Hankinson, R. J. (1992). "Galen's Philosophical Eclecticism." *Aufstieg und Niederlang der Römischen Welt* II.36.5: 3505–3520.

Harnack, A. von (1892). *Medizinisches aus der Älteren Kirkengeschichte*. Leipzig, J. C. Hinrichs.

Harnack, A. von (1904–1905 rpt 1972). *The Mission and Expansion of Christianity in the First Three Centuries*. James Moffatt, New York, G. P. Putnam's Sons.

Harvey, S. (1988). "The Sense of a Stylite: Perspectives on Simeon the Elder." *Vigiliae Christianae* 42: 376–394.

Hauke, E. (1937). *Dass die Vermögen der Steele eine Folge der Mischungen des Körpers sind*. Berlin, Ebering.

Helms, J. (1966). *Character Portrayal in the Romance of Chariton*. The Hague, Mouton and Co.

Hennecke, E. and W. Schneemelcher (1992). *New Testament Apocrypha* trans. R. M. Wilson. 2 vols. Philadelphia, Westminster.

Hijmans, B. L. (1959). *ASKESIS: Notes on Epictetus' Educational System*. Assen, Van Gorcum.

Hills, J. (1990). "Tradition, Redaction, and Intertextuality: Miracle Lists in *Apocryphal Acts* as a Test Case." *Society of Biblical Literature: Seminar Papers*: 375–390.

Hooff, A J. L. van (1990). *From Autothanasia to Suicide*. London, Routledge.

Hopkins, K. (1983). *Death and Renewal*. Cambridge, Cambridge University Press.

Hopkins, K. (1993). "Novel Evidence for Roman Slavery." *Past and Present* 138: 3–27.

Hopwood, K. (1989). "Bandits, Elites and Rural Order." *Patronage in Ancient Society* ed. A. Wallace-Hadrill. London, Routledge. 171–187.

Hunt, L., ed. (1989). *The New Cultural History*. Berkeley, University of California Press.

Irenaeus (1885 rpt 1967). *Against the Heresies* ed. A. Roberts and J. Donaldson. Rev. ed. A. C. Coxe, *Ante-Nicene Fathers*, Grand Rapids, Wm. B. Eerdmans.

Jameson, F. (1981). *The Political Unconscious*. Ithaca, Cornell University Press.

Jay, E. G. (1981). "From Presbyter-Bishops to Bishops and Presbyters: Christian Ministry in the Second Century." *Second Century* 1: 125–162.

Johnson, R. (1986–1987). "What is Cultural Studies Anyway?" *Social Text: Theory/Culture/Ideology* 16: 38–80.

Joly, R. (1979). *Le Dossier d'Ignace d'Antioche*. Brussels, Editions de l'Université Bruxelles.

Jones, A. H. M. (1963). "The Social Background of the Struggle Between Paganism and Christianity." *The Conflict Between Paganism and Christianity* ed. A. Momigliano. Oxford, Clarendon Press. 17–37.

Jones, C. P. (1978). *The Roman World of Dio Chrysostom*. Cambridge, Harvard University Press.

Jones, F. S. (1993). "Principal Orientations on the Relations Between the Apocryphal Acts." *Society of Biblical Literature Seminar Papers* 32: 484–505.

Joplin, P. K. (1991). "The Voice of the Shuttle is Ours." *Rape and Representation* ed. L. Higgins and B. R. Silver. New York, Columbia University Press. 35–64.

Julian (1930). *The Works of the Emperor Julian* trans. W. C. Wright. Loeb Classical Library, Cambridge, Harvard University Press.

Junod, E. and J. D. Kaestli (1983). *Acta Iohannis*. Corpus Christianorum Series Apocryphorum Turnhout, Brehols.

Justin (1915). *Die ältesten Apologeten* ed. E. J. Goodspeed. Göttingen, Vanderhoeck and Rupprecht.

Justin (1930). *The Dialogue with Trypho* trans. A. L. Williams. London, Society for Promoting of Christian Knowledge.

Justin (1948). *Saint Justin Martyr* ed. and trans. T. Falls. The Fathers of the Church New York, Christian Heritage.

Kaestli, J. D. (1981). "Les Principales Orientations de la recherche sur les actes apocryphes des Apôtres." *Les Actes apocryphes des Apôtres* ed. F. Bovon. Geneva, Labor et Fides. 49–67.

Kahn, C. H. (1983). "Arius as Doxographer." *On Stoic and Peripatetic Ethics* ed. W. W. Fortenbaugh. New Brunswick, Transaction Books. 3–13.

Kahn, C. H. (1985). "Democritus and the Origins of Moral Psychology." *American Journal of Philology* 106: 1–31.

Kahn, C. H. (1988). "Discovering the Will: From Aristotle to Augustine." *The Question of "Eclecticism"* ed. J. Dillon and A. A. Long. Berkeley, University of California Press.

Kerferd, G. B. (1972). "The Search for Personal Identity in Stoic Thought." *Bulletin of the John Rylands University Library* 55: 177–196.

Kerferd, G. B. (1978). "What Does the Wise Man Know?" *The Stoics* ed. J. Rist. Berkeley, University of California Press. 125–136.

Kermode, F. (1979). *The Genesis of Secrecy: On the Interpretation of Narrative*. Cambridge, Harvard University Press.

Kidd, I. G. (1971). "Stoic Intermediates and the End for Man." *Problems in Stoicism* ed. A. A. Long. London, Athlone Press. 150–172.

Klign, A. F. J. (1962). *The Acts of Thomas*. Leiden, Brill.

Konstan, D. (1994). *Sexual Symmetry: Love in the Ancient Novel and Related Genres.* Princeton, Princeton University Press.

Kudlien, F. (1981). "Galen's Religious Belief." *Galen: Problems and Prospects* ed. V. Nutton. London, Wellcome Institute.

Kudlien, F. and R. J. Durling, eds (1991). *Galen's Method of Healing: Proceedings of the 1982 Galen Symposium.* Leiden, Brill.

Kyrtatas, D. (1987). *The Social Structure of Early Christian Communities.* London, Verso.

LaCapra, D. and S. Kaplan (1988). *Modern European Intellectual History.* Ithaca, Cornell University Press.

Lacey, W. K. (1986). *"Patria Potestas." The Family in Ancient Rome: New Perspectives* ed. B. Rawson. Ithaca, Cornell University Press. 121–144.

Lake, K. (1917). *The Apostolic Fathers.* Loeb Classical Library, New York, G. P. Putnam's Sons.

Lamberton, R. and J. J. Keaney, eds (1992). *Homer's Ancient Readers.* Princeton: Princeton University Press.

Lampe, P. (1987). *Die stadtrömischen Christen in den ersten beiden Jahrhunderten.* Tübingen, J. C. B. Mohr.

Lane Fox, R. (1987). *Pagans and Christians.* New York, Alfred A. Knopf.

LeGlay, M., ed. (1978). *Les Martyrs de Lyons (177).* Paris, Centre national de la recherche scientifique.

Leitch, V. (1992). *Cultural Criticism, Literary Theory, Post-Structuralism.* New York, Columbia University Press.

Lent, F. (1915–1917). "Life of St. Simeon Stylites." *Journal of American Oriental Society* 35: 103–198.

Lévi-Strauss, C. (1969). *The Elementary Structures of Kinship* trans. J. H. Bell. Boston, Beacon.

Liebeschuetz, J. H. W. G. (1979). *Continuity and Change in Roman Religion.* Oxford, Oxford University Press.

Lietzmann, H., ed. (1908). *Leben des heiligen Symeon Stylites.* Leipzig, J. C. Hinrichs.

Lieu, S. N. C. (1992). *Manichaeism in the Later Roman Empire and Medieval China.* Wissenschäftliche Untersuchungen zum Neuen Testament 63. Tübingen, J. C. B. Mohr.

Lipsius, R. A. and M. Bonnet, eds (1891–1898 rpt 1959). *Acta Apostolorum Apocrypha.* Darmstadt, George Olms.

Lloyd, G. (1988). "Scholarship, Authority and Argument in Galen's *Quod Animi Mores.*" *Le Opere psicologiche di Galeno* ed. P. Manuli and M. Vegetti. Napoli, Bibliopolis. 9–41.

Long, A. A., ed. (1971). *Problems in Stoicism.* London, Athlone.

Long, A. A. (1982). "Soul and Body in Stoicism." *Phronensis* 27: 34–57.

Long, A. A. (1983). "Arius Didymus and the Exposition of Stoic Ethics." *On Stoic and Peripatetic Ethics* ed. W. Fortenbaugh. New Brunswick, Transaction Books. 41–65.

Long, A. A. and D. N. Sedley (1987). *The Hellenistic Philosophers.* 2 vols. Cambridge, Cambridge University Press.

Lucian (1936). *Lucian with an English Translation* trans. A. M. Harmon. Loeb Classical Library, Cambridge, Harvard University Press.

Lukacs, G. (1971). *The Theory of the Novel.* Cambridge, MIT Press.

Lutz, C. E. (1947). "Musonius Rufus: The Roman Socrates." *Yale Classical Studies* 10: 3–147.

MacDonald, D. R. (1983). *The Legend and the Apostle.* Philadelphia, Westminster Press.

McGowen, R. (1989). "Punishing Violence, Sentencing Crime." *The Violence of Representation* ed. N. Armstrong and L. Tennenhouse. London, Routledge. 140–156.

MacMullen, R. (1966). *Enemies of the Roman Order.* Cambridge, Harvard University Press.

MacMullen, R. (1974). *Roman Social Relations.* New Haven, Yale University Press.

MacMullen, R. (1981). *Paganism in the Roman Empire.* New Haven, Yale University Press.

MacMullen, R. (1984). *Christianizing the Roman Empire.* New Haven, Yale University Press.

MacMullen, R. (1986). "What Difference Did Christianity Make?" *Historia* 35: 322–343.

MacMullen, R. (1988). *Corruption and the Decline of Rome.* New Haven, Yale University Press.

Macro, A. D. (1980). "The Cities of Asia Minor under Roman Imperium." *Aufstieg und Niederlang der Römischen Welt* II.7.2: 658–697.

Magie, D. (1950). *Roman Rule in Asia Minor to the End of the Third Century after Christ.* Princeton, Princeton University Press.

Magoulias, H. J. (1964). "The Lives of the Saints as Sources for the History of Byzantine Medicine in the Sixth and Seventh Century." *Byzantinische Zeitschrift* 57: 127–150.

Manuli, P. and M. Vegetti, eds (1988). *Le Opere psicologiche di Galeno.* Napoli, Bibliopolis.

Maraval, P., ed. (1971). *Vie de Sainte Macriné: introduction, texte, critique.* Sources chrétiennes 178. Paris, Editions du Cerf.

Meeks, W. (1974). "The Image of the Androgyne: Some Uses in Earliest Christianity." *History of Religions* 13: 165–208.

Meeks, W. (1983). *The First Urban Christians.* New Haven, Yale University Press.

Meeks, W. (1993). *The Origins of Christian Morality.* New Haven, Yale University Press.

Meredith, A. (1984). "A Comparison Between *Vita S. Macrina* of Gregory of Nyssa, the *Vita Plotini* of Porphyry and the *De Vita Pythagoria* of Iamblicus." *The Biographical Works of Gregory of Nyssa* ed. A. Spira. Cambridge, Philadelphia Patristic Foundation. 181–195.

Merkelbach, R. (1962). *Roman und Mysterium in der Antike.* Munich, Beck.

Merquior, J. G. (1979). *The Veil and the Mask: Essays on Culture and Ideology.* London, Routledge and Kegan Paul.

Mertens, C. (1986). "Les Premiers martyrs et leur rêves." *Revue d'histoire ecclésiastique* 81: 5–46.

Meyer, R. T. (1965). *Palladius: The Lausiac History.* New York, Newman Press.

Michenaud, G. and J. Dierkens (1972). *Les Rêves dans les discourses sacrés d'Aelius Aristide: essai d'analyse psychologique*. Brussels, Université de Mons.

Miles, M. (1989). *Carnal Knowing: Female Nakedness and Religious Meaning in the Christian West*. New York, Random House.

Millar, F. (1964). *A Study of Cassius Dio*. Oxford,

Millar, F. (1965). "Epictetus and the Imperial Court." *Journal of Roman Studies* 55: 141–148.

Millar, F. (1973). "The Imperial Cult and the Persecutions." *Le Culte des souverains dans l'empire Romain* ed. W. Den Boer. Geneva, Foundation Hardt. 11–63.

Millar, F. (1977). *The Emperor in the Roman World*. Ithaca, Cornell University Press.

Miller, N. (1988). *Subject to Change: Reading Feminist Criticism*. New York, Columbia University Press.

Misch, G. (1951). *A History of Autobiography in Antiquity* trans. E. W. Dickes. Cambridge, Harvard University Press.

Molinié, G., ed. (1979). *Le roman de Chairéas et Callirhoé*. Paris, Les Belles Lettres.

Momigliano, A. (1985). "Marcel Mauss and the Quest for the Person in Greek Biography and Autobiography." *The Category of the Person* ed. M. Carrithers *et al.* New York, Cambridge University Press. 83–122.

Momigliano, A. (1986). "The Disadvantage of Monotheism for a Universal State." *Classical Philology* 81: 285–297.

Morgan, J. (1981). "History, Romance and Realism in the Aithiopika of Heliodoros." *Classical Antiquity* 1: 221–265.

Morton, D. and M. Zavarzadeh, eds (1991). *Theory/Pedagogy/Politics*. Urbana, University of Illinois Press.

Most, G. W. (1989). "The Stranger's Stratagem: Self-Disclosure and Self-Sufficiency in Greek Culture." *Journal of Hellenic Studies* 109: 114–133.

Muchow, M. D. (1988). "Passionate Love and Respectable Society in Three Greek Novels." Unpublished dissertation, Johns Hopkins University.

Musurillo, H., ed. (1972). *Acts of the Christian Martyrs*. Oxford, Oxford University Press.

Nautin, P. (1961). *Lettres et écrivains chrétiens des IIe and IIIe siècles*. Paris, Les Editions du Cerf.

Nesbitt, J. W. (1969). "A Geographical and Chronological Guide to Greek Saint Lives." *Orientalia Christiana Periodica* 35: 443–489.

Newman, B. (1990). "Gender, Narrative and Gaze in *Wuthering Heights*." *PMLA* 105: 1029–1041.

Newman, R. (1989). "*Cotidie Meditare*: Theory and Practice of the *Meditatio* in Imperial Stoicism." *Aufstieg und Niedergang der Römischen Welt* II.36.3: 1473–1517.

Nock, A. D. (1933). *Conversion: The Old and the New in Religion from Alexander the Great to Augustine of Hippo*. Oxford, Clarendon Press.

Nutton, V. (1972). "Galen and Medical Autobiography." *Proceedings of the Cambridge Philological Society* 18: 50–62.

Nutton, V. (1973). "The Chronology of Galen's Early Career." *Classical Quarterly* 23: 158–171.

Nutton, V. (1985). "Murders and Miracles: Lay Attitudes toward Medicine in Classical Antiquity." *Patients and Practitioners* ed. R. Porter. Cambridge, Cambridge University Press. 23–53.

Nutton, V. (1991). "Style and Context in the Method of Healing." *Galen's Method of Healing* ed. F. Kudlien. Leiden, Brill. 1–25.

Origen (1953). *Contra Celsum* trans. H. Chadwick. Cambridge, Cambridge University Press.

The Oxyrhynchus Papyri (1898–) ed. B. P. Grenfell and A. S. Hunt. London, Egypt Exploration Fund.

Pagels, E. (1980). "Gnostic and Christian Views of Christ's Passion." *The Rediscovery of Gnosticism* ed. B. Layton. Leiden, Brill. Vol. 1. 262–283.

Papanikolaou, A. D. (1964). "Chariton und Xenophon von Ehesus: zur Frage der Abhängigkeit." *Kharis: Kōnstantinos I. Bourberēs.* ed. A. Anastassiou *et al.* Athens, 305–320.

Papanikolaou, A. D. (1973). *Xenophontis Ephesii Ephesiacorum Libri V De Amoribus Anthiae et Abrocomes.* Leipzig, Teubner.

Patlagean, E. (1976). "L'Histoire de la femme deguisée en moine et la évolution de la sainteté feminine à Byzance." *Studi Medievali* 17: 595–623.

Patlagean, E. (1983). "Ancient Byzantine Hagiography and Social History." *Saints and Their Cults* ed. S. Wilson. Cambridge, Cambridge University Press.

Pavlovskis, Z. (1976). "The Life of Saint Palagia the Harlot." *Classical Folia* 30: 138–149.

Pearcy, L. T. (1988). "Theme, Dream, and Narration: Reading the Sacred Tales of Aelius Aristides." *TAPA* 118: 377–391.

Perkins, J. (1985). "The Apocryphal Acts of the Apostles and Early Christian Martyrdom." *Arethusa* 15: 211–230.

Perkins, J. (1992a). "The Apocryphal Acts of Peter: A Roman à Thèse." *Arethusa* 25: 445–455.

Perkins, J. (1992b). "The 'Self as Sufferer.'" *Harvard Theological Review* 85: 245–272.

Perkins, J. (1993). "The Social World of the Acts of Peter." *The Search for the Ancient Novel* ed. J. Tatum. Baltimore, Johns Hopkins University Press. 296–307.

Perkins, J. (1994). "Representation in Greek Saints Lives." *Greek Fiction: The Greek Novel in Context* ed. J. R. Morgan and R. Stoneman. London, Routledge. 255–271.

Perkins, J. (1994). "The Passion of Perpetua: A Narrative of Empowerment." *Latomus* 53: 837–847.

Perry, B. E. (1967). *The Ancient Romances.* Sather Classical Lectures 37. Berkeley, University of California Press.

Pervo, R. (1987). *Profit with Delight: The Literary Genre of the Acts of the Apostles.* Philadelphia, Fortress.

Pervo, R. (1994). "Early Christian Fiction." *Greek Fiction* ed. J. R. Morgan and R. Stoneman. London, Routledge. 239–254.

Peterson, D. W. (1977). "Observations on the Chronology of the Galenic Corpus." *Bulletin of the History of Medicine* 51: 492–495.

Peterson, L., ed. (1992). *Emily Brontë: "Wuthering Heights."* Case Studies in Contemporary Criticism. Boston, Bedford Books.

Petit, P. (1957). *Les Etudiants de Libanius*. Paris, Nouvelles Editions Latines.

Petitmengin, P. (1981). *Pélagie la pénitente: métamorphoses d'une légende*. Paris, Études augustiniennes. Vol. 1.

Philostratus (1922). *Lives of Eminent Philosophers* trans. W. Wright. Loeb Classical Library, New York, G. P. Putnam's Sons.

Philostratus (1949). *The Letters of Alciphron, Aelian and Philostratus* trans. F. H. Forbes. Loeb Classical Library, Cambridge, Harvard University Press.

Pigeaud, J. (1989). *La Maladie de l'âme*. Paris, Les Belles Lettres.

Pinault, J. R. (1992). *Hippocratic Lives and Legends*. Leiden, Brill.

Pleket, H. W. (1975). "Games, Prizes, Athletes and Ideology." *Arena* 1: 165–208.

Pliny (1963) *Epistularum Libri Decem* ed. R. A. B. Mynors. Oxford, Clarendon Press.

Plutarch (1928). *Moralia (De Tuenda Sanitate Praecepta)* trans. F. C. Babbitt. Loeb Classical Library, Cambridge, Harvard University Press.

Poupon, G. (1988). "Les Actes de Pierre et leur remaniement." *Aufstieg und Niedergang der Römischen Welt* II.25.6: 4363–4383.

Praet, D. (1992–1993). "Explaining the Christianization of the Roman Empire." *Sacris Erudiri* 33: 1–119.

Price, R. M. (1985). *Theodoret of Cyrrhus: A History of the Monks of Syria*. Kalamazoo, Cistercian Studies 88.

Price, S. (1984). *Rituals and Power: The Roman Imperial Cult in Asia Minor*. Cambridge, Cambridge University Press.

Proudfoot, W. (1985). *Religious Experience*. Berkeley, University of California Press.

Radway, J. A. (1978). "Phenomenology, Linguistics, and Popular Literature." *Journal of Popular Culture* 12: 88–98.

Reardon, B. P. (1969). "The Greek Novel." *Phoenix* 23: 291–309.

Reardon, B. P. (1971). *Courants littéraires des IIe et IIIe siècles après J.C.* Paris, Les Belles Lettres.

Reardon, B. P. (1974). "The Second Sophistic and the Novel." *Approaches to the Second Sophistic* ed. G. W. Bowersock. University Park, PA., American Philological Asssociation. 23–29.

Reardon, B. P. (1982). "Theme, Structure, and Narrative in Chariton." *Yale Classical Studies* 27: 1–27.

Reardon, B. P., ed. (1989). *Collected Ancient Greek Novels*. Berkeley, University of California Press.

Reardon, B. P. (1991). *The Form of Greek Romance*. Princeton, Princeton University Press.

Reardon, B. P. (1994). "Achilles Tatius and Ego Narrative." *Greek Fiction: The Greek Novel in Context* ed. J. R. Morgan and R. Stoneman. London, Routledge. 80–96.

Riddle, D. (1931). *The Martyrs: A Study in Social Control*. Chicago, University of Chicago Press.

Rist, J. (1969). *Stoic Philosophy*. Cambridge, Cambridge University Press.

Rist, J. (1978a). "The Stoic Concept of Detachment." *The Stoics* ed. J. Rist. Berkeley, University of California Press. 259–272.

242

Rist, J., ed. (1978b). *The Stoics.* Berkeley, University of California Press.

Rist, J. M. (1982). "Are You A Stoic? The Case of Marcus Aurelius." *Jewish and Christian Self-Definition* ed. B. F. Meyer and E. P. Sanders. London, SCM. Vol. 3, 23–45.

Rives, J. B. (1994). "The Priesthood of Apuleius." *American Journal of Philology* 115: 273–290.

Robert, L. (1982). "Une Vision de Perpétue." *Comptes rendus de l'académie des inscriptions et belles lettres*: 228–276.

Rogers, G. M. (1990). *The Sacred Identity of Ephesus: Foundation Myths of a Roman City.* London, Routledge.

Rohde, E. (1914). *Der griechische Roman und seine Vorlauder.* 3rd ed. Leipzig, Breitkopf und Hartel.

Rousselle, A. (1986). *Porneia.* Oxford, Basil Blackwell.

Rutherford, R. B. (1989). *The Meditations of Marcus Aurelius: A Study.* Oxford, Oxford University Press.

Rutter, T. (1993). "Recent Scholarship on the Hippocratic Pseudepigrapha." *Society for Ancient Medicine Review* 21: 148–160.

Ruttimann, R. J. (1986). "Asclepius and Jesus." Unpublished dissertation, Harvard University.

Said, E. (1979). *Orientalism.* New York, Random House.

Said, S. (1993). "The City in the Greek Novel." *In Search of the Ancient Novel* ed. J. Tatum. Baltimore, Johns Hopkins University Press. 216–236.

Salzman, M. R. (1989). "Aristocratic Women: Conductors of Christianity in the Fourth Century." *Helios* 16: 207–220.

Salzman, M. R. (1993). "The Evidence for the Conversion of the Roman Empire to Christianity in Book 16 of the *Theodosian Code*." *Historia* 42: 362–378.

Scarborough, J., ed. (1985). *Symposium on Byzantine Medicine.* Dumbarton Oaks Papers 38. Washington, Dumbarton Oaks Library.

Scarcella, A. M. (1977). "Les structures socio-économiques du roman de Xénophon d'Ephèse." *Revue des études Grecques* 90: 249–62.

Scarry, E. (1985). *The Body in Pain.* Oxford, Oxford University Press.

Schmeling, G. (1974). *Chariton.* Twayne's World Authors Series, New York, Twayne.

Schmeling, G. (1980). *Xenophon of Ephesus.* Twayne's World Authors Series, Boston, Twayne.

Schneider, P. G. (1991). "A Perfect Fit: The Major Interpolation in the Acts of John." *Society of Biblical Literature Seminar Papers*: 518–532.

Schoedel, W. R. (1985). *A Commentary on the Letters of Ignatius of Antioch.* Philadelphia, Fortress Press.

Schofield, M. (1991). *The Stoic Idea of the City.* Cambridge, Cambridge University Press.

Schofield, M., *et al.*, eds (1980). *Doubt and Dogmatism: Studies in Hellenistic Epistemology.* Oxford, Clarendon Press.

Scobie, A. (1973). *More Essays on the Ancient Romance and its Heritage.* Meisenheim am Glan, Anton Hain.

Segal, C. (1984). "The Trials at the End of Achilles Tatius' *Clitophon and Leucippe:* Doublets and Complementaries." *Studi Italiani di Filologia Classica* 2: 83–91.

243

Seneca, L. (1920–1925). *Epistulae Morales* trans. R. G. Gummere. Loeb Classical Library, New York, G. P. Putnam's Sons.

Seneca, L. (1928–1935). *Moral Essays* trans. J. W. Basore. Loeb Classical Library, New York, G. P. Putnam's Sons.

Sextus Empiricus (1933). *Outline of Pyrrhonism* trans. R. G. Bury. Loeb Classical Library, Cambridge, Harvard University Press.

Shaw, B. (1984). "Bandits in the Roman Empire." *Past and Present* 105: 3–52.

Shaw, B. (1985). "The Divine Economy: Stoicism as Ideology." *Latomus* 64: 16–54.

Shaw, B. (1993). "The Passion of Perpetua." *Past and Present* 139: 1–45.

Sherwin-White, A. N. (1966). *The Letters of Pliny: A Historical and Social Commentary.* Oxford, Clarendon Press.

Siegel, R. (1973). *Galen on Psychology, Psychopathology, and Function and Diseases of the Nervous System.* Basel, S. Karger.

Skarsaune, O. (1976). "The Conversion of Justin Martyr." *Studia Theologica* 30: 53–73.

Smelser, N. J. (1962). *Theory of Collective Behavior.* New York, Free Press.

Smith, J. (1969–1970). "Birth Upside Down or Right Side Up!" *History of Religions* 9: 281–303.

Smith, R. (1884). "Misery and Mystery: Aelius Aristides." *Pagan and Christian Anxiety: A Response to E. R. Dodds* ed. R. Smith and J. Lounibas. Lanham, MD., University Press of America. 53–86.

Smith, W. D. (1979). *The Hippocratic Tradition.* Ithaca, Cornell University Press.

Smith, W. D. (1989). "Notes on Ancient Medical Historiography." *Bulletin of the History of Medicine* 63: 73–109.

Smith, W. D. (1990). *Hippocrates: Pseudepigraphic Writings.* Leiden, Brill.

Söder, R. (1932). *Die apokryphen Apostelgeschichten und die romanhafte Literatur der Antike.* Stuttgart, W. Kohlhammer.

Stadter, P. A. (1980). *Arrian of Nicomedia.* Chapel Hill, University of North Carolina Press.

Stallybrass, P. (1989). "Drunk with the Cup of Liberty: Robin Hood, the Carnivalesque, and the Rhetoric of Violence in Early Modern England." *The Violence of Representation* ed. N. Armstrong and L. Tennenhouse. London, Routledge. 45–76.

Stallybrass, P. and A. White (1986). *Politics and Poetics of Transgression.* Ithaca, Cornell University Press.

Stead, G. C. (1981). "Conjectures in the Acts of John." *Journal of Theological Studies* 32: 152–153.

Stephens, J. C. (1982). "The Religious Experience of Aelius Aristides: An Interdisciplinary Approach." Unpublished dissertation, University of California at Santa Barbara.

Stephens, S. A. (1994). "Who Reads Ancient Novels." *In Search of the Ancient Novel* ed. J. Tatum. Baltimore, Johns Hopkins University Press. 405–418.

Stobaeus, J. (1884). *Anthologii* ed. C. Wachsmuth. Berlin, Weidmanns.

Stoops, R., Jr. (1982). "Miracle Stories and Vision Reports in the Acts of Peter." Unpublished dissertation, Harvard University.

Stoops, R., Jr. (1986). "Patronage in the Acts of Peter." *Semeia* 38: 91–100.

Stoops, R., Jr. (1987). "If I Suffer: Epistolary Authority in Ignatius of Antioch." *Harvard Theological Review* 80: 161–178.

Stoops, R., Jr. (1991). "Christ as Patron in the *Acts of Peter*." *Semeia* 56: 143–157.

Stowers, S. K. (1981). *The Diatribe and Paul's Letter to the Romans*. Chico, Scholars Press.

Stowers, S. K. (1986). *Letter Writing in Greco-Roman Antiquity*. Library of Early Christianity. Philadelphia, Westminster.

Stroumsa, G. G. (1990). "*Caro Salutis Cardo*: Shaping the Person in Early Christian Thought." *History of Religions* 30: 25–50.

Stuart, Z. (1958). "Democritus and the Cynics." *Harvard Studies in Classical Philology* 63: 179–191.

Suleiman, S. (1983). *Authoritarian Fictions*. New York, Columbia University Press.

Swatley, W (1973). "The *Imitatio Christi* in Ignatian Letters." *Vigilae Christianae* 27: 81–103.

Tacitus, C. (1937). *The Annals* trans. J. Jackson. Loeb Classical Library, Cambridge, Harvard University Press.

Tacitus, C. (1925 rpt 1980). *The Histories* trans. C. F. Moore. Loeb Classical Library, Cambridge, Harvard University Press.

Tatian (1982). *Discourse to the Greeks and Fragments* ed. and trans. M. Whittaker, Oxford, Clarendon Press.

Taylor, C. (1989). *Sources of the Self.* Cambridge, Harvard University Press.

Temkin, O. (1973). *Galenism: Rise and Fall of a Medical Philosophy*. Ithaca, Cornell University Press.

Tennenhouse, L. (1982). "Representing Power: Measure for Measure in its Time." *Genre* 15: 139–156.

Tertullian (1960). *Treatise on the Resurrection* ed. E. Evans. London, Society for Promoting Christian Knowledge.

Tertullian (1931). *Tertullian* trans. T. R. Glover. Loeb Classical Library, New York, G. P. Putnam's Sons.

Thomas, C. M. (1992). "Word and Deed: the *Acts of Peter* and Orality." *Apocrypha* 3: 125–164.

Thornton, T. (1986). "The Destruction of Idols: Sinful or Meritorious." *Journal of Theological Studies* 37: 121–129.

Toohey, P. (1990). "Some Ancient Histories of Literary Melancholia." *Illinois Classical Studies* 15: 143–161.

Toohey, P. (1992). "Love, Lovesickness, and Melancholy." *Illinois Classical Studies* 17: 265–286.

Turner, B. (1984). *The Body and Society: Explorations in Social Theory*. Oxford, Blackwell.

Turner, C. H. (1931). "The Latin Acts of Peter." *Journal of Theological Studies* 32: 118–133.

Turner, V. (1969). *The Ritual Process: Structure and Anti-Structure*. Ithaca, Cornell University Press.

Turner, V. (1972). "Betwixt and Between; The Liminal Period in *Rites des Passages*." *Reader in Comparative Religion* ed. W. Lessa and E. Vogt. New York, Harper Row, 3rd ed. 338–347.

Turner, V. (1980). "Social Dramas and Stories About Them." *Critical Inquiry* 7: 141–168.

van der Ven, P., ed. (1962). *La Vie ancienne de S. Syméon Stylite le Jeune (521–592)*. Brussels, Subsidia Hagiographia 32.

Veeser, H. A., ed. (1994). *The New Historicism Reader*. New York, Routledge.

Veilleux, A. (1980). *Pachomian Koinonia*. Kalamazoo, *Cistercian Studies* 45.

Vernant, J. P. (1980). *Myth and Society in Ancient Greece* trans. J. Lloyd. Atlantic Highlands, Humanities Press.

Veyne, P. (1987). "The Roman Empire." *A History of Private Life*, vol. 1 *From Pagan Rome to Byzantium* ed. P. Veyne. Cambridge, Harvard University Press. 6–233.

Veyne, P. (1990). *Bread and Circuses* trans. B. Pearce. London, Penguin.

Vouaux, L. (1922). *Les Actes de Pierre*. Paris, Librairie Letouzey.

Walzer, R. (1949). *Galen on Christians and Jews*. London, Oxford University Press.

Walzer, R. (1962). "New Light on Galen's Moral Philosophy." *Classical Quarterly* 43: 82–96.

Watson, G. (1966). *Theriac and Mithridatium: A Study in Therapeutics*. London, Wellcome Library.

White, H. (1980). "Literature and Social Action: Reflections on the Reflective Theory of Literary Art." *New Literary History* 11: 363–380.

Whitehorne, J. E. G. (1977). "Was Marcus Aurelius a Hypochondriac?" *Latomus* 36: 413–421.

Wilken, R. L. (1984). *The Christians as the Romans Saw Them*. New Haven, Yale University Press.

Wilson, S. (1983). *Saints and Their Cults*. Cambridge, Cambridge University Press.

Winkler, J. (1980). "Lollianus and the Desperadoes." *Journal of Hellenic Studies* 100: 155–181.

Winkler, J. (1982). "The Mendacity of Kalasiris and the Narrative Strategy of Heliodoros' *Aithiopika*." *Yale Classical Studies* 27: 93–158.

Wolff, J. (1992). "Excess and Inhibition: Interdisciplinarity in the Study of Art." *Cultural Studies* ed. L. Grossberg, C. Nelson and P. Treichler. London, Routledge. 706–718.

Zeitlin, F. I. (1982). "Cultic Models of the Female: Rites of Dionysus and Demeter." *Arethusa* 15: 129–157.

Zïzek, S. (1988). *The Sublime Object of Ideology*. London, Verso.

INDEX